MAYBE IT'S ME

MAYBE

Looking Inward

IT'S

to Create Real Change

ME

Through Conscious Choices

Erika Alessandrini

www.amplifypublishinggroup.com

Maybe It's Me: Looking Inward to Create Real Change Through Conscious Choices

©2026 Erika Alessandrini. All Rights Reserved. No part of this publication may be reproduced, stored in a retrieval system or transmitted in any form by any means electronic, mechanical, or photocopying, recording or otherwise without the permission of the author.

The advice and strategies found within may not be suitable for every person or situation. This work is sold with the understanding that neither the author nor the publisher is held responsible for the results accrued from the advice in this book.

For more information, please contact:
Amplify Publishing, an imprint of Amplify Publishing Group
620 Herndon Parkway, Suite 220
Herndon, VA 20170
info@amplifypublishing.com

Library of Congress Control Number: 2025926004

CPSIA Code: PRV0126A

ISBN-13: 979-8-89138-848-2

Printed in the United States

For those who've carried the weight of the world for far too long—may you find the courage to exhale, release what was never yours to carry, and discover the peace that's been waiting for you all along.

CONTENTS

INTRODUCTION

Thank you for joining me on this journey. Reaching this moment—where I hold a fully published book in my hands—has been no easy task. God placed this book on my heart and called me to stay the course, but I won't sugarcoat it: I wanted to quit more times than I can count. So. Many. Times. God knows that I thrive on tackling hard things, yet He has also witnessed my struggles when I start to question whether I can truly do those hard things well.

Like so many authors who have come before me, I used you as an excuse to write the book I needed to read. But I genuinely care about you, and I believe we have a lot in common—enough to share my journey and insights with you.

I hope you found this book on your own, but my instincts tell me that it's more likely someone gifted it to you. Perhaps you're taking too long to recognize that your impact on others is eroding your relationships and blocking your potential—factors that may be limiting your success and satisfaction in various areas of your life.

You might be wondering, *What qualifies you to write this book?* That's a fair question. I'm a college dropout with no fancy credentials to my name. If that disqualifies me in your eyes, I completely understand. No hard feelings, truly.

What I do have is a wealth of life experience and a passion for coaching, which I hope will resonate with you as we explore the themes of this book together.

God doesn't call the qualified; He qualifies the called.

I'm excited to share a bit about myself as we get started. After spending most of my twenty-five years in the automotive aftermarket at the executive level, I found myself spiraling into burnout. It was a wake-up call that led me to walk away from the corporate world and start my own business—a decision that transformed my life. Today, I am a certified professional coach with over ten thousand hours of practical experience in life, leadership, and business coaching, and I genuinely love what I do.

I am a white, Christian, conservative woman who cherishes my faith and my family. My husband and I reside in Michigan, and we've recently embraced our new identity as empty nesters, navigating this exciting chapter of life.

As a card-carrying member of Generation X, I grew up in the 1970s and '80s with very little supervision. I weathered a few storms and came out stronger. I developed a killer work ethic and a healthy skepticism, all while enjoying what I believe to be the best music ever made.

My family background includes its share of hardship. We didn't have much money growing up, and I faced significant loss when my father was killed in a car accident when I was just fourteen. Since then, I've lost my mother and a sister to cancer. My personal life has had its ups and downs as well—I've been married twice and divorced once, and I have one child, two stepchildren, and three delightful grandchildren so far. Interestingly, I was the oldest of three on my father's side, the middle of five on my mother's, and somewhere in the lower middle of eight with my stepfather's family. And, as fate would have it, I'm not even my father's oldest or second-oldest child! ☺

I share these details for two important reasons: first, to normalize the idea that we all have our own unique forms of dysfunction that contribute to our life stories; and second, to illustrate how my upbringing and experiences shape the examples and references I use throughout this book. While you may not relate to my specific life events (or my Gen X pop culture references), I hope you find resonance in the concepts and lessons they convey. They are not meant to exclude or diminish your lived experiences. Feel free to swap in your own experiences; the concept should still ring true.

You should know that we have a lot in common. I'm someone who gets shit done. I've never met a dragon I couldn't slay, and I used to take pride in that—until I realized the true cost of doing so. A recurring theme in my life is my tendency to hyperfocus on what I need to do during difficult situations, often neglecting the more important question of who I'm being in those moments.

I suspect you might relate. On a good day, people love being around you. But on a bad day—when stress is high and pressure mounts—they tend to avoid you or push back. More often than not, they simply tolerate you because they know you mean well or they are afraid to be without you. But let's be honest: They deserve better, and so do you. If you recognize that your most important people deserve the best of you but are only getting what's left of you, then please read on. You're not alone, and I'm here to help.

I wrote this book as a conversation between friends—but not just any friend. I'm the one who loves you enough to tell you what others won't. This might feel confronting, but I hope you won't let that stop you. I won't hide my own struggles from you; instead, I'll invite you to learn alongside me through my experiences. I will get straight to the point, and it won't be coated in sugar—because let's face it, who has time for that? I don't, and if you're where I think you are—at, or near, the end of your rapidly fraying rope—neither do you.

I believe in practical, proven methodologies that you can implement right now—not just theories. I won't share or recommend anything that I haven't personally tried and successfully used with my clients. This book is for those who are ready to look inward and commit to creating meaningful change. It's written for leaders already familiar with the concepts of conscious leadership. If you're new to this work, that's okay too—you shouldn't have any trouble keeping up.

If you're ready for what's inside, I hope you'll stay the course and revisit these pages from time to time for your ongoing development. This isn't a book you'll outgrow; rather, it's a reference guide you can turn to throughout your life. Keep in mind that you don't have to consume everything at once. Take your time, and allow yourself the space to reflect, absorb, and apply what resonates with you. I'm here to support you every step of the way. If you find yourself resisting what's inside or forming strong objections, don't rush to conclude that it isn't for you. Instead, take a pause. Come back again later with a fresh perspective. You might discover insights that resonate more deeply upon a second look.

I invite you to visit maybeitsmebook.com to access bonus content and digital downloads that are specifically designed to enhance your reading experience. These resources will provide additional support as you work through the exercises and reflections in each chapter.

Let's dive in with curiosity and openness, ready to uncover the potential that's been waiting within you all along. I'm truly honored to be part of your journey.

One last thing—I'm not here to judge you.

I see you.

I get you.

I am you.

Let's go!

Chapter 1

WELCOME TO THE END OF YOUR RAPIDLY FRAYING ROPE

If you've found your way to this book, it's likely because you feel stuck and are struggling to move forward in some aspect of your life—whether it's your relationships, your career, or your life. You might even be at a breaking point, teetering on the edge of losing something big—or worse, watching something unravel right before your eyes.

You've tried everything in your power to solve your problems in the way you know how: pushing through, working harder, and doing more. Yet despite your efforts, things seem to be getting worse. This doesn't make sense to you, because you've always been able to work your way out of a problem. As you look to the future, you're starting to realize that what got you here won't get you there.

I know this from personal experience. I was the kind of leader who was so sure I could solve every problem by working my way out of it (and usually I did). But solving problems this way left me at the edge of burning out and asleep to how my results-oriented behavior was impacting others.

For much of my adult life, I was chasing an elusive goal, not fully aware of what I was seeking—I only knew I believed it was *there*. I thought that once I reached this distant, ideal version of my life, the pressure would ease, and I could finally enjoy the fruits of my labor. I envisioned focusing on what truly mattered and becoming the person I knew I was meant to be. So I settled for good, convincing myself that eventually I would work my way to great.

I was wrong.

What I was truly chasing was a sense of peace and fulfillment. What I didn't realize was that peace and fulfillment could only be found *here*—in the present moment. It was available all along; I just needed to learn where to look. I came to understand that by simply stopping when I felt a moment of relief, I was missing the opportunity to experience true peace, which requires a fundamentally different mindset and skill set.

I see this same cycle in many of my clients: They know they aren't achieving the outcomes they desire, yet they continue the same patterns because it's all they know. Meanwhile, they believe that the problem—the thing that's keeping them from what they really want—is some external factor that's working against them: an overbooked calendar, a demanding client or boss, an incompetent team, or a family who just doesn't understand.

Sound familiar? If I know you like I think I do, you're starting to wonder if maybe the problem isn't them.

Maybe it's you.

Coming to this realization can be challenging, but it has the potential to change your life. I'm here to guide you through it. In my coaching business, I focus on working with highly responsible, well-meaning, results-driven individuals who often believe that the issues they face stem from everyone and everything else.

In my decades of leading and coaching, I've discovered a better approach—one that won't cost you your job, your marriage, your health, your relationships, or your sanity. In fact, it has the potential to improve all of them and more.

What do you have to lose by giving this approach a try? All I'm asking is that you read this book and put in some effort—something that comes naturally to you. The truth is, if you don't make a change, you have a lot to lose.

And if you're one of the fortunate few who aren't at the end of your rope, the work is still relevant for you too. The same principles apply, and the next level of results is just on the other side of this effort.

Before I ask you to do some hard things, let's confront the reality of your situation and explore how your current approach may be creating problems across your life. As you review the upcoming sections, I encourage you to actively engage with the material: Mark up the pages, underline what resonates with you, strike through statements that don't apply, and put question marks next to anything you're unsure about. Those questions are excellent opportunities to seek perspective later from someone you trust.

You Mean Well, but You Know You're Rubbing People the Wrong Way

You set out to have a positive impact, but—quite frankly—you know some people think you're kind of an asshole (or a control freak, tough cookie, bossy pants, firecracker, or straight shooter). One of my clients once said she was aware that working with her felt like touching a hot stove. You're convinced that the good intentions you hold excuse any behavior that makes it really hard for people to connect with you, work with you, and feel supported by you. You get good out of yourself and others, but you're struggling to achieve great consistently because you're not convinced that changing your ways is worth it.

Your Loved Ones Notice How Out of Alignment You Are

Your fingers are crossed, hoping your loved ones don't notice how bad things have gotten—but they do. They see how stressed you are, they watch you take on more, and they suffer the consequences of your lack of time and energy. When they bring up how your actions are impacting your relationship, it makes you feel exposed and raw. You might get defensive, shut down completely, or live in a state of denial; you're convinced you'll get it under control if they'll just give you another shot to make things right.

You've Exhausted the Patience of Those Closest to You

At best, your loved ones are frustrated with what they experience as your mismanagement of your time, energy, and priorities; at worst, they've had enough. Checking emails during family dinner, missing the kids' soccer games, and canceling plans with friends have become the expectations, not the exceptions.

Everything You Do Is in Service of Those You Love, but Something Is Getting Lost in Translation

The greatest irony of all is that you continue to push yourself toward your breaking point in service of the people you love and care about. You take on the extra project because you know your team member is already overworked; you put in the late hours because your next promotion means you can afford that vacation for your family. But your overcommitment is leaving you drained of time and energy, and those closest to you can feel it.

You Resent Others for Not Understanding

You become frustrated when those around you don't give you grace for how much you're taking on. Can't they see how much you're carrying around? The truth is, they can't. You haven't let them in, so they have no idea how much your responsibilities are weighing on you. All they can feel is the lack of connection that's resulted from your near-constant burnout.

You're Smart, Successful, and Woefully Unsatisfied

You're struggling to get to the next level and can feel the weight of the world on your shoulders—and it's crushing you. You're constantly overcommitted, have high value for responsibility and achievement, and have become the poster child for busy. Despite having something to do nearly every minute of the day, you struggle to find meaning or satisfaction in any of it. Your life is passing you by.

You Refuse to Admit Defeat, but You Can't Get It All Done

You're terrified of letting others down, but you can't bring yourself to ask for help. Your drive for results and enthusiasm for control leaves you trying to do everything yourself; it doesn't help that you love a challenge and say yes to nearly every opportunity to solve a problem that comes your way.

Your Relationships Are at Risk—or Actively Falling Apart in Front of Your Eyes

For me, this was the hardest pill to swallow and the catalyst for changing my own life.

It was 6:00 p.m., and I was on the phone having another (urgent) after-hours conversation with the company president, pacing around the kitchen while my fifteen-year-old son was waiting for me to pick him up from my parents' house. He texted to see if I wanted his papa to bring him home. I said no; picking him up was my job. "I'll be there soon," I replied.

What felt like the most important thing in the moment—the conversation with my boss—was preventing me from my duties as a mom, yet that conversation is now so inconsequential that I can't even remember what we were talking about. All I know is that more than an hour after I told my son I'd be right there, I was still on the phone when he walked through the front door.

Shit. I finally ended the call. "I said I'd come get you," I barked, as if the problem was that he didn't wait long enough.

I could tell something was wrong. Naturally, I made it all about me and assumed he was upset that I was so late (again). I started talking about me and my day in a shameful attempt to gain some sympathy.

Then his eyes welled up.

"What's up?" I asked.

"I don't want you to be mad, but . . ." he said.

After a long silent pause, he continued, "I want to transfer to a different school."

I was baffled. Why would he think I'd be mad about this? I couldn't wrap my mind around why my son was scared to tell me about his life and desires. "Oh, honey," I said, "why would I be mad about that?"

"I know it's important to you," he said.

"*You're* what's important to me. Let's back up. What's going on? How did you get here?"

Long story short, he made a really courageous decision to leave the Catholic school he was attending and transfer to a public school and, more importantly, had decided that today was the day he was going to tell me about it. And instead of being there for him when he needed me, I'd left him waiting.

And it wasn't the first time. It was becoming a habit for me to barely get to a high school basketball game in time for the national anthem just to duck into a quiet hallway to take an urgent call. I'd said yes to so much that I was stretched unreasonably thin. In trying to be invested in everything, I was invested in nothing.

How many deadlines have you missed because you were overcommitted? How many ball games or band recitals have you missed because something seemingly more important came up? How many times have you gotten upset with your kids because, well, they're kids, and they were noisy in the back seat while you were taking a phone call after hours? This kind of behavior can only go on for so long before you cause long-term damage to the relationship.

WHAT'S STANDING IN YOUR WAY

The problem you've likely faced when trying to change your situation on your own is that it's hard—and for good reason. There's a lot standing in your way, and frankly, most of it isn't your fault. But it is your responsibility. Let's explore three things that have led you to believe that the problem isn't you:

1. The many things you've been conditioned to believe but didn't know you could challenge
2. The illusion of control
3. The five self-sabotaging beliefs harming your life, relationships, and results

BUILDING AWARENESS AROUND WHAT WE'VE BEEN CONDITIONED TO BELIEVE

Part of what's holding you back (and what is now your duty to overcome) is that you've learned or inherited some beliefs and habits that are actively contributing to your suffering. This is completely natural. As humans, we are heavily influenced by those around us, particularly authority figures, as we absorb what they say and do without question. Psychologists call this phenomenon introjection: the unconscious internalization of values, attitudes, beliefs, and personality traits learned from authority figures, often as a defense mechanism or coping strategy.

Consider this relatable example for high achievers: Perhaps growing up, you absorbed the belief that working tirelessly and sacrificing personal time is the only way to succeed, because you observed a parent or mentor who consistently prioritized work over everything else. This belief, though intended to drive success, can lead to overcommitment and burnout if not consciously examined and adjusted.

Introjection is a natural part of psychological development, but in some cases, it can create lasting negative consequences, like the ones we'll explore on the next few pages. I encourage you to treat the next few pages like a workbook; take notes, circle or put checkmarks next to what resonates, and mark up the pages.

We've Been Taught That Problems Exist Outside Ourselves, Not Within Ourselves

When asked what causes stress, most people will point to an external factor, person, or circumstance: an unrelenting boss, an ungrateful child, a bank account balance. Similarly, we point to external factors when asked what would bring us joy: a raise, your boss's recognition, your family's appreciation.

The problem with that thought process is that it reinforces the biggest lie we are told—that circumstances outside us are the cause of how we feel. And since most of us want to feel better than we do, it makes perfect sense that we would set out to control the things we believe are contributing to the stress we feel.

We Were Taught to Place High Value on Achievement, and We've Been Rewarded for It

Even as a child, you were likely a high performer. Your motivation to perform could have been fear of judgment from others (you wanted to appear to have it all together and not draw attention to yourself or your family) or fear of uncertainty (you might have grown up in an unstable household and responsibility could have been a coping mechanism you used to create a sense of predictability).

You were likely praised for your accomplishments as a child; as your parents, teachers, or coaches celebrated your report card and sense of responsibility, they were unknowingly instilling in you a high value for (and sometimes obsession with) success, performance, and results. Now, your identity is mostly fueled by a job well done and the praise that comes along with it.

We Were Taught to Have High Concern for Others—but Higher Value for Personal Responsibility

Everything you do is in service of the people you love and care about. But in moments of stress, you prioritize your responsibilities (meeting your sales quota, hitting a deadline, providing for your family) over the people in your life. You might be frustrated by how hard you're working to enrich the lives of those you care about as you look around and see how many important relationships in your life are struggling.

We Were Told That Asking for Help Is a Sign of Weakness

Because you have high concern for others and an identity fueled by responsibility, you don't want to burden others with your problems. Even when you're struggling, you'd rather continue to shoulder more than reach out for support. This can leave you feeling both overworked and isolated as you try to do it all by yourself.

We Were Told That Underperforming Isn't an Option

You are known as someone who will never drop the ball, no matter how many of them you're trying to keep in the air at once. For you, not living up to your commitments isn't an option, so you'll find a way to fulfill them, no matter the cost to yourself or those around you.

We Were Told That Getting Things Done Right Is the Ultimate Goal

You'd love other people to believe you have it all together, so you strive to create an outward identity that leaves people amazed at how much you can handle. Meanwhile, on the inside you're drowning under your responsibilities and gasping for air. You're harder on yourself than anyone else is, and even if you wouldn't call yourself a perfectionist, your personal goal for yourself is excellence—so you're constantly striving to do more, be better, and improve.

We Were Encouraged to Be the Best

And the reality is, you are probably better than most people at many things. At this point, your ability has become your greatest liability. You're quick to jump at every opportunity to contribute because you're a highly capable individual who can achieve outcomes faster and better than most. The result is that you are carrying a huge burden—and even though it's become nearly impossible to carry it all, you continue to say yes and inch closer to the edge of burnout. Meanwhile, you're hoping the important people in your life don't notice.

We Were Taught to Persevere

You truly believe that if you can just get through this milestone (the new project, the merger at work, this abnormally busy season), everything will sort itself out; you'll find your footing and finally be able to prioritize what's really important once things calm down. The problem is that once these pressures ease up, new pressures are in the queue, ready to replace them.

We Were Told That We Could Control Things That Are Outside Our Control

It is completely human to get caught up in things we can't directly control—especially other people and what they think, say, and do. When we set out to control these things, we create power imbalances that invite powerlessness and defensiveness in others. Learning to identify what we can and can't control is a crucial skill for anyone wanting to experience a high degree of life satisfaction. You may not have been taught this critical skill, but it isn't too late to learn. Let's start now.

COMING TO TERMS WITH THE ILLUSION OF CONTROL

I don't know about you, but I'm not a great passenger in most situations. I don't want to be on the back of a Jet Ski—I want to drive. Feeling as if we are in control provides a certain sense of security, so it makes sense that we might overreach when something that matters to us (a project, a person, our reputation, winning) is at risk.

But most of that risk is manufactured. Yes, there's real risk associated with getting on the back of a Jet Ski while someone else is driving. But the risk in relinquishing control and letting someone else manage the important client relationship is relatively low.

But many of us can't help ourselves. Leaders like us have a high degree of responsibility, and what often follows is an overreliance on control. You're more likely to reach a goal if you have control, right? Not quite.

In the short term, control may get you the results you want. But in the long term, control (and its not-so-distant cousins manipulation and force) spark mere tolerance, avoidance, and resistance in others. Eventually they'll just give up.

How Your Use of Control Is Impacting Those Around You

The real issue you face isn't just a tendency to default to control, force, or manipulation; it's that, in seeking control, you're inadvertently hurting those you care about. Your peers, employees, spouse, children, and friends may be experiencing your need for control in the following ways:

- They feel as though they don't get to have the freedom to learn, fail, and grow.
- They're scared of what might happen if they disappoint you.
- They feel like they need to please you.

- They won't tell you what they really think.
- They don't believe you respect their ideas, thoughts, or opinions, so they save their best thinking for other projects and people.
- They're overreliant on you and don't feel empowered to make even small decisions without your input or approval.

In these ways and more, your decisions and actions are eroding your relationships and, in turn, negatively impacting your quality of life. This is what is contributing to chronic dissatisfaction and relief that never lasts.

I encourage you to take a moment to reflect on the points mentioned above and honestly evaluate how applicable each one is to your situation. Consider dog-earing this page as a reminder to pay closer attention to these aspects. For a more impactful approach, you might also ask a handful of people in your life who will answer truthfully—such as peers, your spouse, family members, or direct reports—how true these statements resonate with them. Their insights could provide valuable perspectives.

EXPOSING THE FIVE SELF-SABOTAGING BELIEFS UNDERMINING YOUR DECISIONS, RELATIONSHIPS, AND RESULTS

While it's important to understand your conditioned beliefs and recognize the control issues you may face, it's more crucial to realize that these issues often stem from self-sabotaging beliefs. This book will help you identify and address how these limiting beliefs promote overcontrol and negatively impact your decisions and relationships. By doing so, you can break free from the patterns that hold you back and move closer to the life you've been chasing.

A self-sabotaging belief is a deeply ingrained assumption or mindset that undermines our potential and hinders us from achieving our goals. Over my decades of experience in leadership and coaching, I have identified five particularly common self-imposed roadblocks that many leaders face. I have also witnessed how working to understand and shift these beliefs can lead to profound and lasting change, resulting in greater satisfaction and success.

At this point, these beliefs may be so embedded in your psyche that you might not even realize you're choosing to hold on to them. They exist as an integral part of your reality, as undeniable as the air you breathe. However, the work we will do together will illuminate how these beliefs contribute to challenges in your life and affect those you care about most.

As you dig into these beliefs, you might notice the similarities between them. Like in a Venn diagram, there will be ways in which these beliefs overlap and distinct unique qualities about each of them. If you find yourself connecting the dots and recognizing those overlaps, know that's all by design.

If you find yourself becoming defensive while reading about these beliefs, ask someone who knows you well for their feedback before discarding what you've read. Your resistance to a belief might indicate there's something to dig into.

Self-Sabotaging Belief #1: You Know What's Right

You likely believe you know what's right—the right way to approach a project, the right choice to make, the right highway to take on your family road trip. You're probably the first person in the meeting to propose a solution, and you likely insist that your idea wins.

You're as equally committed to being right as you are to doing what's right; you have a strong sense of right and wrong and may tend to insist that your idea, opinion, or perspective is the right one.

But what you may not yet see is how your commitment to being right ends up shutting down everyone around you. When you're right, you give others no choice but to be wrong, which leaves the people you care about feeling dejected, inadequate, and unimportant. Not only that, but your rigidness has made you blind to new ideas and perspectives that might improve outcomes.

Self-Sabotaging Belief #2: You Believe the Ends Justify the Means

You're likely an extremely goal-oriented leader—so much so that, in your mind, nothing is more important than achieving your desired outcome. You may justify your bad behavior for the sake of reaching the goal; that's what we're all here for, after all, isn't it?

The problem with this belief is that in the process of working to achieve a result, you end up sacrificing your own character. You do and say things you know you shouldn't so you can get the job done, you become defensive when challenged, and you steamroll or undermine those around you.

When you excuse your behavior ("I had to jump in to take over the project—it was the only way to ensure we'd meet the deadline"), you're justifying your actions in the moment. But deep down, you know you're not living and leading with integrity and are actively causing long-term harm to your relationships and reputation.

Self-Sabotaging Belief #3: You Believe You Can Do Things Better Than Others

You likely think you know better and can perform better than most people—and you probably can. If you're a high-achieving, highly responsible high performer, you can probably run circles around others.

The problem is that when you put your talent on display and demonstrate your capabilities every chance you get, you make everyone around you feel inferior. This behavior positions you as superior to others, which means everyone else is inferior. On top of that, it means you take on a disproportionate amount of work, which adds to your already full plate.

You overwork yourself, but somehow you feel like you're never doing enough; meanwhile, whether you know it or not, your behavior makes other people feel like nothing they do is ever good enough.

Self-Sabotaging Belief #4: You Believe You're Helping

"Helping" is your middle name. You're wildly gifted at seeing the gaps in people, projects, and plans and are quick to offer up advice and ideas, even when not asked. But when you set out to help, you might be doing more harm than good. Before you object, just consider the following.

While well intended and seemingly focused on others, protecting others from the natural consequences of their decisions and actions is not helping—it's enabling. Further, your motivation to help is more about you; you seek to fix what you see as broken or insufficient. Even if you're not aware of it, the people around you likely experience you as a know-it-all, which can invite helplessness and resistance. When you solve all their problems, there's no need for them to learn, think, or grow themselves, and when you push your opinion hard enough, eventually you'll be met with opposition, pitting you against those you care about.

Self-Sabotaging Belief #5: You Believe It's Temporary

And now for the most distressing belief on this list: You believe all this is temporary. You've convinced yourself that all the energy and hard work you're putting in now will eventually lead to some big payoff that will result in your feeling satisfied in the life you've created.

But what you're sacrificing is the life you actually have and the chance at being happy and fulfilled *now*. You settle for *fine* and *good enough*, claiming that once you finish this project / get a promotion / win that big client, things will calm down.

But you've been saying that for a while now, and it's never proven true. Meanwhile, the people you love get pushed to the back burner while you wait for your circumstances to improve, clinging to the belief that eventually things will be different.

INTRODUCING SEVEN CONSCIOUS QUESTIONS TO TRANSFORM YOUR LIFE

Now, let's get to the good news: Your beliefs are not set in stone; they are fluid, and you have the power to influence them. I'm going to introduce you to seven conscious questions that will help you retrain your brain and counteract the negative impact of those five sabotaging beliefs on your decisions, relationships, and results.

But what exactly is a conscious question? A conscious question is one that invites deep reflection and awareness, encouraging you to explore your thoughts, feelings, desires, and experiences with intention. Unlike surface-level inquiries, conscious questions prompt you to deeply examine your situation, helping you gain clarity about your options and the impact you want to have on your life and those around you. They serve as tools for self-discovery, guiding you toward insights that can transform your perspective and your life.

These questions have been carefully curated from over a decade of coaching high-performing leaders. Each question holds the potential to accelerate your best life, and together, they are a superpower. From my personal experience and observing the transformation of so many others, I have seen how these questions enable leaders to get out of their own way and expand what is possible in their lives. The best part? You can achieve this without needing to change your spouse, kids, boss, or job.

These questions serve as tools for both looking forward—helping you navigate unresolved issues and moments of feeling stuck—and looking backward to learn from past experiences. By applying this assessment to past situations, you can discern what went well and should be repeated as well as identify opportunities for growth in similar future scenarios. Simply adjust the questions to past tense for retrospective analysis.

Later in this book, we will delve deeper into each of these questions—why they are important, why they deserve your time and attention, and how to master them. For now, I'll simply list them.

1. What am I feeling, and what are my emotions signaling?
2. What is true for me?
3. What might be true for others?
4. What is the whole truth, even if it's inconvenient?
5. What do I want for myself, and why is that important to me?
6. What impact do I want to make?
7. What does it look like to take 100 percent personal responsibility, no more, no less?

WHAT TO EXPECT NEXT

I wrote this book for well-meaning leaders like you who are sometimes (maybe often) referred to as assholes. I say that with all the love in the world; I am one of you, after all. And while we are usually well intentioned, often our impact is harmful—and it's time to change.

I'm not suggesting that you *completely* change who you are. The world needs people like us: well-meaning people who are willing to do what others won't, who get the job done, who advance things that would otherwise be stalled. I want you to continue leveraging your greatest strengths. But I also want to show you how you can achieve great results, experience more satisfaction, and leave a positive, lasting impact on others.

Imagine a life where you're as effective as you are now, but not at the cost of your health, happiness, and relationships. That life is possible, and I'm here to show you how to create it for yourself.

The first truth I'm going to ask you to accept is one of the hardest to swallow: There's no one to blame for the issues you're experiencing in your life. Your life and all your results are of your own creation. While I recognize that most of us have our fair share of imperfect circumstances—and maybe some more than others—your life is the sum total of your decisions and actions. You have likely convinced yourself that if you could just work harder, find more hours in the day, or learn more life hacks, things would get better. But if you continue to try to outwork yourself from this mess, you will find yourself worse off a year from now. You don't have a *how* problem. What you have is a *who* problem, and that *who* is you.

It's critical that you accept this truth in order for the rest of the work we do to take root. If you continue reading with the belief that other people or your circumstances are the source of your suffering, I can't help you. And quite frankly, no one else can either.

Here's a second, more uplifting truth: When you are the problem, you are also the solution.

Most of the problems you're experiencing are a construct of your own mind. Your decisions are the products of what you think and believe—both of which are within your direct control. This book will teach you how to influence your beliefs in a way that will drastically change how you experience your life—and how others experience you too.

Through the rest of this book, I'm going to help you come to terms with and create awareness around the five self-sabotaging beliefs that are undermining your success despite your best intentions and hard work. Becoming aware of these beliefs is critical to your transformation, which is only sustainable when done from the inside out.

You might identify with some more than others, and that's okay. Don't get hung up if a few sentences don't apply to you. Focus on what does, and carry that forward. I also advise getting a second opinion before dismissing an idea—the people closest to us often see us more clearly than we see ourselves. If you find yourself becoming defensive or resistant, that's a sign something is hitting a nerve. If you're not ready to examine it, put down the book and come back later when you're able to.

I invite you to approach this section with an open mind and a sense of optimism. Remember, every discovery you make about these self-limiting beliefs is a step toward understanding and growth. By identifying and confronting these patterns, you're setting the foundation for what comes next.

After exploring those five beliefs, we'll dive into the seven conscious questions that have the potential to transform your life. I understand that's a bold statement, but I've witnessed their impact firsthand. These questions address the core of your challenges, empower you to create lasting change, and guide you from self-sabotage—where you currently find yourself—to self-mastery, where your best life awaits. This approach is grounded in neuroscience, positive psychology, cognitive behavioral therapy, and my personal experience coaching hundreds of leaders like you.

The work you do in this book will amplify your results, turn pressure into purpose, and help you find levels of peace and satisfaction you didn't know were possible. In doing so, you will finally feel like you've done enough, have enough, and are enough.

One of my all-time favorite quotes by Maya Angelou perfectly summarizes what I'm asking of you:

Do the best you can until you know better.
Then, when you know better, do better.

I'm going to help you make positive, lasting changes in your life. Let's get to work. Together, we'll work through the obstacles and lay the groundwork for lasting success and fulfillment.

Chapter 2

SELF-SABOTAGING BELIEF #1

You Believe You Know What's Right

Tony is generous and hardworking. He's the first to pick up the tab and the last to ask for help. He considers himself highly responsible and hasn't relied on anyone but himself since he was a teenager. He's proud of his independence, which means he tends to struggle in partnership at work and at home.

At work, he has been passed over for promotions because at the next level, they need leaders, not managers. Tony refuses to deal with the drama that comes with those people—you know, the ones from the generation that doesn't have a work ethic. Who has time for all their feelings?

Tony has a reputation for leading with an iron fist. When people do (reluctantly) collaborate with him, they're frustrated by his lack of clarity: It's nearly impossible to know what he wants, but it's very clear when he's displeased because they didn't get it right.

When shit eventually hits the fan, he has ample evidence—documentation, saved emails—that prove the failure wasn't his fault. Eventually he resorts to doing the work himself, leaving him buried and bottlenecking other projects.

At home, his wife feels more like a dependent than a partner. He doesn't include her in big decisions, seek her opinion, or disclose his needs and challenges. As far as he's concerned, it's not her problem or, quite frankly, any of her business.

He loves his wife, but she wants more, and Tony can't figure out how to give her what she wants. For Tony, emotional unavailability is a source of power and control; showing emotion is a sign of weakness, and he can't figure out how to give his wife what she wants without being vulnerable—which he refuses to do.

His marriage has suffered from his behavior for a while, but this time there's a real consequence on the line: Tony's wife is threatening to leave if something doesn't change.

But here's the problem: Tony is convinced he's right. Not just with his wife but in every situation. For Tony, being right is a form of control, and since lack of control makes him feel insecure, he finds a way to feel right in every situation—which leaves everyone around him no place to be but wrong. Despite working so hard to feel secure, Tony has created this win-lose arrangement in most of his relationships—and he's about to lose all of them.

We've all been around people like Tony—morally superior leaders who are insistent that their perspective, idea, or opinion is the right one. Operating in a state of self-righteousness, these leaders tend to ignore or diminish the inputs of others and, even worse, get defensive or activated when challenged about their own opinions. They will often weaponize results, data, facts, or their beliefs to do what is right, just, or fair.

Focused on winning at all costs, leaders like Tony unfortunately (and ironically) set themselves up to lose; their self-orientation and hyperfixation on proving their own point (even when no one is asking them to) leaves them rigid and inflexible to being influenced by others. They tend to force their own outcome and justify their actions because of their status or position without concern for how their behavior impacts others.

But here's the question: Are you one of them?

Leaders who believe it is most important to be right and do what is right end up being rigid and righteous, overpower others, and sacrifice their relationships and long-term effectiveness by inviting resistance.

Most leaders who think this way do so because it served them well up to a certain point. After all, being results oriented and self-righteous aren't inherently mean-spirited traits. In fact, this approach is so popular because it produces immediate results, moves things forward, and creates momentum. Leaders who rely on these tendencies are driven by a set of beliefs that are rooted in moral integrity. If you are motivated to be right and do what is right, you might believe the following:

- Accuracy, accountability, and justice are important values.
- Admitting fault is a sign of weakness.
- Sometimes it's easier to just do things yourself, especially when they need to be done right.
- You need to do whatever it takes to drive results and move things forward.
- If people just see the evidence you have, it will persuade them to think differently.
- A competitive spirit is helpful.
- There will always be winners and losers.
- It's important that other people agree with you and your opinion.
- It is your job to know or have the answers.

Trouble arises when these beliefs become a liability—when they stop working for you and start working against you. Leaders who exhibit these tendencies often feel an intense pressure to perform. Backed into a corner with no other options, they become threatened by anything or anyone who stands in their way.

In order to get what they want and need (support, buy-in, action, results), leaders are under the impression that they must fight for it or force it. As much as this approach can deliver temporary results, it's not sustainable. Even *the good fight* is still a fight—and every fight bears a cost.

THE COSTS OF THINKING IN TERMS OF RIGHT AND WRONG

There is always a cost when you think you're right, exert power over others, or use force to get your way. In the moment, you might get what you want—which helps justify your actions and reinforce your behavior. But in the long term, you're wreaking havoc on your life, your relationships, and your results. Here's how:

You're Jeopardizing Your Reputation

Operating from a moral high ground often feels overly direct or abrasive on the receiving end. When you're more committed to being right than being effective, you end up undermining your own goal of being positively seen by others and instead are perceived as egocentric, smug, and downright difficult.

Your Relationships Are Crumbling

When you insist on proving that you're right, what you're also doing is proving that others are wrong. This is most damaging when being right or proving a point doesn't add value and only serves to shut down or diminish the contributions of others. Your fear-based leadership style strips power from others and likely makes them feel inferior, insecure, and intimidated.

Other People Are Resistant to Your Ideas

When you resist alternate perspectives and attempt to convince others that your ideas and beliefs are the right ones, you invite resistance in return. Even if your idea is better, people don't like things being forced upon them. People around you likely feel like they have to fight you to be heard or valued, and when that becomes too exhausting, they simply avoid or just tolerate you.

You're Damaging Your Mental and Physical Health

The best way to characterize the emotional experience of this approach is cross. You may find yourself living in a near-constant state of annoyance or irritation, which shows up in your body as an increased heart rate or blood pressure, a clenched jaw, perspiration, and tightness in your chest. Harboring feelings of fear, worry, obsession, anger, frustration, and hostility can feel like living your day-to-day life under a black cloud of bitterness and resentment. And you're not alone: A survey I conducted years ago asked respondents to reflect on being frequently agitated, frustrated, or moody. A whopping 40 percent reported, "Yes! All the time, and I don't know why," while only 9 percent disagreed or couldn't relate.

You're Stifling Innovation, Creativity, and Discovery

Another reason this approach is widely used is that humans crave certainty—it puts a leader's mind at ease to think they know or can predict an outcome. Sadly, knowing shuts down learning and curiosity and invites resistance to anything to the contrary. This puts you in opposition to any perspective that's different from your own and prioritizes *your* outcome over the *best* outcome.

You're Forcing Others to Lose

You likely enjoy fierce competition and embrace binary thinking (win-lose, right-wrong, good-bad), but this black-and-white mentality means anything that isn't working with you is working against you. When you label other people and ideas as a threat, you naturally take on a protective posture, and you end up being surrounded by people who are too afraid to act, share their ideas, or create meaningful change. Proving that you're right feels good in the moment, but the inherent result is that someone else is always wrong—and that leadership style isn't productive or effective.

You've Stopped Learning and Growing

Failure is a breeding ground for growth, and when you pass up an opportunity to admit to a mistake or be wrong, you're also passing up an opportunity to learn from those situations. You likely also have a reputation for being a my-way-or-the-highway kind of leader, which means others are less likely to share their input for fear of interrogation, rejection, or humiliation. When you're convinced your idea is the right idea, you pass up the opportunity to learn from or be influenced by others.

You're Not Leading; You're Commanding

No matter how powerful you think your facts, data, and logic are, you're failing to influence others. You may be getting the results you want, but when you already have all the answers, you're failing to develop and get the best out of others. And worse, you condition others to defer to you instead of thinking for themselves, which adds to the increasingly uneven distribution of tasks.

REFLECT ON YOUR LEARNING

As you conclude your exploration of this belief, take a moment to reflect on your insights. Confronting these beliefs can feel uncomfortable and may evoke feelings of vulnerability. Remember, this experience is a shared human struggle, and recognizing the costs associated with these beliefs is a vital step toward personal growth.

Use the prompts below to guide your self-reflection. Approach these questions with kindness and without judgment.

Self-Assessment: To what degree is this belief causing problems in your life? *Make notes about where this belief shows up in your life or relationships.*

- ☐ Not at all.
- ☐ I can see it in a few places, but it's not creating issues as far as I can tell.
- ☐ It's actively causing stress in my relationships or hindering results.
- ☐ I'm about to lose something big if I don't make changes soon.

Key Insights: What resonated with you in this chapter?
Note any specific ideas or realizations that stood out to you.

Personal Impact: Where do you see this belief holding you back?
Reflect on specific areas or situations in your life.

Relationships at Risk: Which relationships are most affected by this belief and its associated behavior? *Consider how this belief impacts your interactions with others.*

Consequences of Inaction: What is at risk if you choose to ignore this problem? *Think about the potential outcomes of maintaining this belief.*

If this chapter felt heavy for you, allow yourself some time to digest it before moving forward. Remember, personal growth is not a race; it's about becoming better—for yourself, your relationships, and the world around you.

Chapter 3

SELF-SABOTAGING BELIEF #2

You Believe the Ends Justify the Means

Jeremy might be the best salesperson you've ever met. He's motivated, charming, and brilliant. He's broken just about every sales record (and perhaps a few rules along the way). He's intent on being the company's top sales performer and isn't letting anything stop him.

Jeremy's identity is tightly wound around his work, so when closing a sale is in jeopardy, he takes it personally and becomes desperate. His approach with his customers quickly devolves to include flattery, control, and force; naturally, it repels people rather than winning them over. They can feel the shift in his demeanor—they hear his sarcastic, smug tone; they smell his desperation; they sense his focus on his own needs, commission, and ego.

Jeremy knows he shouldn't behave this way, but he can't help himself. Luckily, he has enough charm and charisma to restore relationships with his customers when he goes too far.

Jeremy's behavior stems from his laser focus on winning. He won't let anyone stand in the way of what he wants, regardless of the cost. When he pays the price, he justifies the impact he has on those around him as a necessary part of the process.

Jeremy has been passed over for a promotion into leadership on more than one occasion; other candidates were less accomplished, maybe even less talented, but they knew how to be team players. Jeremy doesn't see his coworkers as teammates; he sees them as pawns and uses them to his advantage.

Jeremy's home life regularly takes a back seat. At any time, you might find him going in to work early, staying late, working weekends, and taking sales calls on vacation. He knows this hurts his family, but he believes what he is doing is necessary to provide for them.

He is involved in his son's life as his soccer coach but regularly finds himself in the hot seat with other parents who think he needs to focus more on camaraderie and less on winning. His son has noticed the tension and has started to withdraw from the sport he used to love, and his wife is embarrassed every time she hears parents talking about his temperament.

Jeremy is on thin ice in every facet of his life. He doesn't know it yet, but unless something changes, he's going to feel what it's like to lose big.

You can likely think of someone in your life who displays behavior like Jeremy's—someone who is often so laser focused on the task at hand that they justify their own poor behavior and even act out of alignment with their own values for the sake of achieving the goal. These leaders are often in a state of self-deception, convinced that what they are doing is acceptable and ignoring or rationalizing any evidence to the contrary.

Leaders like Jeremy have usually earned opportunities in their careers because of their productivity; at the end of the day, they know how to get shit done. But the experience of working with self-deceived leaders doesn't always feel like a victory; these leaders often display controlling behaviors, avoid accountability, and blame others for shortcomings or failures.

Leaders who believe reaching a goal is more important than anything else justify their bad behavior for the sake of reaching the outcome and end up sacrificing their own character and become defensive when challenged.

As you were reading Jeremy's story, did you see a little (or a lot) of yourself in his experience? If so, you likely got to this point because, like Jeremy, something about this belief was working for you. Leaders who are willing to get the work done at all costs are highly prolific and are often praised and trusted for their ability to produce results. If you're one of them, you are likely driven by a sense of duty to achieve a goal and live for that sweet yet fleeting moment of satisfaction when you've achieved it. That emotional payoff, while temporary, justifies the journey to getting there, however hellish it was.

If you saw yourself in Jeremy's story, you might believe the following:

- You perform better under pressure.
- You are responsible for your life and your results.
- High-pressure situations are opportunities to shine.
- Your stakeholders don't care how you get it done, just that you do.
- You have to scramble some eggs to make an omelet.
- Creating disruption and challenging the status quo produce innovation and big thinking.
- As long as you're in control, everything will be fine.

But at some point, those beliefs started limiting you rather than empowering you, and your ability to perform became a liability. The constant pressure to produce the results you were known for mutated into an unmanageable amount of stress. To compensate, you started justifying behavior that you knew wasn't in alignment with who you are because it propelled you toward the goal faster. You figured that once you reached the goal, the pressure valve would release. When it didn't, you continued to focus on winning despite the high-stress, high-pressure environment you've created for yourself.

But eventually, something had to give—and it couldn't be the goal. You'd become known for your ability to deliver, and you were unwilling to compromise that. Instead, you started to compromise other important parts of your life—your values, your relationships, your well-being—justifying behaviors that were out of character for the sake of achieving. When the pressure is so intense that you need relief, you find control by taking charge, taking on more than you should, and exerting power over others—all of which leave you feeling morally conflicted and come with serious costs.

THE COSTS OF DOING WHATEVER IT TAKES TO REACH THE GOAL

Every competitor knows that winning comes at a price. The Herculean effort it takes to perform with intensity and consistency may feel worth it in the short term, but the damage your win-at-all-costs orientation is having on you and those around you is likely jeopardizing your relationships, your happiness, and your health. Here's how:

You're Emotionally Out of Touch with Yourself and Others

Your tendency to disconnect from emotion means you often miss important emotional cues in yourself and others. When you fail to pick up on the emotional experiences of those around you, you're unable to express empathy and build rapport and trust. You may come across as disinterested and unresponsive to others. Your failure to tune in to your own emotional needs negatively impacts your decisions, relationships, and physical and mental health.

Other People Experience You as Cold

When you take a goal-oriented approach to people and problems, you run the risk that others will experience you as cold, detached, and transactional, and they may feel used in the process. This has likely made it difficult for you to forge deep, meaningful relationships or is putting the relationships you do have at risk.

You Aren't Getting the Best Out of Others

When you are hyperfixated on results and see people as projects or problems (instead of humans filled with potential), those around you will work below their potential as they defer to you. At the office, this behavior could be impacting your team and peers; at home, it could be limiting your kids' development. Even worse, this issue is self-perpetuating—with everyone else working below their potential, you'll never shed the need to do more and pick up the slack, leaving you and everyone else stuck.

You're Out of Integrity

Your focus on doing, doing, doing comes at the expense of finding joy and satisfaction on the way there. Life is simultaneously crushing you and passing you by. On top of that, your pattern of compromising your values, standards, and reputation means you're living out of alignment with who you really are, adding to the undercurrent of dissatisfaction in your life.

REFLECT ON YOUR LEARNING

As you conclude your exploration of this belief, take a moment to reflect on your insights. Confronting these beliefs can feel uncomfortable and may evoke feelings of vulnerability. Remember, this experience is a shared human struggle, and recognizing the costs associated with these beliefs is a vital step toward personal growth.

Use the prompts below to guide your self-reflection. Approach these questions with kindness and without judgment.

Self-Assessment: To what degree is this belief causing problems in your life? *Make notes about where this belief shows up in your life or relationships.*

- ☐ Not at all.
- ☐ I can see it in a few places, but it's not creating issues as far as I can tell.
- ☐ It's actively causing stress in my relationships or hindering results.
- ☐ I'm about to lose something big if I don't make changes soon.

Key Insights: What resonated with you in this chapter? *Note any specific ideas or realizations that stood out to you.*

____

____

Personal Impact: Where do you see this belief holding you back? *Reflect on specific areas or situations in your life.*

____

____

Relationships at Risk: Which relationships are most affected by this belief and its associated behavior? *Consider how this belief impacts your interactions with others.*

Consequences of Inaction: What is at risk if you choose to ignore this problem? *Think about the potential outcomes of maintaining this belief.*

If this chapter felt heavy for you, allow yourself some time to digest it before moving forward. Remember, personal growth is not a race; it's about becoming better—for yourself, your relationships, and the world around you.

Chapter 4

SELF-SABOTAGING BELIEF #3

You Believe You Can Do Things Better Than Others

Ellie might be of the most talented leaders in her firm. She consistently receives high marks for both her skills and her ability to create results—yet equally as consistently, she receives peer feedback about her inability to connect and collaborate with her team. While everyone at the office knows she is the firm's top performer, no one trusts her. She appears self-motivated and out to prove herself, but no matter what she accomplishes, it is never enough for her.

On the surface, her behavior appears to be selfish: Under stress, she routinely takes on the majority of the responsibility, which suggests that she doesn't trust others to get the job done. When she does bring others into the work, she micromanages. She is rarely satisfied with anyone's performance and is quick to criticize. On her worst days, she claims victory for the team's results and casts blame on others when the work falls short.

Underneath the surface is a different story. Ellie is an anxious, insecure leader who is deeply scared of falling short. That fear drives her to obsessively focus on proving she is valuable and competent—which meant she's completely lost sight of the human part of work: developing and working through others.

When challenged, she claims she is sparing her teammates the burden of responsibility. But in reality, she isn't alleviating a burden; she is causing one. When a deadline or goal is threatened, Ellie pushes everyone—especially herself—to a breaking point. Failure is not an option.

In those high-stress moments, Ellie becomes overly direct and unreasonably demanding. At first, her team forgives her behavior and tolerates her control issues because when not under stress, Ellie is a pleasant and wickedly talented peer. But because her behavior persists, her team has been passed over for challenging and important projects. Her behavior is now impacting their opportunities and can no longer be tolerated.

Her personal life doesn't tell a much better story. Ellie's best friend, June, has become her dumping ground for her self-disappointment. Ellie is constantly complaining to June about all the ways she isn't enough: Her body, her relationship, and her home aren't satisfactory, and they've become all June hears about.

So here is Ellie: a track record of success a mile long, expecting to get promoted, and on the edge of losing her job, her best friend, and the life she's worked so hard to build.

You can likely think of someone like Ellie: a superstar at work who is equally focused on performing and *proving* they can perform. Leaders like Ellie are laser focused on delivering results and let very little get in their way. Outwardly, high performers like Ellie appear extremely confident and highly capable. They might even be indispensable. These leaders provide immense value, and while they sometimes act out of character under stress, they're dependable. You can count on them to have everything under control.

But underneath that confident exterior is a world of bitterness, insecurity, and obligation. People like Ellie live dutifully compliant lives in service of the external authority figures (bosses, parents, rules, deadlines, policies) that govern their expectations of themselves. They frequently take on more than they can reasonably handle as they chase the emotional satisfaction of feeling valued and needed by those around them.

But that emotional satisfaction is fleeting, and what inevitably follows is a sea of *should*—"I should do this; I should be doing more; I shouldn't slow down"—leaving people like Ellie perpetually dissatisfied, racing toward burnout, and exhausted by the weight of their (mostly) self-induced pressure.

Still, they overcommit because they believe they can do it faster and better than others—and they might be right. But by choosing themselves, they're stripping power from others and sacrificing both relationships and human potential. While they don't intentionally harm others or behave badly, their decisions are often self-serving and inconsiderate, and they may unintentionally hold others to their own unachievable high standards. And since they're so fixated on their own capabilities, they pass up opportunities to bring others into the work. When they do, their transactional leadership style requires command-and-control measures to get the result they want. When all is said and done, they excuse their behavior by claiming, "It's not personal" and hiding behind their responsibility and results.

What's worse is that this kind of leader causes their own emotional prison: This leader is convinced that their value comes from what they're *doing*, not who they're *being*, so they've created a version of reality where their value hinges on their ability to deliver results. They keep doing, doing, doing: taking action, taking credit, and surviving off the temporary reward of being good enough—for now.

Can you relate?

Leaders who believe they can do things better than others and prove it through their performance aren't good team players and end up overextending themselves while never feeling like they've done enough.

If you believe you know better and can do better than most people—and you enjoy outperforming and outpacing others—you might also believe the following:

- Doing things as well as you possibly can will bring enjoyment or fulfillment.
- Being goal oriented, driven, and committed is how to succeed in life.
- Control provides safety and security, and sharing power weakens your position.
- Goals need to be big and audacious, or they're not worth it.
- Nothing valuable comes from an experience if it didn't produce the desired result.
- It's not personal.
- It will get done better or faster if you do it yourself; deadlines don't care who gets it done.
- It is a waste of time to collaborate when you've already figured it out.
- A leader's job is to have the answers.
- Asking questions makes you look incompetent or disruptive.

THE COSTS OF PROVING YOU'RE BETTER THAN OTHERS

When you think you're better and insist on regularly demonstrating it, you're causing damage throughout your life; while your head's down, getting stuff done, your relationships, reputation, and long-term results are suffering. Here's how:

When You Settle for *Good Enough*, You Forgo *Great*

Relying on outperforming others leaves you overworked and exhausted. If it hasn't already, your performance will eventually deteriorate; your pace simply isn't sustainable. You may believe the pressure helps you perform, but research shows that once pressure exceeds an optimal point, performance suffers.

You're Inviting Shame by Overemphasizing What You *Should* Do

When you *should* on yourself, it triggers a sense of obligation from an external source of authority (a boss, cultural norm, comparison to others, etc.) and implies there will be a consequence if you fail to perform. *Should* is well intended, but it's in opposition with reality; it reinforces what we wish were true but isn't and leads to shame, doubt, overwhelm, guilt, regret, and frustration.

Other People Don't Want to Work with You

Your peers likely find your work ethic and intensity intimidating and would prefer not to work at your pace or strive for your unreasonable standards. While you may go fast working alone, you won't go far—and burnout is waiting for you at the end of the road you're racing down. While you insist that your independent work style or inconsiderate behavior isn't personal, you're rationalizing behavior that marginalizes other people's very real emotional experiences. People likely only work with you as a last resort.

You're Wearing Yourself Out

You must acknowledge the physical, emotional, and social consequences that exist in the cycle you've created for yourself. Physically, you're likely fatigued and experiencing headaches, trouble sleeping, digestive issues, disordered eating, or lowered immunity. Emotionally, the cost is low energy, disinterest, feeling disconnected, and chronic moodiness or irritability. Socially, you may struggle to maintain friendships, finding that you withdraw or distance yourself from social interactions or tolerate less-than-ideal conditions in your work or relationships.

Your Reputation Is Taking a Hit

Because you're obsessed with controlling your image and being seen as highly competent, you're likely known as a control freak, a micromanager, and someone who doesn't care about others. At work, you've probably lost perspective and are in constant pursuit of validation from others. The result is that people don't trust you or see you as a team player.

Your Relationships Are Struggling

At home, people you care about will see you as someone impossible to please, so they'll stop trying. Your intensity and constant judgment will be more than they can handle, so your family and friends will limit their interactions with you . . . unless they need the value only you can provide—in which case, they'll use you.

REFLECT ON YOUR LEARNING

As you conclude your exploration of this belief, take a moment to reflect on your insights. Confronting these beliefs can feel uncomfortable and may evoke feelings of vulnerability. Remember, this experience is a shared human struggle, and recognizing the costs associated with these beliefs is a vital step toward personal growth.

Use the prompts below to guide your self-reflection. Approach these questions with kindness and without judgment.

Self-Assessment: To what degree is this belief causing problems in your life?

Make notes about where this belief shows up in your life or relationships.

- ☐ Not at all.
- ☐ I can see it in a few places, but it's not creating issues as far as I can tell.
- ☐ It's actively causing stress in my relationships or hindering results.
- ☐ I'm about to lose something big if I don't make changes soon.

Key Insights: What resonated with you in this chapter? *Note any specific ideas or realizations that stood out to you.*

Personal Impact: Where do you see this belief holding you back? *Reflect on specific areas or situations in your life.*

Relationships at Risk: Which relationships are most affected by this belief and its associated behavior? *Consider how this belief impacts your interactions with others.*

Consequences of Inaction: What is at risk if you choose to ignore this problem? *Think about the potential outcomes of maintaining this belief.*

If this chapter felt heavy for you, allow yourself some time to digest it before moving forward. Remember, personal growth is not a race; it's about becoming better—for yourself, your relationships, and the world around you.

Chapter 5

SELF-SABOTAGING BELIEF #4

You Believe You're Helping

Dana is known for her keen eye for detail. Her gift for discernment is part of the reason she's been successful at work: She's the person people go to when something needs to be tested and vetted. If there's a mistake or problem, she'll find it.

Drawing from a lifetime of experience and learning, she can contribute something of value in almost any situation. As a matter of fact, it's a bit of a sport for her to show off what she knows, whether invited or not. She doesn't just know a little about a lot of things; she knows a lot about a lot of things, and if you're unsure, just ask her.

Dana's favorite words are should *and* shouldn't. *You can't be around her long before the should and shouldn't guns come out firing.*

To her daughter: "You know, you shouldn't let your kids boss you around. They're going to grow up to be disrespectful."

To her coworker: "You shouldn't go to so much trouble—no one is going to read that memo."

To her son, who just finished his MBA: "You really should have done that right after college."

To her grandson, who just scored 100 percent on his test: "That's great, sweetie, but you should have done the extra credit too!"

And even to the stranger in front of her at the grocery store: "You should grab another one of those. They're on sale—two for one."

Dana has not one but two ex-husbands who couldn't handle her shoulding *anymore. While she loved them both, she was more in love with their potential than with who they were in reality. In the end, both of them said her actions made them feel inadequate and incompetent. They couldn't be themselves around Dana without fear of judgment and felt their spark for life had been beaten out of them, so eventually they left.*

Yet two failed marriages later, Dana can't figure out why she doesn't have many close friends, why she doesn't get included in the fun after-work events, or why her adult children don't call more often. She tries so hard to help those around her and loves them all so much, but she can't figure out why they don't seem to want her around. Everything's starting to fall apart, and she looks to the future and sees herself alone—but she isn't sure what to do to change it.

I'm guessing you know a few people in your life who remind you of Dana: people who can't seem to pass up an opportunity to jump in, share an opinion, solve the problem, and save the day—even when they're not asked to. People like Dana are usually high performers. Their motivation to meddle in other people's lives is rooted in the fact that they're truly gifted at solving problems. When they see others struggling to solve their own problems or not solving their problems quickly or well enough, they step in to help—and why not? The solution is so obvious to them; it would be heartless to withhold it.

While these individuals truly think they're helping by running interference and protecting others from the consequences of their choices, what they're actually doing is creating drama, adding to the difficulty of the situation, and enabling. And while their motivation isn't malicious—people who truly want to help often feel a high degree of concern for others and want to help relieve the emotional discomfort of those around them—their way of helping is just a kinder version of control: When they're helping others solve their problems, what they're really doing is solving for their own emotional discomfort and imposing their own solution. They're attached to a specific outcome rather than allowing or empowering the other person to solve their own problem. This me-oriented approach is crippling for relationships, especially when the help wasn't desired or asked for in the first place.

Leaders who believe they are helping others by using their gift—a critical eye—to spot problems and propose solutions end up imposing their opinions or ideas onto others, stifling autonomy, trust, and critical thinking.

When you were reading Dana's story, did you see a bit of yourself in her behavior? If so, you might also believe the following:

- Problems should be solved, even if they're not your problems.
- Suffering and conflict are bad.
- If you try hard enough, you can control how other people feel and behave.
- *Urgent* and *important* are two valid reasons for jumping in and taking over.
- Other people's performance is an extension of you.
- Your job is to help, fix, save, or protect others (your family, friends, coworkers, customers).
- When you help, you'll be liked, approved of, and appreciated.
- Your identity includes that of peacemaker, cheerleader, protector, provider, and advocate.

THE COSTS OF IMPOSING YOUR HELP ONTO OTHERS

At their best, people who aim to help those around them come across as judgy know-it-alls, and at their worst, they're insufferable to be around. If you're imposing your need to help by chronically solving other people's problems, your relationships are either at risk or crumbling in front of your eyes—and you might not yet know why. Here's why:

You're Breeding Your Own Resentment

When you tell others what they should and shouldn't do, it invites them to reject your help, ideas, suggestions, and comments—and ultimately, it feels like they end up rejecting you. Rejection is a surefire path to resentment, especially given all you've done to help them. By continuing to force your opinion on those around you, you're ensuring that you'll resent them later for not taking your advice or appreciating your gestures of help.

Others Feel Judged by You

While you think you're delivering a beautifully wrapped package of solutions, other people often experience your help as judgment, criticism, and manipulation. Even the little things—like trying to improve someone's work or commenting in a way that demonstrates your disapproval—makes a giant statement. People around you may think your standards are unreasonable and that nothing is ever good enough for you, which leaves them feeling broken, insufficient, or incapable.

You're Preventing Others from Learning and Growing

While you may think your genuine offers to help are serving those you love, you're actually reinforcing learned helplessness. Your interference in others' problem-solving processes creates a dependency on you, which adds undue responsibility to your already full plate. Even worse, if your solution does provide temporary relief for the person experiencing it, the real problem isn't truly solved: The person you helped didn't learn how to solve the issue on their own because you intervened. This is particularly problematic when you interrupt emotional discomfort that could have led to their own healing and growth.

You're Fighting Against Reality; in the End, You're Going to Lose

When you seek to control things outside yourself (other people, their emotions and decisions), you're operating beyond your span of direct control. Not only is this battle futile—nothing outside yourself is ever within your direct control—but it also delays your own progress because you're trying to alter reality rather than work within it.

REFLECT ON YOUR LEARNING

As you conclude your exploration of this limiting belief, take a moment to reflect on your insights. Confronting these beliefs can feel uncomfortable and may evoke feelings of vulnerability. Remember, this experience is a shared human struggle, and recognizing the costs associated with these beliefs is a vital step toward personal growth.

Use the prompts below to guide your self-reflection. Approach these questions with kindness and without judgment.

Self-Assessment: To what degree is this belief causing problems in your life?

Make notes about where this belief shows up in your life or relationships.

- ☐ Not at all.
- ☐ I can see it in a few places, but it's not creating issues as far as I can tell.
- ☐ It's actively causing stress in my relationships or hindering results.
- ☐ I'm about to lose something big if I don't make changes soon.

Key Insights: What resonated with you in this chapter?

Note any specific ideas or realizations that stood out to you.

Personal Impact: Where do you see this belief holding you back?

Reflect on specific areas or situations in your life.

Relationships at Risk: Which relationships are most affected by this belief and its associated behavior?
Consider how this belief impacts your interactions with others.

Consequences of Inaction: What is at risk if you choose to ignore this problem?
Think about the potential outcomes of maintaining this belief.

If this chapter felt heavy for you, allow yourself some time to digest it before moving forward. Remember, personal growth is not a race; it's about becoming better—for yourself, your relationships, and the world around you.

Chapter 6

SELF-SABOTAGING BELIEF #5

You Believe It's Temporary

Nina is one of the highest performers at the agency. She raises her hand for the really tough projects no one else wants to take on and volunteers to come in on the weekends to help with tight deadlines. She's a boss's dream; her tenacity and commitment to getting the job done know no bounds.

On top of that, Nina is engaged to a successful entrepreneur, and they just bought a stunning new home in the ritzy part of town. Love, talent, financial success: Nina has it all.

At least that's how it seems on the surface.

Peel back the curtain and you'll see someone who desperately wants to feel satisfied in her life but experiences daily life as something to be endured. Eventually it will be worth it: Her reward for all this hard work—satisfaction, serenity, a moment to rest—will come after this next big wave of client work.

Nina's been telling herself that for six years now as she's sacrificed her personal time, relationships, and well-being to be everything to everyone at the office. She's so committed to this belief that she can't see how disillusioned she is; the reality is, the work is never going to slow down. There will never be a lack of projects to say yes to.

But she can't help herself—when one project wraps up, she fills its place with two more, creating an even bigger gap between her and the sense of satisfaction (and the vacation) she desperately needs.

Her unproven promises that things will slow down soon are impacting her at home too. She's been engaged to her fiancé, Marcus, for nearly three years, not because they're not ready to get married but because she can't find time to plan the wedding. She says she'll focus on the wedding when things slow down at work, but it's been three years, and things still haven't slowed down.

Speaking of her fiancé, he's frustrated by what he experiences as Nina neglecting their relationship. Nina leaves for work at 6:00 a.m. and doesn't get home until after dinner. She reassures him it's temporary, but Marcus is starting to wonder if he wants to sign up for always coming in second place.

Until she's able to live the life she's working so hard for (whenever that is), Nina lives like a hamster on a wheel: working herself to death, hoping to reach her destination, but getting nowhere.

Nina isn't alone in her perpetual feelings of slight dissatisfaction in her life. One Gallup poll found that only 78 percent of people were very or somewhat satisfied with their personal lives, meaning that 22 percent of people—or one in five—aren't.*

While dissatisfaction can stem from many places, for Nina, and possibly for you, the undercurrent of malaise stems from something that was once hopeful: a quest for happiness. The problem for people like Nina is that they're searching for joy in all the wrong places.

---

* Gallup, "Mood of the Nation 2024: Life Satisfaction" (poll conducted Jan. 2–22, 2024), https://news.gallup.com/topic/category-life-satisfaction.aspx

People who believe that their situation, unsustainable pace, and general discontent are temporary end up struggling to find satisfaction in the present moment because they're always yearning for a different, future version of reality. They cope with their current situation, tolerating less-than-ideal situations and relationships, because they believe it's only going to be this way a little longer; things will get better *eventually* if they just persevere. This is a true strength of someone with this belief: reframing a negative situation into something more temporarily tolerable. But it's also a rationale they use to excuse the poor habits that undermine their success. They're thinking, *It's temporary, and once it's over, things will be different.*

The problem with that mentality is that the life they want is constantly *there* and never *here*. They're living for later and chasing external measures of success—achieving goals, buying new toys, people pleasing—in the hope that their actions will bring them satisfaction.

Worst of all, the accomplishments they believe will cure their emotional ailments never pay off in the ways they think they will; they lose the weight, get the promotion, or win the award, and they still feel dissatisfied. This cycle of low satisfaction governs their lives and leaves them resisting reality; neglecting their own needs, dreams, and desires; and constantly searching for *more* while never truly feeling like they're enough.

Leaders who believe the situation is temporary are motivated to reach future, more accomplished versions of their lives but end up perpetually settling for *fine* and *good enough*, never experiencing true satisfaction in the lives they have.

You can spot this leader when they claim, "If I could just _____, I'd be able to rest / be happy / feel content." People who believe it's temporary love to manufacture finish lines, but once they approach or reach one, they create another one even further away. For this leader, chasing happiness is a lifelong endeavor, but experiencing it is a pleasure they never grant themselves.

If you believe your situation is temporary like Nina, you might also believe the following:

- If you can just get *there*, it will all work out.
- Customary markers of success bring life satisfaction.
- Your value is wrapped up in what you do, what you have, and what you give.
- You earn rest or play when the work is done.
- Being busy on behalf of others is the same as being with others.
- Feeling dissatisfied means you need to try harder.
- You can outwork or outachieve negative emotions.
- Generosity is a virtue.
- In giving, you receive.

THE COSTS OF BELIEVING IT'S TEMPORARY

Perpetually living in a version of reality that doesn't exist (*there*) rather than being present (*here*) has a high price; the costs are your relationships, your integrity, and—most distressingly—your mental health and happiness. If you tend to believe your situation is temporary, you might be paying the price in these ways:

You're Never Going to Find Happiness Because You're Looking in All the Wrong Places

At this point, you've likely convinced yourself that with enough money, status, titles, power, treasures, toys, and vacations, you will finally get to experience *enough*. But each time you achieve something—lose the weight, get the promotion, finish your MBA, start your own business—happiness doesn't follow. You feel a temporary lift, but it's fleeting, and you quickly refocus on the next goal. The problem with this orientation is that happiness and satisfaction are goalposts that perpetually exist outside of you, not within you.

When You Obsess over Being Happy in the Future, You Choose to Be Dissatisfied in the Present

You tend to spend a disproportionate amount of your time and energy focused on the places you can't control—the past and the future—and neglect the one place where you do have power: *here*. *Here* is the only place that exists, and when you're stuck rethinking and ruminating over what you should have done in the past or will do differently in the future, it keeps you from doing better now. You convince yourself that things can still be perfect in the future, so you spend too much time thinking about it—but what that creates is disappointment in the present, because the perfect life you dream of is always *there*, not *here*. Your overemphasis on the future limits your ability to enjoy the rewards of your hard work or experience simple pleasures that come with being present in the moment.

You Conflate Geography with Connection

Being physically near others is not the same as building connections. When you're in the same room as your spouse or kids, you believe you're connecting with them, even though your mind is elsewhere. You might even treat fun and play like tasks on your to-do list and miss the joy and intrinsic reward that comes from being present and in communion with others, which is known to be a key indicator of life satisfaction.

You Overgive, and It Leads to Burnout

You likely love to show your loyalty to others by giving, and that's a virtuous quality in moderation. But when you give more than you receive, it builds an energy deficit that eventually leads to the burnout of your career, marriage, relationships, or passions. Overgiving can also stem from a darker place; you may be overgenerous with others because you're searching for praise, appreciation, absolution, or control—all of which will leave you mentally and emotionally depleted and resentful of yourself and others.

You're Trying to Please Everyone, but in the End, You're Pleasing No One—Not Even Yourself

When your actions are driven by the need to please others, you're up against an uncomfortable truth: You can't control what other people think or feel. Basing your behavior on how you hope others will respond means you're not just seeking approval—you're attempting to manage their perceptions to fulfill your own need to be liked, valued, or accepted. This cycle pulls you out of alignment with yourself. It erodes your trust in your own intuition, distances you from your inner wisdom, and leaves you feeling disconnected from what truly matters to you.

REFLECT ON YOUR LEARNING

As you conclude your exploration of this limiting belief, take a moment to reflect on your insights. Confronting these beliefs can feel uncomfortable and may evoke feelings of vulnerability. Remember, this experience is a shared human struggle, and recognizing the costs associated with these beliefs is a vital step toward personal growth.

Use the prompts below to guide your self-reflection. Approach these questions with kindness and without judgment.

Self-Assessment: To what degree is this belief causing problems in your life? *Make notes about where this belief shows up in your life or relationships.*

- ☐ Not at all.
- ☐ I can see it in a few places, but it's not creating issues as far as I can tell.
- ☐ It's actively causing stress in my relationships or hindering results.
- ☐ I'm about to lose something big if I don't make changes soon.

Key Insights: What resonated with you in this chapter? *Note any specific ideas or realizations that stood out to you.*

____

____

Personal Impact: Where do you see this belief holding you back? *Reflect on specific areas or situations in your life.*

____

____

Relationships at Risk: Which relationships are most affected by this belief and its associated behavior? *Consider how this belief impacts your interactions with others.*

Consequences of Inaction: What is at risk if you choose to ignore this problem? *Think about the potential outcomes of maintaining this belief.*

If this chapter felt heavy for you, allow yourself some time to digest it before moving forward. Remember, personal growth is not a race; it's about becoming better—for yourself, your relationships, and the world around you.

Chapter 7

COULD IT BE YOU?

I have read countless self-help books, and almost all of them try to convince their readers that they aren't the problem. "It's not you," they say—but then they go on to share any number of reasons you aren't where you want to be in life, all of which are *actually you* in some way. Their message isn't helpful, and someone should tell it to you straight. Whether you agree with me or not, it's time to stop hiding behind your intentions and your imperfect circumstances and at least consider that it might be you.

To help you understand where you could be if you choose to explore answers to the seven conscious questions in the second half of this book, I invite you to read the statements below and reflect on the degree to which they ring true for you:

- *You are a high-value, high-impact player who sees beyond yourself. Serving as a role model in your personal pursuit of greatness, you lift others, amplify their potential, and compassionately call them to their own greatness.*

- *You give of yourself freely, making a difference because you set out to help ensure that things go well. You don't keep score, but you know you are making a difference; you focus on improving yourself instead of obsessing about changing or improving your circumstances.*

- *You consciously and steadily take action toward your goals, and even when you're tempted to quit, you keep your priorities in focus and celebrate progress along the way. You never outsource your happiness or motivation to something or someone outside yourself.*

- *You champion change and do what it takes to succeed by focusing on possibilities over problems, staying focused on what is within your direct control, bouncing back quickly when there are setbacks, and learning from successes and failures.*

- *You account for how you've contributed to your results through what you did or didn't do, and you invite others to do the same through powerful questions that lead to action.*

- *Your relationships are healthy, effective, and marked by trust, respect, compassion, and support. The needs of each partner (spouse, family member, colleague, etc.) are honored, and there is no imbalance of personal power.*

- *You are at peace with who you are, what you have, and where you are in life. While satisfied and generally happy, you continually entertain possibilities for what's next for you.*

Sounds pretty amazing, right? It's attainable; this can be your personal biography if you choose to move forward *as if it's you*—especially if conventional methods are no longer working.

For me, entertaining the idea that it was me was particularly painful because I was *certain* it was everyone else. Get ready to swallow your pride and take the first step. It might be the most impactful decision you make; transforming your life from the inside out is only one courageous decision away.

As It Turned Out, It Was Me

The moment I began to realize it was me was when I got called a bitch in the middle of the Tampa airport.

I was flying home after visiting the headquarters of the company that had recently acquired the business where I had worked for eighteen years. As I navigated my transition from vice president of my old company to director of outside sales for the larger organization, I was also still serving as vice president of our brand and managing much of the postacquisition integration. In a very short time, my responsibilities had effectively doubled.

To put it simply, I was exhausted.

But I was convinced it was worth it. I thought the burnout was short term—once we got the integration figured out, things would settle down, right? On top of that, I was very protective of my team that had transitioned with me through the acquisition and felt a deep personal responsibility to advocate for them as we navigated the future together. For me, pushing through was the right thing to do for myself and for others.

As I pushed through, I pissed a lot of people off. I was unapologetically focused on results—which I always got. The scoreboard was my justification for my actions, and the praise I got from my team, customers, and vendors—"Thank God you're here! What would we do without you?"—reinforced my belief that I was helping and was my fuel to keep fighting.

What I couldn't see at the time was that the way I was showing up was harming not only myself but also my reputation and my team. Looking back, I can recognize the deep internal conflict I was experiencing: I didn't like who I was becoming, and I had no clarity on what I truly wanted. Instead of addressing these feelings, I kept my head down and focused on the work at hand—and there was certainly plenty of it! While I believed I was protecting my team by running interference and shielding them from political pressures, I was actually undermining their position. They weren't learning to adapt to the new environment or preparing for our inevitable future.

My team understood that I was a well-intentioned person with a big heart who would fight for them. However, to everyone else, I came across as a self-righteous bitch, determined to get my way and utterly insufferable when I didn't. It was my responsibility to work effectively with all colleagues, yet I was selective about whom I chose to help and partner with. To the rest, I appeared critical, judgmental, and indifferent to how my results-oriented behavior affected them. As a result, my intentions and my impact were far from aligned.

I learned this while reviewing my 360 feedback with my executive coach in the Tampa airport. My people, the people who knew my heart, praised me: “We’d be lost without her.” “I’d follow her into fire.” “She’s got our back.”

But others shared feedback and opinions that are indelibly imprinted on my soul: “Bitch.” “She thinks she’s the VP of the world.”

I was paralyzed with emotion; if I opened my mouth to respond to my coach, I was going to lose it. I was angry. (If I’m honest, the first response I felt to this feedback was “F ’em.”) I was embarrassed and hurt. And I was certain that I wasn’t the problem. These people didn’t know me. How could they be so cruel?

I choked back my emotions, headed to my boarding gate, and spent my entire flight contemplating my response—none of which helped, by the way. After I conferred (and commiserated) with my husband, he shared five words that brought me some peace. “They just don’t know you,” he said. It was then that I realized we were on to something—they didn’t know me, but it wasn’t because they were unwilling. It was because I hadn’t let them. I’d become so focused on getting shit done that I’d completely pushed people and relationships to the side. This was business, after all. It wasn’t personal, or so I thought. In doing so, I’d become the asshole in their story, and their behavior was the justification for mine.

I had a choice. I could keep pushing through as an unemotional workhorse with an overinflated sense of duty, or I could let my guard down, stop hiding behind the scoreboard, and let people get to know me as a human. I decided to test the latter; if people weren’t going to like me, they should at least make an informed decision, right?

Shortly thereafter, I decided to engage in my own form of personal therapy: making hundreds of homemade, hand-wrapped caramel candies. When I returned to headquarters, I greeted each person I encountered with a heartfelt “Merry Christmas!” and offered them a homemade treat. To be honest, many were surprised to see me as something other than the workaholic machine I had become. As we interacted in this more personal manner, free of the constraints of our roles, the walls began to come down, and genuine connections started to form.

From then on, I slowly (and painfully) started to realize the difference between managing and leading. Despite spending most of my career at the executive level, I had received absolutely no leadership training. I realized that the skills that had carried me this far would not be sufficient for the journey ahead, and it became clear that I needed to acquire new skills. However, before even developing this skill set, I needed to shift my mindset and challenge the beliefs that were the source of my suffering—particularly the distinction between reality and my perceptions of it.

I wasn't operating from reality; I was resisting it and trying to control everything within my orbit. This perceived control is what gave me the security I craved in such uncertain times. Yet this illusion of control is deceptive. When you push against reality, it may seem effective at first, but it inevitably pushes back, and you find yourself losing—every single time. Part of me wants to share the chaos and challenges of this period in my life, but ultimately those details don't matter. The truth is, they never did.

I continued to sit with my 360 feedback and brush off all the unhelpful thoughts that raced through my mind—"This process is bogus. They're just out to get me. What do these people know about me, anyway?"—and tried to find the lesson. As they say, you can have a testimony without a test. And anytime my focus went back to those imperfect circumstances, it weakened my position and took me further from what I wanted most, which was to relieve the pressure and find some peace.

Not knowing where to begin, I committed to being more supportive and less critical. I set out on a journey to really get to know my colleagues and turn them from perceived enemies into allies. What I discovered was that I had been completely unaware of their needs and challenges, and they were just as oblivious to mine. But underneath, we weren't all that different. The more I understood what others were up against, the more I began to see how I was showing up as an obstacle, not an asset.

I'd been pretending my problems were the only ones that mattered; meanwhile, everyone around me was suffering, and my behavior was making it worse. I recognized that my true value was determined not only by my results but also by the unintended negative impact I had on others. With this understanding, I set out to improve my relationships, one connection at a time.

My work woes were just the beginning of my trouble. My behavior was impacting the people I loved most at home too. My teenage son had been silently observing the way I was showing up—working twenty-four seven, coming home bitter and resentful with little left to give to my family—and was beginning to see my experience as what it takes to achieve financial success. If this was the cost of success, it was too expensive. Seeing how my choices were impacting my son during his most developmental years crushed me.

In preparing this story, I asked my son to reflect on his experience during this particularly difficult time. Here's what he had to say:

> *She was the vice president of a multimillion-dollar company—and that came with demands. But she would bring that home with her, and we were all caught in the cross fire. I saw her make a lot of money, but at what cost? I could see the cost. Being around her felt like walking on eggshells; I was afraid to make mistakes or share information with her. There was a reason why I started to be home less often, spend more time at my dad's, and bury myself in extracurricular activities and sports.*

Ouch. Any parent reading this can empathize. Our children are often our greatest motivation for success, and when we hear firsthand that we're failing them, it's devastating.

I started to realize that the problem wasn't my job or the coworkers who gave me feedback or the company that bought us—it was me. My choices were causing my son to actively form unhelpful beliefs about building a successful future, taking a toll on my personal well-being, and harming the people I thought I was protecting. While I thought I was helping, I had actually created an environment of learned helplessness and an us-versus-them mentality—none of which would add value or prove helpful.

I'm hoping that if you've gotten this far, you're starting to open your mind to the possibility that it might be you too. Your signals will look different from mine—perhaps instead of impacting your son, you're slowly watching your marriage erode—but the signals are there. And even if your intentions are pure and good, no amount of good intention can change the very real impact you are having on yourself and others.

The beauty here is that if you are the problem, you are also the solution. If you're not the problem, you have absolutely no power to create a different result. But when you can do the brave work of opening your eyes to the ways you're creating your own suffering, you reclaim the ability to change course and create a more desirable outcome.

Over time, I learned and used many of the evidence-based tools in this book to operate within my zone of control and find my personal power. I was determined to get my shit together. Regardless of whether I stayed with the company or left, I wanted to learn something from this experience and do the work of intentionally moving toward something different rather than running away or ignoring the problem.

I grew to operate in a way that felt good to me and brought out the best parts of me. I learned that I was completely out of touch with what I actually wanted and worked my way toward understanding what was important to me. I went from being at the mercy of circumstance to making things happen in my life that I didn't even know were possible. In doing so, I discovered peace, freedom, and fulfillment—without sacrificing my passion for my work or my commitment to being a responsible person. Perhaps most rewarding of all, my son witnessed these changes in me as well.

> *I remember I wanted to transfer schools. She worked hard to put me in an expensive Catholic high school, but I wanted to go to public school. It took pretty much everything in me to have that tough conversation with her, to the point that I was in tears. That's where I started to see changes happening in her. That conversation went way better than I thought it would. I expected her to get mad and defensive, but she was very supportive. She told me I could make my own decisions and that she'd support me. I always knew she loved me—that was never in question—but at that point I stopped feeling like I was walking on eggshells. I wasn't afraid to have tough conversations with her and felt supported. She let me make my decisions,*

good and bad. I felt more freedom, and she was more open-minded, happier, and less stressed. At that point, she was doing things more on her terms.

With the support of my husband, I made the conscious decision to leave the company and start my own business. I realized that the environment was not aligned with my inner compass, and although it meant leaving behind an organization I had dedicated over twenty years to building and saying goodbye to many friends, it was the right choice for my family and me. This book is not an endorsement to quit your job; rather, it is a call to develop self-mastery. By cultivating this skill, you will be better equipped to navigate imperfect circumstances in your current environment, and any situations you may encounter in the future, with intention, clarity, and some valuable tools.

In this brief glimpse into my life, you can see all five limiting beliefs at play. You might be wondering, *What happened next? How long does it take to see results? Is the transformation lasting?*

As you might imagine, I'm a work in progress—just like everyone else. There's no final destination in this work; it's a lifelong practice. Like most things, results don't last if you fall back into old habits that don't support your goals.

What I've discovered is that my clients' journeys often mirror my own. Change can occur rapidly—sometimes even immediately—but maintaining that change requires ongoing discipline and commitment to the principles I'm about to share with you. When I work with clients, I believe my greatest value lies in helping them navigate their biggest obstacle: themselves.

This book was inspired by the numerous requests I've received from clients seeking to deepen their practice without the need for continuous enrollment in a coaching or leadership development program. They wanted a single reference point for the concepts and strategies they learned, one that would help them stay on track through self-coaching. They desired a resource they could annotate, make notes in, and revisit time and again.

Before we proceed, let's clarify what I mean by self-coaching. As a coach, I view coaching—including self-coaching—as distinct from other modalities such as therapy, counseling, mentoring, or consulting. While some of these approaches focus on healing past experiences, coaching is primarily about taking action toward the future. It empowers clients to discover their own answers rather than relying on prescribed solutions. In many cases, a combination of modalities may be beneficial. For instance, it's common for someone to work with a therapist to process past trauma while simultaneously engaging with a coach to facilitate forward movement.

And finally, if you haven't already visited www.maybeitsmebook.com to snag your bonus content and digital downloads, don't forget to do that. These additional resources are designed to support you with this work.

Let's get started and put you on a path to peace and possibilities.

Chapter 8

CONSCIOUS CHOICES REQUIRE A PAUSE

The quality of your life is intrinsically linked to the quality of your decisions—and making great decisions requires knowing when to pause before taking action. My seven conscious questions are going to help you do just that.

You are not a product of your circumstances; you are a product of your decisions. Improve your decisions—improve your life.

A leader's ability to make sound and confident decisions is not merely a nice-to-have skill; it is a fundamental responsibility of their role. Unlike individual contributors, managers are compensated more because they are expected to exercise strong judgment and make choices that can significantly impact their teams and organizations. Effective decision-making involves analyzing complex information, weighing potential outcomes, and considering the needs of various stakeholders.

This is no small feat. If it were straightforward, everyone would excel at it. Leaders must navigate uncertainty and often make tough calls that require balancing short-term pressures with long-term vision. Ultimately, the quality of a leader's decisions can determine the success of their team and the organization as a whole.

Just as business leaders must make critical decisions that affect their teams, we all face choices in our personal lives that ripple out to impact those around us. Whether it's deciding on a career path, choosing where to live, or determining how to allocate our time, the ability to weigh options and anticipate potential consequences is crucial.

There are many factors that can complicate the decision-making process: too much or too little information, limited resources, emotional blocks, conflicting demands, unclear priorities, distractions, and cognitive biases. Recognizing these complexities is vital for improving our decision-making skills both at work and at home.

Let's take a moment to reflect on some of the *significant decisions* you've made in your adult life. As you consider those decisions and their outcomes, how many would you classify as quality, confident choices? How many had a positive impact on others?

While major choices—such as getting married, accepting a new job, or relocating to a new city—carry higher stakes, my work with clients shows that it's often the everyday decisions that profoundly impact our day-to-day quality of life. These are the choices we make in the blink of an eye, often without much thought. If you overlook the opportunity to make thoughtful, impactful choices in these moments, you may find it more challenging to lead a rich and rewarding life.

Maybe you can relate to a few of these seemingly short-term decisions that left a lasting impact:

- *During a team brainstorming session, you dismiss a colleague's idea without consideration, believing it's not worth your time. This quick dismissal can lead to resentment and discourage collaboration, causing others to feel undervalued and less likely to share their ideas in the future.*

- *You notice that a team member has done excellent work but choose not to acknowledge it, thinking they should know better than to seek validation. This lack of recognition can diminish their motivation and lead to a disengaged team culture.*

- *You choose to avoid addressing a conflict with a peer, hoping it will resolve itself. By doing so, you allow the issue to fester, leading to increased tension and communication breakdowns in the long run.*

- *In an effort to be helpful, you agree to take on additional responsibilities at work without considering your current workload. This decision can lead to burnout, missed deadlines, and a decline in the quality of your work, ultimately affecting your reputation and relationships with colleagues.*

Now, let's pause once more and honestly reflect on *your everyday decisions* and the results they've created. With the outcomes of those decisions top of mind, you may have noticed that they share certain characteristics. Take a moment to review the following hallmarks of poor decision-making and check which ones seem to be a pattern in your life and choices:

- [ ] They produced unintended consequences for you or others.
- [ ] They weren't grounded in sufficient data or facts.
- [ ] They were made from a place of fear or force.
- [ ] They primarily focused on your own needs, wants, or challenges.
- [ ] They were made too late or too quickly.
- [ ] They ignored emotional or instinctual cues.
- [ ] They optimized the short term but neglected the long term.
- [ ] They didn't produce the desired results.
- [ ] They underutilized your full potential and intelligence.

In my work with organizations across various industries, I have consistently observed that teams value leaders who are decisive—especially in the face of uncertainty or high-risk situations. These leaders do not freeze when challenges arise, nor do they simply buy time until conditions improve. Instead, they thoughtfully assess risks, weigh their options, and make informed decisions with confidence. Importantly, they consider the potential impact of their choices on their team and the organization as a whole, fostering a sense of trust and collaboration. Their confidence stems from knowing they can (1) make the next-best decision when more information becomes available, and (2) adapt if things don't go as planned, ensuring that they remain responsive to the needs of those around them.

While not everyone has the privilege of working under such leaders, each of us has the potential to become one ourselves. By cultivating the qualities that inspire others to follow us, we can enhance our ability to make quality, confident decisions. Conscious choices elevate this process, allowing us to consider the broader implications of our decisions, align them with our values and goals, and ultimately deliver positive outcomes.

A conscious choice is made intentionally, with an awareness of the context, options, and consequences involved. It involves a deliberate process of discovery and expanding one's perspective to enhance understanding, aligning with a bigger picture or goal, and taking personal responsibility while remaining responsive to the needs of others. While conscious choices may not always be what's immediately needed in every situation, striving to make them more often can significantly enhance our effectiveness and improve our relationships. This process requires pausing to reflect on our values and goals, ensuring that our actions align with the bigger picture. I invite you to make more conscious choices, and I will teach you a framework to facilitate this process. But first, you must learn to pause.

The Critical Moment Between a Stimulus and Your Response

It should come as no surprise that the moments demanding the most composure and critical decision-making often occur when our minds and emotions feel the most out of control—and this is entirely natural. As humans, we are instinctively wired to scan our environment for potential threats, relying on our survival instincts during high-stakes situations. This instinct kicks in whenever we face a threat, whether physical (like an oncoming car) or psychological (like when your boss makes an inappropriate joke in front of the team, leaving you feeling uncomfortable and unsure of how to respond).

While we shouldn't ignore our instincts when confronted with physical danger—such as taking immediate action to avoid a merging vehicle—psychological threats provide a unique opportunity. In these moments, we can pause our instinctive reactions and engage in critical thinking to determine the best choice for achieving our desired outcome. Instead of reacting defensively or laughing it off to avoid discomfort, you might take a moment to breathe, assess the situation, and decide whether to address the comment directly or discuss it with your boss later.

That brief moment between stimulus and response is where you have the power to choose the outcome and impact you want in any given situation and make a more conscious choice. It all begins with a pause.

> Between stimulus and response there is a space. In that space is our power to choose our response. In our response lies our growth and our freedom.
>
> —VIKTOR FRANKL, AUTHOR OF *MAN'S SEARCH FOR MEANING*

While you may not succeed every time, you will likely find success more often than you expect. Here are some key indicators that you may need to pause before making a decision or taking action:

- **The stakes are high:** Significant consequences are on the line.
- **The pressure is intense:** You feel overwhelmed by demands or expectations.
- **Your emotions are charged:** Strong feelings are clouding your judgment or creating blind spots.
- **You feel stuck:** You're unsure of how to proceed or feel trapped in your situation.
- **You don't see viable options:** You either can't identify alternatives or find them unappealing.
- **You're hesitant to ask for help:** You know you need assistance but fear reaching out.
- **You're struggling to achieve desired results:** Your efforts aren't yielding the outcomes you want.
- **You're contemplating giving up:** You feel ready to abandon the situation altogether.

When you recognize these conditions, I have a plan for how to use that pause in the most powerful way. The seven questions we will explore together throughout this book fit into a framework designed to help you intentionally and thoughtfully choose your response in any situation. The good news is that time isn't as much of a barrier as you might think; you can complete these steps in as little as two to three minutes.

PAUSING WITH PURPOSE

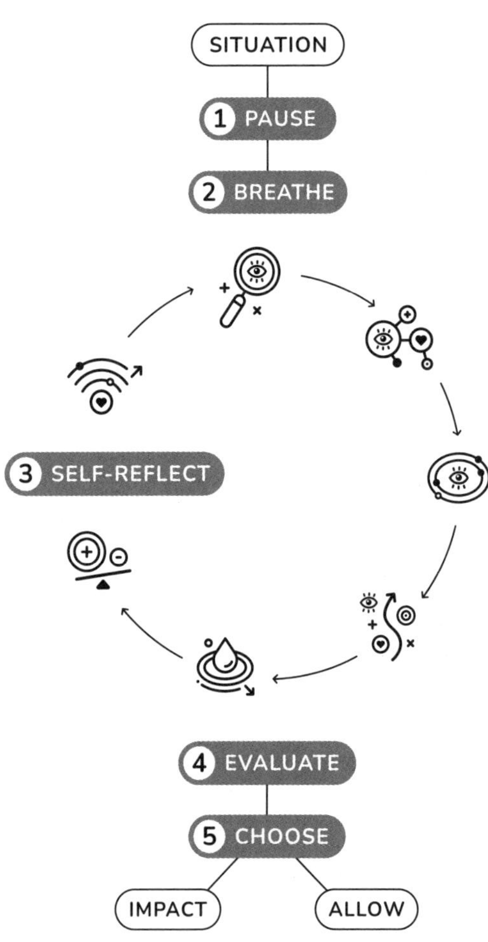

*The **7 Conscious Questions** help you arrive at a conscious choice.*

Pausing With Purpose

While you may not have all the answers right away, by consistently following this framework, you will gradually move closer to making conscious choices and reprogram your mind to overcome the self-sabotaging patterns that can undermine your results, even when your intentions are good. To achieve this, it's essential to make this practice a habit, regardless of the circumstances you encounter.

Step 1: Pause

That's it. Just stop. Stop before you do or say something you can't undo.

Step 2: Breathe

Regulating your emotions and actions begins with regulating your breath. It reconnects you to your body and slows you down. Take one full breath. Inhale through your nose for four seconds, hold it for four seconds, and exhale for eight seconds. Repeat until you feel composed.

Step 3: Self-Reflect

Cycle through the seven questions, and compassionately scan your mind, body, and environment for the answers. To get the most from this framework, it's important that you narrow your focus to your current problem or situation. Clearly articulate it, and keep it at the forefront of your mind as you approach each question with honesty and sincerity. Once you have an answer you are satisfied with, proceed to the next question, and continue this process through all seven questions. You might find a need to make multiple passes through these questions as you uncover new insights.

1. What am I feeling, and what are my emotions signaling?
2. What is true for me?
3. What might be true for others?
4. What is the whole truth, even if it's inconvenient?
5. What do I want for myself, and why is that important to me?
6. What impact do I want to make?
7. What does it look like to take 100 percent personal responsibility, no more, no less?

If you find yourself struggling to answer fully or honestly, take it as a cue to dig deeper—this could be the root of your feeling stuck. You can always reference the corresponding chapter within the book for additional guidance on overcoming any blocks.

Step 4: Evaluate

When making a choice, you have infinite options. When making a *conscious choice*, you have only two potential paths forward to consider:

1. **Allow it.** Change your perspective of the situation and/or move on in peace.
2. **Impact it.** Work within your span of control to make a difference.

Reflect on what you are—and aren't—able and willing to do in this situation. Continue making passes through the seven questions until you find the best decision for you in the moment.

When neither working with it nor working to impact it feels right, it can be tempting to indulge in the illusion of alternative choices, such as fighting against the situation, forcing outcomes, manipulating circumstances, trying to control everything, or avoiding the issue altogether. While these approaches may seem appealing in the moment, they are not conscious choices and often fail to provide sustainable, positive solutions. Engaging in such so-called options is much like shifting your car into neutral and revving the engine—it expends energy but ultimately gets you nowhere. Instead, it's essential to recognize these distractions for what they are and seek more constructive pathways forward.

You might notice yourself believing you've made a choice, only to find that it's difficult to honor the choice. This is normal—just reengage the process and keep working it. For complex or chronic issues, there might be a lot to work through. When the process becomes challenging—and it will—there are many strategies in this book to support you at this step. I encourage you to use them.

Make the *best* decision, not the *right* decision.

And remember, you don't have to make a conscious choice, but I encourage you to ensure that you are comfortable with your reasons for choosing differently and to take ownership of the consequences that arise from your decision.

Step 5: Choose and Commit

Provide your brain with clear direction by selecting your next move and committing to a plan of action. Typically, you don't need to map out every step—just focus on your immediate next move. Since this is your action step, your commitment should begin with a strong verb that clearly defines what you will do.

While you may not have all the answers right away, by consistently following these steps, you will gradually move closer to making conscious choices and reprogram your mind to overcome the self-sabotaging patterns that can undermine your results even when your intentions are good. To achieve this, it's essential to make this practice a habit, regardless of the circumstances you encounter.

INTRODUCTION TO THE SEVEN CONSCIOUS QUESTIONS

Now, let's explore the questions—this is where the real work begins.

Each question has a specific purpose and is crafted to encourage reflection and insight. Engaging with these questions will not only enhance the quality of your decisions and relationships but also improve your overall quality of life.

Important note: These questions should be asked and answered in the context of specific situations, circumstances, or stimuli. They are not meant for broad or generalized use; the depth of insight comes from applying them to real-life scenarios.

To get the most from these questions, you might need to strengthen some of your leadership skills. I will provide you with multiple strategies for building these skills, paving the way for you to navigate your decision-making with confidence and intention. Below you will find a snapshot of what's ahead—the seven conscious questions, their purpose, and their importance. In the following chapters, we will explore each question in depth, examining its significance and how it applies to your unique circumstances.

Question 1: What Am I Feeling, and What Are My Emotions Signaling?

Purpose: *Understanding your emotions and their underlying messages provides the gift of emotional maturity. By recognizing, understanding, and learning from your emotions, you can more effectively connect your inner world with your outer goals and strategies.*

Why It Matters: Emotions carry important signals that can guide your decisions and actions. When you fail to read and respond to these emotional signals, both in yourself and others, you risk addressing surface-level issues rather than the underlying problems. Prioritizing emotional comfort without truly processing emotions can lead to recurring challenges, often surfacing at inconvenient times. Emotional maturity empowers you to maintain personal agency in emotionally triggering situations. By understanding and harnessing your emotions, you create a bridge between your internal experiences and external achievements.

Question 2: What Is True for Me?

Purpose: *Uncovering the mental constructs that shape your reality provides the invaluable gift of a managed mind. By identifying how your conscious and unconscious thoughts influence your experiences and outcomes, you gain the power to redirect or reframe them to serve your best interests.*

Why It Matters: What is true for you is the collective of how you think and feel. Your thoughts and beliefs wield immense power, quietly shaping your reality and influencing your outcomes, often without your conscious awareness. It's important to recognize that you don't have to believe everything you think. Left unchecked, certain thoughts can distort your perception of what's possible, trapping you in cycles of self-sabotage and missed opportunities. By consciously choosing and directing your thoughts, you gain the power to break free from these limiting patterns. This active management of your mind allows you to align your thoughts with your goals, empowering you to create a reality that truly reflects your potential and aspirations. Understanding that you have the choice to reframe your thinking is a transformative step toward shaping a life that serves your best interests.

Question 3: What Might Be True for Others?

Purpose: *Compassionate curiosity offers the gift of an expanded perspective. By setting aside judgment and engaging in meaningful inquiry—especially under pressure or in challenging situations—we open ourselves to a broader understanding of others' experience.*

Why It Matters: What's true for others is the collective of what they think and feel, based on their mental models and life experiences. No two people see things the exact same way. Embracing compassionate curiosity is essential for conscious leadership, as it encourages us to set aside what we believe to be true, look beyond ourselves, and genuinely seek to understand the experiences of others. This deeper engagement goes beyond merely asking questions; it requires us to pause our personal judgments and narratives to listen with empathy and compassion. By considering external perspectives without the intent to control, persuade, or manipulate, we not only broaden our understanding but also equip ourselves with a fuller context for decision-making. In doing so, we strengthen our relationships rather than weaken them.

Question 4: What Is the Whole Truth Here, Even If It's Inconvenient?

Purpose: *Seeing and accepting the whole truth provides the gift of being grounded in reality. By distinguishing your thoughts and emotions from the facts, you achieve a clear understanding of the situation at hand. This clarity allows you to embrace the truth, even when inconvenient, positioning you in your most powerful stance for taking meaningful action.*

Why It Matters: What you believe to be true can blind you to the actual truth. Conscious choices require that we not only see the truth; we must also accept it. The mind's tendency to create stories and the ego's attraction to drama can cloud your perception, allowing narratives to masquerade as logic and facts. Without a clear picture of reality (the truth), you might incorrectly attribute your circumstances to be the cause of your suffering or struggle, distorting your sense of personal responsibility. The clarity that comes from seeing and accepting the truth strengthens your ability to take full personal responsibility in any situation.

Question 5: What Do I Want for Myself, and Why Is That Important to Me?

Purpose: *Understanding what you truly want for yourself offers the gift of directional clarity. By pinpointing your personal desires and the reasons they matter, you can establish priorities that move you steadily and consciously toward what is most important to you.*

Why It Matters: Having in-the-moment awareness of what you truly want is essential for living a successful and fulfilling life. When you lack clarity about your immediate desires and priorities, you risk being swayed by external pressures and short-term distractions that don't align with what you want most in life. This misalignment can lead to a sense of aimlessness and dissatisfaction, as you may find yourself investing time and energy into pursuits that ultimately leave you unfulfilled. By cultivating directional clarity in the present moment, you create an "inner compass" that guides your decisions and actions, ensuring they consistently reflect your authentic goals. This real-time alignment empowers you to live with purpose, making each step meaningful and contributing to a life of true satisfaction and success.

Question 6: What Impact Do I Want to Make?

Purpose: *Thoughtfully identifying the impact you want to make provides the gift of making a difference with your decisions. By focusing on making conscious choices that positively affect yourself and others, you align your words and actions with meaningful outcomes, contributing to a better world.*

Why It Matters: The quality of your life is intrinsically linked to the quality of your relationships and decisions. Your success and ability to lead effectively are marked by your capacity to pause and thoughtfully respond to life's circumstances with decisions that support your goals and positively impact others. Leaders often fall short of making a difference in favor of making a point, making things happen, or making a profit. When push comes to shove and the pressure is high, the most successful leaders operate from their fullest potential by making quality, conscious choices. These decisions not only support personal and collective goals but also foster a positive impact on the world around them.

Question 7: What Does It Look Like to Take 100 Percent Personal Responsibility, No More, No Less?

Purpose: *Taking full personal responsibility and allowing others to do the same provides the gift of shared power. When both sides take 100 percent ownership of thoughts, feelings, actions, results, and impact, it fosters an environment of mutual respect and accountability.*

Why It Matters: Sharing power with others and understanding what you can and can't control is crucial for effective leadership and personal growth. When you overextend your sense of responsibility, it becomes unsustainable and can lead to burnout. Conversely, underestimating your responsibility can hinder progress and accountability. By taking precisely 100 percent responsibility for your own thoughts, feelings, actions, and impact while allowing others to own theirs, you create a balanced environment.

A Peaceful, More Satisfied Life Awaits You

I hope you feel inspired to read on. In the next seven chapters, you'll discover how to pair these powerful questions with dozens of practical strategies to coach yourself toward **greater peace and satisfaction, all without compromising your results**. These tools will guide you beyond short-term fixes, amplifying your success and enabling you to achieve things you never thought possible. To maximize the benefits of this book, it's helpful to have an unresolved challenge in mind. This approach will enable you to move beyond theoretical understanding and apply your learning in real time. Remember that this is a process, and it's perfectly okay to take your time with each question. Let them guide you toward deeper understanding and transformation. This is your opportunity to become your own coach, unlocking your full potential.

Chapter 9

QUESTION 1

What Am I Feeling, and What Are My Emotions Signaling?

Purpose: *Understanding your emotions and their underlying messages provides the gift of emotional maturity. By recognizing, understanding, and learning from your emotions, you can more effectively connect your inner world with your outer goals and strategies.*

There are hidden messages inside every emotion. When we identify them and learn to act upon them intentionally, there isn't anything we can't create in our lives.

After reading the first half of this book, you might have experienced a host of negative emotions—especially if you started judging yourself. Part one might have left you feeling the following:

- Exposed, because you feel called out
- Guilty, because you started calculating the cost of your behavior
- Afraid of what you stand to lose if you don't change
- Exhausted, because you're resisting your natural reaction, and it's hard
- Resentful that you didn't know this earlier
- Worried that it's too late

- Defeated at the thought that you can't be yourself (which isn't true, by the way)

Whatever you're feeling, take a moment to acknowledge it and understand that you are exactly where you need to be. You are in the messy middle: the space between awareness and acceptance, where judgment often runs high. It can be uncomfortable here, but the journey is worthwhile, and something amazing awaits you on the other side.

You might be tempted to skip this chapter, but I urge you not to—especially if you've been conditioned to prioritize thinking over feeling. Even if you consider yourself more action oriented or data driven, you still possess the ability to recognize and respond to emotions in yourself and others. You may believe you're an exception to this rule, but I assure you, you are not. As long as you can open your mind and heart, there is relief waiting for you on the other side of this work.

A Tangled Web of Emotions

I live in the small town of Luna Pier, Michigan, which is situated on the southwest shore of Lake Erie. Like most neighborhoods on the water, we have our share of spiders. I'm reminded of them when I take my regular sunrise stroll up to the public beach and fishing pier and walk face-first into a web.

An onlooker would laugh at my utterly unhelpful behavior as I wave my arms around wildly and attempt to swat the webs away. It's irrational, I know, but even though I know the webs are there, they leave me startled and annoyed every time I walk into them.

Emotions are kind of like that for me. Even though I can't see them, I know they're there, waiting for me to acknowledge them. Intellectually I understand that they have a role (see how I prefer to think even when it comes to feeling?), yet I often struggle to understand what my emotions are trying to tell me—and might over- or underreact to them.

I've had to do significant work on my emotions to become the leader I aspired to be, both at home and at work. I once believed that if I ignored uncomfortable emotions, they would simply fade away without consequence. However, that approach ultimately held me back personally and professionally. It's a common pattern I observe among many leaders I coach—those who aren't where they want to be but struggle to understand why. If you can relate, you might recognize these common behaviors in others who grapple with their emotions:

- They don't know what they are feeling or why, and they can't put language to their emotional experiences.
- They are unaware of how they're displaying their inner emotions outwardly.
- They make excuses or defend their emotional dysfunction.
- When emotions come up, they hide behind responsibility and results instead.
- They routinely avoid and resist uncomfortable emotions.
- They don't know what to do with emotions in others, so they often dismiss or resist them.

Sound like you? You're in the right place.

WHY EMOTIONAL MATURITY MATTERS

There is a four-letter word that begins with *F* that might be the biggest obstacle to your continued success. Fear is just one of many emotions, but I find it's the biggest thief of our dreams. Learning what to do with fear is essential for anyone who wants to move past *good enough*. Before you tell me that fear isn't a problem for you, consider that you might not recognize the many faces of fear.

Fear is the natural response when you sense a threat. When something that matters to you is perceived to be at risk, your protective mechanisms kick in. The problem is that when fear is in charge, you aren't. Letting fear take the lead can cause destruction in your life. Understanding the primary drivers of fear will help keep the *conscious you* in the driver's seat so you can get in front of your fear response and choose something *less protective*.

According to licensed psychologist Kelly Crace, a common source of fear for highly responsible individuals like you and me is the fear of failure.* More specifically, this fear often stems from concerns about being judged by others, the potential costs of failure, and the uncertainty of unknown outcomes. In simpler terms, when no one is watching, when there's nothing at stake, or when the outcome is guaranteed, there's little to fear. (Crace's work also connects personal values as a means to manage fear more effectively, and I highly recommend exploring it if this section resonates with you.)

In my own experience, I've found that a leading cause of dysfunction in families and relationships is a lack of emotional skills—specifically, difficulty in understanding, controlling, and expressing emotions. Many people go through life without truly grasping their emotions or recognizing the power they hold to create the feelings they crave. They often miss the opportunity to learn from uncomfortable emotions and grow through the process.

There is immense power to be found in emotional maturity, and through the work in this chapter, you're going to learn to harness it.

Before we dig in, let's rally around a shared definition of emotions. For our purposes, we'll choose to define them most simply as *the felt experiences of our thoughts*. This definition works for multiple reasons: It acknowledges the connection between our thoughts and our emotions (what we think directly influences our emotional response), and it assigns ownership over our emotions to us (if how you feel can be determined by what you think, not external circumstances, you have direct influence over your emotions).

And since there's a lot of lies you've been told about emotions through social conditioning, let's set the record straight.

- *Emotions are a human biological response that help the body and mind regulate and cope with life's circumstances. They serve as signals designed to inform us, connect us, alert us, and help us make sense of the world around us. They are a significant input into our decisions and actions.*

---

* R. Kelly Crace and Robert L. Crace, *Authentic Excellence: Flourishing and Resilience in a Relentless World* (Routledge, 2019).

- *Most people can't hide their emotions successfully.*
- *Men experience just as many emotions as women.*
- *Emotions have energy, and that energy cannot be destroyed; it can only be processed or converted.*
- *Your emotional energy will attract similar energy. Resistance invites resistance, anxiousness invites anxiousness, etc.*
- *Emotions are not excuses to behave poorly, and you have more control over them than you realize.*
- *Denying your emotions and your needs is not noble.*
- *You can't outthink or out-rationalize your emotions.*
- *You are human, and as such, you were built to feel the full range of emotion across your life.*
- *Every human needs to feel compassion.*
- *All emotions have value, even the negative ones.*

That last bullet point is the source of much human suffering. The belief that we should feel good most of the time and avoid negative or uncomfortable experiences isn't only false; it's also unattainable. It simply isn't possible to be a human and experience only positive emotions—nor should you want to.

Even worse, when we hyperfixate on feeling good all the time, we miss the opportunity to learn from what our negative emotions are trying to tell us. Learning to decode negative emotions and turn them into allies can increase the richness of life and spark personal growth and change.

The work we'll do in this chapter will be frustrating and potentially exhausting, but stay motivated as you anticipate what you can gain from fully investing in being able to answer this question.

Before we dive into the work, take a moment to reflect on these prompts designed to deepen your emotional self-awareness. Consider the emotions that arise in various situations and how they influence your actions:

- **Make difficult decisions:** What emotions support you in navigating challenging choices?

- **Take action on a goal:** Which feelings motivate you to pursue your goals and ambitions?
- **Do something new for the first time:** What emotions surface when stepping outside your comfort zone, and how do they affect your willingness to try?
- **Tackle something difficult:** How do your emotions guide you when confronting tough tasks or challenges?
- **Act in the face of uncertainty:** What feelings help you remain calm and focused amid uncertainty?
- **Grow closer to somebody you love:** Which emotions foster connection and intimacy in your relationships?
- **Be kind and respectful to someone you don't care for:** What emotions can you tap into to show compassion, even when it feels challenging?
- **Maintain grace under fire:** What emotion is most likely to help you respond with composure in high-pressure situations?
- **Give feedback or have candid conversations:** What emotions can help you approach difficult conversations with openness and honesty?
- **Receive feedback gracefully:** Which feelings allow you to accept constructive criticism without defensiveness?
- **Follow through on a commitment:** What emotions drive you to honor your commitments and responsibilities?

Take your time with these questions. Write down your reflections, or discuss them with a trusted friend or coach. Understanding the emotions that influence your actions can empower you to respond more effectively and authentically in various situations.

Envisioning the Change: The Power of Working with Your Emotions

Lacking Emotional Maturity

- You display disruptive outbursts and impulsive behavior, often reacting without thinking.
- You have dysfunctional relationships characterized by conflict, low trust, and chaos.
- You struggle to address disagreements constructively, frequently resorting to blame, avoidance, or passive-aggressive tactics.
- You find it difficult to express your needs clearly, leading to misunderstandings and unresolved issues.

Displaying Emotional Maturity

- You think critically and consider the consequences before speaking or acting, allowing for thoughtful responses.
- You foster strong, healthy relationships marked by trust, empathy, and open communication.
- You navigate conflict constructively, taking personal responsibility for your contributions and seeking resolutions.

- You read emotional signals effectively and can express and advocate for your needs, promoting understanding and connection.

- You recognize and manage your emotional triggers, enabling you to respond rather than react impulsively.

- You utilize healthy coping strategies to deal with stress, such as mindfulness or seeking support, rather than resorting to unhealthy behaviors.

THE PATH TO EMOTIONAL MATURITY

In this next section, you'll learn very practical strategies for overcoming some common barriers to displaying emotional maturity. In doing so, you will positively impact your capacity for answering the questions "What am I feeling, and what are my emotions signaling?"

BARRIER	OVERCOMING STRATEGY	DESCRIPTION
DIFFICULTY IDENTIFYING EMOTIONS	Strategy 1.01: Expand Your Emotional Vocabulary	If you struggle to recognize what you're feeling, strategy 1.01 can help you expand your emotional vocabulary, allowing you to articulate your experiences more clearly.
AVOIDANCE OF UNCOMFORTABLE EMOTIONS	Strategy 1.02: Develop Your Emotional Response Skills	If you tend to shy away from negative emotions, strategy 1.02 encourages you to develop emotional response skills, helping you address emotions constructively and embrace the full human emotional experience.

FEAR OF EMOTIONAL EXPOSURE	Strategy 1.03: Learn from Your Negative Emotions	If you find it hard to sit with your emotions, strategy 1.03 will help you learn from negative emotions, fostering resilience and clarity around your true concerns and desires.
OVERTHINKING OR RUMINATING	Strategy 1.04: Don't Figure It Out—Feel It Out Instead	If you lean toward analyzing your feelings rather than experiencing them, strategy 1.04 will assist you in feeling your emotions fully, leading to greater emotional clarity.
UNAWARENESS OF TRIGGERS	Strategy 1.05: Understand Your Emotional Triggers	If you are unaware of what triggers your emotional reactions, strategy 1.05 will help you identify these triggers, allowing you to manage your responses more effectively.
RESISTANCE TO PAINFUL EMOTIONS	Strategy 1.06: Turn Pain into Power	If you avoid confronting painful emotions, strategy 1.06 will help you embrace uncomfortable feelings to harness their potential for information and transformation.
EMOTIONAL REACTIVITY	Strategy 1.07: Control Your Emotional Impulses	If you struggle with impulsive reactions to stressors, strategy 1.07 teaches you to regulate your emotional impulses through breath control and mindful awareness, enabling you to respond thoughtfully and align your actions with your desired outcomes.

Strategy 1.01: Expand Your Emotional Vocabulary

Imagine that a friend asks how you're feeling. Without hesitation, you reply, "I'm fine—just looking forward to the weekend." It's a typical response, but have you really stopped to reflect on how you actually feel? In reality, you might be feeling anxious about an upcoming deadline or excited about plans with family. This scenario highlights how often we default to generalities rather than doing the work of checking in with ourselves and putting language to our emotional experience.

Most of us want the same thing: to feel *better*. Yet if asked what *better* feels like, we would likely share thoughts, not emotions. Let's play out a few common responses to the question "What would better *feel* like to you?"

"It would feel like my family and friends were taken care of."

"Like everything at work was going smoothly."

"Better would feel like waking up knowing that things are moving in the right direction."

While these examples capture beautiful ideals about a future state, they serve as examples of the way many people answer questions about how they feel: They default to thoughts.

If we take a moment to truly answer the question with a feeling, not a thought, the answers above might change to the following:

"I'd feel confident and safe knowing my family and friends are being cared for."

"I'd feel secure in my job and free to take time off."

"Better would feel exciting and hopeful."

Take a moment to reflect on how you typically respond when someone asks how you're feeling. Do you take the question seriously, or do you dismiss it? If you do answer, is your response honest, or do you default to replies like "Fine," "Okay," or "Good"? Are you using genuine emotional language, or do you tend to respond with thoughts instead?

As you consider these questions, ask yourself this: Do you even recognize your default response? If you're unsure, take a few minutes to pause and think deeply about how you usually answer that question.

Learning to speak the language of emotions is the gateway to fully trusting and embracing them, and you need an emotional vocabulary that has an adequate level of specificity to do that—which means knowing the difference between anger and hurt, annoyance and disgust, happiness and ecstasy.

> The limits of my language mean the limits of my world.
>
> —LUDWIG WITTGENSTEIN

While there are several theories regarding human emotions and how they break down into a set of universally recognizable basic emotions, there is consensus among researchers that there are five basic emotions: anger, fear, sadness, disgust, and enjoyment. Other emotions are derivatives of these five basic emotions that add specificity and degrees of intensity to our experiences. For example, anxiety is a version of fear with worry mixed in, and misery is a more intense version of sadness.

Most of us don't inherently have the ability to name and talk about our emotions, so we must intentionally develop that skill—which can feel messy and confusing. That work is worth it; putting language to what you feel and understanding why you're feeling it helps you control and regulate your emotions and your responses to them. Without this skill, you're at the mercy of your emotions—which is a one-way street to unproductive and unbecoming behavior.

The chart below is a framework for the five basic emotions and the different ways we can experience them. I invite you to use this as a guide to start putting more specific words to your emotions. If you outgrow this basic list, there are abundant, free resources you can access online.

ANGER	When you sense an injustice; when needs or expectations are not met	Annoyed, Frustrated, Tense, Bothered, Resentful, Bitter, Infuriated, Irritated, Mad, Cheated, Vengeful, Insulted, Outraged, Critical, Skeptical	Often felt in the head, jaw, neck, and shoulders
FEAR	When you sense any sort of real or perceived threat, physically or psychologically	Worried, Doubtful, Hesitant, Nervous, Anxious, Terrified, Panicked, Attacked, Horrified, Desperate, Confused, Suspicious, Guarded, Edgy, Concerned	Often felt in the abdomen
SADNESS	When you experience loss or rejection	Lonely, Heartbroken, Gloomy, Disappointed, Hopeless, Grieved, Unhappy, Lost, Troubled, Resigned, Miserable, Discouraged, Devastated, Down, Helpless	Often felt in the eyes, face, and chest
DISGUST	When you are faced with unwanted or unpleasant situations	Disapproving, Loathsome, Offended, Horrified, Uncomfortable, Nauseated, Disturbed, Withdrawn, Evasive, Appalled, Embarrassed, Judgmental, Awful	Often felt in the mouth, throat, stomach, and face
ENJOYMENT	When you experience sensory pleasure and safety	Happy, Grateful, Relieved, Content, Amused, Joyful, Proud, Excited, Peaceful, Satisfied, Calm, Cheerful, Confident, Optimistic, Delighted	Often felt in the eyes, face, and chest

In my personal experience with this practice, here's what I learned:

- I had no real awareness of positive emotions.
- I described my emotions using thoughts.
- Anger came way too easily for me.
- The title of my emotional playlist was "Under Pressure."
- My signature emotions were annoyance, resentment, and frustration.

Most of my negative emotions were correlated to very specific people and situations. My stressors were relatively isolated.

To build your emotional vocabulary and better understand your emotions, try one or more of the following:

- **Emotion journal:** Dedicate a few minutes each day to journaling about your emotions. Use the chart to identify and label the specific emotions you experience throughout the day. Reflect on what triggered these emotions and how they influenced your reactions. Over time, observe any patterns and how your emotional awareness evolves.

- **Build your emotional vocabulary:** Challenge yourself to expand your emotional vocabulary by learning and using new emotion words each week. Aim to incorporate at least three new words into your conversations or journaling. Reflect on how these words help you articulate your feelings more precisely and how they impact your understanding of your emotional experiences.

- **Emotion check-ins:** Set aside three moments each day to pause and perform an emotion check-in. Ask yourself how you're feeling at that moment, and use the chart to identify the specific emotion. Consider what might have triggered the emotion and how you can respond constructively. This practice will help you become more attuned to your emotions and improve your emotional regulation skills.

Strategy 1.02: Develop Your Emotional Response Skills

Imagine you're in a meeting, and a colleague challenges your ideas. You feel your face flush with emotion, but instead of responding, you brush it off and focus on your phone. Later, you find yourself dwelling on the encounter, replaying it in your mind, and wishing you had addressed it. Now you worry that it's too late, but you haven't let it go, and it's about to impact future interactions. You've transitioned from avoidance to indulgence, and understanding these responses is key to developing emotional intelligence.

There are six common responses to emotions. Each of them has productive use cases, but when used unproductively, they can deteriorate our mental and physical health.

Avoidance

When we manipulate a situation in order to escape a feeling or dismiss it entirely, we're practicing emotional avoidance. It's common to pair avoidance with distractions that help fix the physical discomfort in the body and convince ourselves that what we're experiencing is no big deal.

Resistance

When we overregulate an emotion, push against it, or refuse to process it, we're practicing resistance. Resistance is a common response to feeling vulnerable; rather than sitting in discomfort, we may stuff the emotion down. The problem with this response is that the emotion will continue to fester below the surface and reappear later, often at the most inconvenient time.

Indulgence

When we hold on to an unproductive emotion for longer than is necessary or helpful, we're practicing indulgence. Indulging an emotion buys us time when we don't know what to do with it; this response masquerades as useful but is kind of like being in neutral and revving the engine: We don't go anywhere, but we're still using gas.

Reacting

When we are not in control of how we display an emotion, positive or negative, we're reacting to it. Reacting is a common response when we're stressed, we're not seeing things clearly, and we feel unable or unwilling to get in front of the emotional charge and regulate it.

Allowing

When you are present with your emotion and observe it with compassion, you are allowing the emotion to exist. It's that simple.

Seeking

When you intentionally find, create, and leverage situations that produce a desired emotional state, you are seeking emotional experiences that will improve your life.

Building your awareness of these six common responses to emotional experiences can significantly enhance your emotional intelligence. By identifying which responses you tend to overuse, you can gain insights into your default emotional reactions. This understanding allows you to explore and leverage new types of responses, expanding your emotional repertoire. Additionally, recognizing your default responses helps you identify and address potential triggers, ultimately giving you more control over your emotional behavior.

The goal here is to—over time—**allow** all emotions to exist and to develop your skill for **seeking** emotional experiences that enhance your life, relationships, and results.

I have seen this practice reveal transformational insights in my work with clients. One client learned which emotions had the most power over her and found out she was most afraid to feel insecure; her insecurity manifested as outward overconfidence. She compensated for her lack of security by being overbearing and controlling.

In my personal exploration with this practice, I discovered that I resisted feeling weak or vulnerable with every fiber of my being. This awareness opened my eyes to the lengths I would go to and the damage I would inflict on myself to avoid experiencing those emotions.

I'm excited for you to experience equally powerful takeaways. Your work ahead is to grow your emotional self-awareness as you reflect and find answers to the following prompts:

- *When it comes to the emotions you are most likely to avoid, what are you doing instead? How are those distractions helping or hurting you?*
- *What are you protecting yourself from by resisting certain emotions?*
- *What are you most afraid or resistant to feel?*
- *What do you gain from the emotions you seek? Why is this important to you?*
- *What is the cost of indulging in emotions that keep you from taking action and making decisions?*
- *Which emotions do you allow, and which do you resist? What can you learn from that?*

> Let everything happen to you: beauty and terror. Just keep going. No feeling is final.
>
> —**RAINER MARIA RILKE, "GO TO THE LIMITS OF YOUR LONGING"**

Strategy 1.03: Learn from Your Negative Emotions

Imagine you're at home when your partner mentions an unexpected job opportunity that would require relocating across the country. As everyone else excitedly discusses the possibilities, you feel a knot of fear and insecurity tighten in your stomach. Thoughts race through your mind about leaving your current job, uprooting your family, and the uncertainty of starting over in a new place. Emotions—like fear, worry, and anxiety—fight for your attention, and they're all trying to tell you something.

All emotions, both positive and negative, are trying to get our attention and tell us something. In a way, it's their job to be messengers, and they carry out their job by traveling to our body where we *feel them*.

Consider the following negative emotions and the insights they might reveal:

IF YOU ARE FEELING	IT MIGHT SUGGEST
ANGER, BITTERNESS, RESENTMENT, FRUSTRATION, ANNOYANCE	You have an unmet need; something that matters to you is at risk; you feel trapped.
SADNESS, GRIEF, DISAPPOINTMENT	You have experienced a loss or rejection.
FEAR, WORRY	You sense a physical or psychological threat.
ANXIETY	You have a desire to control something you can't; something needs attention; you're experiencing a false sense of urgency.
DISGUST	You may be in an unpleasant situation.

Emotions are complex, yet they serve a vital purpose. When we encounter negative emotions, we often overlook the opportunity to uncover their messages. These feelings exist for a reason, and by taking the time to listen, we can gain valuable insights. While sitting with uncomfortable emotions can feel daunting, it is often in these moments of discomfort that we discover profound truths about ourselves.

Reflecting on uncomfortable emotions allows us to peel back the layers and explore their origins. For instance, anger might reveal deeper frustrations related to unmet expectations, while sadness can signal a loss that needs to be acknowledged and processed. By taking the time to understand what these emotions are trying to communicate, we can gain clarity about what truly matters to us. This reflective practice can help us recognize patterns in our emotional responses and identify recurring themes in our lives, ultimately guiding us toward healthier choices and interactions.

As we learn to understand our emotions, we become more equipped to extend compassion to those around us, recognizing that they, too, may be grappling with their own struggles.

The next time you find yourself in discomfort, rather than dismissing these emotions as burdens, consider following this guided reflection and see what you uncover. You might discover something valuable about your needs, values, and boundaries.

Strategy 1.04: Don't Figure It Out—Feel It Out Instead

I tend to be more of a thinker than a feeler, and if that resonates with you, then this section is for you.

As a thinker, you naturally rely on logic to overcome obstacles when you encounter a block. This instinctive response can lead you to depend heavily on a single center of intelligence—whether it's your head or your gut—while underutilizing other valuable sources of insight.

Take a moment to reflect on the following questions:

- *In which areas of your life do you most often listen to your heart, and where do you find yourself ignoring this vital source of intelligence?*

- *Can you recall a time when you should have paid attention to your heart? How might your outcomes have differed if you had allowed your feelings to guide you through that situation?*

Believe it or not, your mind isn't more qualified than your heart or gut when it comes to problem solving. When you leverage your heart as a partner in making decisions, you tap into an intelligence center that has the power to significantly improve the overall quality of your decisions. Consulting your heart is a sound strategic move, but you might have to build some trust with your body and be prepared to manage your mind when it chimes in.

To experiment with heart-forward decision-making, don't start with life-altering decisions. Begin by consulting your heart on smaller decisions, like what to wear or what task to tackle on a Saturday morning. Give yourself extra time to sit in a moment of stillness and really tune in to your body and its signals. Consider different options, and scan your body as it responds. When your mind chimes in with what it *thinks* you should do, listen, but don't let it control your next steps.

For my feeling friends, I see you too. Similarly, your heart isn't more qualified than your head or gut. Your path for development here involves learning to turn an emotional situation into a math problem. For example, as a solopreneur feeling stressed about how to generate business, you can approach this challenge mathematically. Start by determining how much revenue you need to sustain your business. Next, identify what products or services you want to offer.

Once you have those figures, divide your revenue target by the price of each product or service to calculate how many sales you need to make. From there, you can craft a detailed plan that outlines your marketing strategies, target audience, and sales tactics.

Getting into your head helps take you away from the overwhelming feelings in your body, allowing for a more rational assessment that provides clarity in a challenging situation. Almost anything can be turned into a math problem. This objective perspective can help you find actionable solutions and regain a sense of control over your business.

Strategy 1.05: Understand Your Emotional Triggers

Imagine yourself in a full-team meeting. As you're leading a discussion with the team on upcoming projects, your manager suddenly questions your approach in an area of your expertise. Instantly, a wave of anxiety washes over you, and you feel your heart race as anger bubbles up inside you.

We all face situations where emotional triggers can surface unexpectedly, catching us off guard and challenging our composure. These triggers are your buttons, and when pushed, they're likely accompanied by emotional symptoms (rage, disgust, anxiety) and physical symptoms (sweaty palms, racing heart, tightness, increased body temperature).

Most people have emotional triggers, but they present differently from person to person. Triggers are people, events, circumstances, sounds, smells, and memories that set off an emotional response. Triggers are informed by our experiences, beliefs, and values and are a signal that a need isn't being met.

Imagine attending a school event, eagerly waiting for your parents to pick you up, only to find yourself waiting alone as time passes by. The anxiety of feeling forgotten can create lasting impressions, leading to heightened fears in adulthood—such as the worry of being overlooked in professional settings or left out of important social gatherings. Similarly, if you struggle with impostor syndrome like I do, being unexpectedly criticized in a public setting can feel particularly crippling, intensifying feelings of inadequacy and self-doubt, especially if you're caught off guard. This can leave you questioning your abilities and fearing that others will discover that you don't belong.

Be grateful for your triggers—
they show you where you have work to do.

Understanding and labeling your emotional triggers empower you to respond thoughtfully rather than react impulsively. For instance, I've learned that when I receive constructive criticism, my best response is to take a deep breath and simply say, "Thank you." If I try to say more, things often don't go well, so I stick to this prepared response. Having set responses for your emotional triggers can help you take better care of yourself in those moments. It comforts me to remember that my uncomfortable emotions are temporary. This awareness allows me to take the necessary time to process my feelings, thoughtfully consider the feedback, and integrate what resonates with me.

To effectively navigate your own emotional triggers in the future, take time to prepare your own playbook of thoughtful responses. When you notice them arise, acknowledge the feelings associated with them. If your reactions affect others, take the time to apologize and share that you are actively working on improving. As you become more attuned to your triggers, practice interrupting them and choosing more constructive responses that are less likely to undermine your goals, reputation, or relationships.

One way to get started is by considering the following prompts to study your emotional triggers:

- *What people, situations, events, and sensations trigger an emotionally unproductive response in you?*
- *In these situations, which of your values feels violated?*
- *What are you afraid will happen if you don't express or honor that value?*
- *What is your current response in these situations?*
- *What would be a more thoughtful or productive response in the future?*
- *How could you better care for yourself the next time you experience this emotional trigger?*

Take your time with these questions, allowing yourself to explore your thoughts and feelings deeply. Acknowledging these triggers is the first step toward gaining control over your emotional reactions. Identify what specifically causes these intense emotions, and use this understanding to create strategic responses that promote your well-being and strengthen your relationships. This is a practical way to transform your interactions and improve your overall quality of life.

Strategy 1.06: Turn Pain into Power

For many, the thought of emotional exposure is intimidating. Personally, I'd prefer a root canal over feeling emotionally exposed. What is your most uncomfortable emotion? How far would you go to avoid feeling it?

Here's the good news: You have an emotional superpower—if you're up for a challenge. This superpower is the antidote to your greatest emotional fear.

There's likely an emotion you'd do anything to avoid experiencing, and you've probably done a good job so far. This avoidance perpetuates the fear of that emotion because you haven't fully felt it, fueling your anxiety.

Encountering a situation that triggers this emotion can also trigger irrational fear that is so overwhelming you'd go to great lengths to avoid it. When avoidance isn't possible, you may find yourself battling the emotion like a heavyweight champion. Here are some ways this might play out:

THE MOST FEARED EMOTION	THE GREAT LENGTHS SOMEONE MIGHT GO TO AVOID THAT EMOTION
REJECTION	People who fear rejection might self-sabotage romantic relationships (or avoid them altogether).
SADNESS	People who run from sadness may numb themselves by abusing alcohol, drugs, or food.

THE MOST FEARED EMOTION	THE GREAT LENGTHS SOMEONE MIGHT GO TO AVOID THAT EMOTION
UNCERTAINTY	People who fear uncertainty may avoid risks of all kinds, even those that could enhance and expand their lives.
JOY	Yes, some people fear joy because they believe it will eventually end. People in this bucket may say no to fulfilling endeavors because of the fear that they'll eventually be taken away.
INSECURITY	People who fear insecurity may turn down opportunities to learn and grow out of fear of not being good enough.
DEPRIVATION	People who fear deprivation may recklessly seek sensation, fun, and stimulation to avoid disappointment, pain, and sadness.
CONTROLLED	People who fear losing control may become overly assertive, willful, self-directed, and confident to compensate.
UNLOVED	People who fear they won't receive love may disregard their own needs and overexpress love and generosity to others in an attempt to earn love in return.
CONFRONTED OR ATTACKED	People who fear confrontation may become so compliant and focused on pleasing others that they lose their sense of self.
UNWORTHY	People who fear not being seen as worthy may respond by being responsible, improvement oriented, and self-controlled to the point that they become judgmental, perfectionistic, and critical.

The challenge lies in the fear of the emotion you're avoiding; this fear can grip you tightly, sabotaging your efforts despite your good intentions. To overcome this fear, you must confront the emotion head-on, accepting that the experience will be uncomfortable.

Exposure therapy is a powerful approach that involves gradually facing what you fear, starting with less daunting situations and working your way up to more challenging ones. This process diminishes the hold the emotion has over you, making it more manageable.

By the end of this chapter, you should be better equipped to identify the emotion that is causing the most disruption in your life. If you're still uncertain, take the time to revisit this section. Exploring your shadow side and inner voice can provide valuable insights.

Your work here is to improve your emotional resilience and, in doing so, open up possibilities that have been blocked by your unwillingness to be emotionally uncomfortable. For each emotion you identify, follow these steps:

- **Identify the emotion:** Use a single emotion word to describe what you're most likely to avoid.

- **Identify the opportunities:** List situations that could promote the emotion you've been avoiding. If these circumstances don't arise naturally, create opportunities to challenge yourself.

- **Identify the actions you'll take:** Plan in advance the actions you will take in these situations.

- **Execute your plan:** Put your plan into action, observe the results, make adjustments as needed, and repeat the process. Keep going until you cultivate emotional resilience.

Strategy 1.07: Control Your Emotional Impulses

Imagine starting your day with an optimistic outlook, only to be met with unexpected challenges: an overflowing inbox, a last-minute schedule change, and a child who refuses to get dressed for school while you're trying to leave on time. As the pressure builds, you feel your composure slipping and the urge to react impulsively intensifies. It's in these moments that the ability to remain poised can define you.

Losing your composure in a public setting is rarely a good look, yet most of us can recall moments when we were pushed to our limits. Such turmoil comes with consequences. As daily demands rise, maintaining poise becomes essential—not just as a hallmark of great leaders, but for anyone looking to navigate life's complexities with greater grace.

You invest significant effort into building trust within your relationships, but when you allow your emotions to take control and act in ways that are out of character, it affects those you care about most and shapes how others perceive you. The bottom line is that without this vital skill, you risk damaging both your relationships and your reputation.

I, too, have faced challenges that impacted my reputation. More times than I'd like to admit, I encountered setbacks due to my lack of emotional intelligence. As a natural protector, I believed that standing up for something or someone I cared about justified my uncharacteristic reactions.

Good intentions do not excuse such behavior, and they won't excuse yours either. While there were moments when it felt justified, a more conscious version of myself recognizes that I would have achieved better outcomes with a more measured emotional response.

The skill that can guide you through these challenges is *self-management*. This involves exercising good judgment and discipline when your environment affects your emotions. It's about being intentional with your reactions to any stimulus.

There are numerous strategies for developing emotional (impulse) control, but for those who struggle with impulsiveness, the following two steps are particularly effective. As soon as you notice emotions swelling inside you or become aware of a known stressor (your personal triggers), try these steps:

- **Step 1: Regulate Your Breath.** Breathe in and out through your nose a few times slowly. Don't skip this part, and don't hold your breath. In moments of stress, your body requires more energy; adequate oxygen levels ensure that your cells have the energy needed for optimal functioning. Breath regulation activates the parasympathetic nervous system, which helps calm the body and mind, giving you the much-needed time to respond thoughtfully rather than react impulsively.

- **Step 2: Tune In to Your Emotional Experience.** Take a moment to accurately name and describe what you are feeling using specific words. For example, instead of simply saying, "Angry," you might describe it as "Frustrated" or "Disappointed." Next, reflect on what these emotions are signaling about your needs or desires at that moment.

From there, consider your desired outcome, both in the short term and long term. Ask yourself whether your current emotion will help you achieve what you want or if it might hinder your progress. For instance, if you feel disrespected and want to communicate effectively with a colleague, recognize that this emotion might lead to a reactive response that could push you further away from a productive conversation.

Finally, based on this understanding, think carefully before making any decisions or taking action. This thoughtful approach will help you align your emotional responses with your goals.

For example, when you've had a challenging day at work and walk into a chaotic home feeling depleted and impatient, longing for some version of peace and quiet, the action of lashing out at your family gives you the opposite: more chaos. If you were to self-manage instead, perhaps when you felt your feelings of impatience perk up, you'd take five minutes to engage in a meaningful pause to collect yourself privately before going back into the shared space with your family.

Your stressors and desired outcomes will vary, but consider how you want to feel, how you want to impact others, and what you want the outcome of your actions to be. Then work backward and behave in a way that will give you what you want *most*.

Try combining this approach with the framework in strategy 2.05 to become a just-in-time architect of your thoughts, which will also help you become a just-in-time architect of your emotions.

FINAL THOUGHTS

Your emotions are powerful messengers that can provide valuable insights into your thoughts, desires, and needs. By fully engaging with your emotional experiences and learning from them, you will take a significant step toward emotional maturity and personal fulfillment.

As you progress through this journey of self-discovery, remember that every emotion is valid and worthy of exploration. Embrace the process and allow your emotional landscape to guide you toward a more meaningful and connected life. Doing so can exponentially increase your capacity for greatness.

APPLY YOUR LEARNING

Take a moment to reflect on what you've learned in this chapter. Use the prompts below to guide your thoughts, and make notes on how you can apply these insights moving forward.

Key Takeaways: What are the most imporant insights or concepts you learned in this chapter? Write down two or three key points that resonated with you.

Areas for Change: What is one thing you are most interested in doing differently as a result of what you learned in this chapter? Consider how this change could impact your decision-making or approach to challenges.

Commitments to Practice: Identify two specific actions or practices you are committed to implementing based on what you learned. These could be new habits, questions to ask yourself, or approaches to decision-making.

Erika's recommendations:

- ☐ Commit to intentionally engaging with difficult emotions; explore what they are trying to communicate and how they can inform your decisions.

- ☐ Dedicate time each week to learn and incorporate new emotional words into your conversations and reflections. Aim to identify at least three specific emotions daily.
- ☐ Engage in open conversations with trusted colleagues, friends, or family about your emotional experiences. Share your feelings, and invite them to do the same, increasing trust and connection.
- ☐ Change the habit of using vague terms (fine or okay) to describe your feelings. Start identifying and articulating specific emotions you experience regularly.
- ☐ Focus on identifying specific situations, people, or events that trigger strong emotional responses. Understanding these triggers can help you manage your reactions better.
- ☐ Change any tendency to suppress or ignore uncomfortable emotions. Instead, practice acknowledging these feelings as valid and worthy of exploration.

Reflection on Impact: How do you believe these changes will affect your life, leadership, or relationships? Take a moment to visualize how acknowledging and engaging with your emotions can improve your decision-making process.

Chapter 10

QUESTION 2

What Is True for Me?

Purpose: *Uncovering the mental constructs that shape your reality provides the invaluable gift of a managed mind. By identifying how your conscious and unconscious thoughts influence your experiences and outcomes, you gain the power to redirect or reframe them to serve your best interests.*

> Every man is what he is, because of the dominating thoughts which he permits to occupy his mind.
>
> **—NAPOLEON HILL, *THINK AND GROW RICH***

Imagine being in a meeting when a colleague dismisses your idea. In that moment, it's natural to label their behavior as rude and disrespectful, which can lead to feelings of frustration and a sense of being undervalued. However, if you stop your analysis at this surface level, you risk overlooking the deeper issues at play—and worse, you may attribute your frustration solely to your colleague's behavior.

By taking a moment to reflect, you may uncover an underlying belief: that all voices deserve to be heard and respected. This belief is anchored in your value of inclusiveness. Recognizing this connection helps you understand why your colleague's behavior impacts you so profoundly.

This increase in self-awareness provides an opportunity to evaluate whether or not your belief is valid and empowers you to learn from the experience. You'll not only have a more constructive interaction in the moment but also improve your interactions in future meetings.

Uncovering *what is true for you* goes well beyond surface insights. To get the most from this question, you must dig deeper into your beliefs, motivations, and emotional responses. Consider the beliefs you hold about yourself and others, as these can significantly influence your perceptions and reactions. Reflect on the expectations you have of yourself and those around you, as it can help uncover any unrealistic or rigid expectations that might create unnecessary pressure and lead to disappointment. Your past experiences also play a crucial role; unresolved issues from earlier in life can shape how you respond to current situations. While you can't change your past, you can modify the way you think about it in the present. Furthermore, consider how the fear of judgment by others affects your choices and emotional state—this fear can often lead you to conform rather than express your authentic self. Lastly, examine any tendencies to exert control over situations or people, as this can create stress and make it hard for you to let go.

Understanding what fuels your concerns empowers you to navigate your challenges with greater focus and clarity. It's not just about identifying problems; it's about articulating why they are significant to you personally. By exploring these dimensions and the underlying reasons that make an issue resonate, you gain valuable insight into the mental constructs that may be at the source of your suffering.

Tales of a Teenager

When I was fourteen, I was hanging out at a friend's house where no parents were home when a teenage boy came by and invited us to ride ATVs. Initially I declined, but my friend pulled me aside and assured me it was okay and that we would be safe. This kid was exactly like you might imagine a sixteen-year-old ATV-owning boy in the 1980s to be: He liked to show off and had very little regard for safety or rules. In short, he wasn't the kind of driver you wanted to be a passenger to—but on one summer day, that's exactly what I was.

You can probably see where this is going. Midride, he misjudged the curve, and we both went flying into the air and landed on a concrete driveway. I knocked out my front tooth and was covered in bloody scrapes. I was so disoriented, I didn't know where I was or how to get home. My physical condition was the least of my concerns because I had just become the very opposite of what I worked relentlessly to be: a good, responsible girl. I went door to door, bloodied and bruised, asking strangers for help, all the while terrified at the thought of having to explain myself to my mother.

Eventually we both found our ways home, and everything turned out okay, but while the physical scars healed, I inherited from this experience three new beliefs:

- ATVs are dangerous and should be avoided.
- If you want to be safe, don't let others control the wheel.
- Trust your gut, not your friends.

Given what I went through, these beliefs were rational, especially for my fourteen-year-old brain. But I carried them with me into adulthood, never stopping to question them. Those thoughts ended up wreaking havoc on my relationships and my life, and it took me a long time to see it.

This is the work of mental models.

Your mind is incredibly powerful and is responsible for perceiving the world around you (with help from bodily sensations), thinking, remembering, imagining, and making choices. It dynamically constructs your unique identity, shapes your reality, and directs your life. Managing your mind is not about deceiving yourself or repeating positive affirmations; rather, it is about raising awareness of your conscious and unconscious thoughts and actively directing them to work in your favor, especially when they are undermining your best intentions or interests.

Getting the most from your mind requires intentional evaluation and maintenance. You accomplish this through observing the way you think and feel, understanding how your mind works, spotting patterns, studying how they limit or expand your potential, and making adjustments.

Easy to say. *Not so easy to do.*

So many of us are unaware of the incredible power we have to influence our results, minimize our suffering, and reduce the drama that seemingly seeps into our lives uninvited. When you are in control of your mind, you are in control of your life.

With practice, you can become more aware of your thoughts, challenge and reframe those that are no longer serving you, curate thoughts that propel you toward what you want, and position yourself to respond better under stress.

You can change your mind and, in doing so, change your life for the better.

In this chapter we will explore conscious and unconscious thoughts, how each impacts your life, and what you can do about it.

WHY MIND MANAGEMENT MATTERS

Humans do a lot of thinking. Research estimates that the average person processes over sixty thousand thoughts per day. As much as 75 percent of those thoughts are negative or critical, and up to 90 percent of them are considered repetitive.

In this chapter we are going to explore the relationship between our thoughts and our results, and you might be shocked to learn how powerful it can be to shift even just one unhelpful thought. Once you see the impact, you're going to want to do more of it.

> “Until you make the unconscious conscious, it will rule your life, and you will call it fate.
>
> —**CARL JUNG**”

Your Unconscious Mind Is Directing Your Life

You might think things outside you (your boss, your bank account, your schedule) are what block your progress or impede your results, but while some obstacles are very real, most of what limits us comes from within—and because they aren't obvious, we have to consciously develop awareness around them.

Contrary to what you might think, your brain doesn't provide a literal, factual readout of reality; it *interprets* reality based on your mental models.

Mental models are the abstract and subconscious thought processes we rely on to make sense of our experiences. My accident, and the trust and control issues that came out of it, are just one example. Your brain houses countless mental models that inform and shape how you experience yourself, other people, and the world around you every day.

Think of your mental models as your personal and unique filing cabinet. You have files on everything from life experiences you've had (dating, job interviews, flying on airplanes) to the people in your life (your mother, your boss, your barista). Your files vary in size; your barista file is small, while your mother file may be unwieldy. This filing system quietly works in the background of your everyday life, informing your experiences and interactions. You rely on your files so that you don't approach every person or situation as if it's the first time. You know to put your seat belt on before you put your car in drive; you know what topics to avoid in conversation with your mother.

Like filing systems, your mental models get an update when you have new experiences and learn new information that relates to them. Eventually I grew to believe it was safe to trust my friends and colleagues.

Your mental models can be incredibly useful; they help you make logical assumptions based on past experiences, allow you to easily make sense of complex information, or empower you to perform everyday tasks on autopilot. For example, you don't have to use all your brainpower to start your car; you have a mental model around how keys work.

While this behind-the-scenes processing makes us efficient, it can also make us lazy and complacent and can harm our relationships and limit our lives—unless we pause to question what's in our files.

In my case, one of the conclusions I formed after my accident—"Trust your gut, not your friends"—would go on to create issues for me in various life roles where I took on more than my share of tasks and responsibilities for fear of trusting someone and having them let me down or, worse, hurt me.

Even more insidious is that our mental models are constantly constructing our reality, even when we're not conscious of them. Our filing systems shape what we see and limit (or expand) what we take into our awareness, and that often happens without our consent. Limiting what we take into our awareness limits the amount of potentially useful data we have access to when making decisions. While reading my ATV story, you yourself might have had any number of subconscious reactions that came naturally to you:

- *"Erika never should have gotten on an ATV with a stranger. She learned a valuable lesson that day."*
- *"ATVs aren't that scary. Accidents happen all the time, and it was fine in the end."*
- *"Children that young should never be allowed to operate an ATV. That's dangerous, and her parents are to blame."*

You likely didn't take time to examine or challenge your reaction; you simply reacted and kept reading. Your reaction was constructed by your own mental models, which are based on your experience with ATVs (if any), your relationships to danger and risk, your childhood experiences, and, if you're a parent, your experiences with your own children, among other factors. All this thought processing happens in the background without your conscious awareness of it.

And that's fine . . . sometimes. It's helpful when our mental models kick in and automate our latte order at the coffee shop. It's not helpful when they create self-sabotaging beliefs that subconsciously govern how we experience ourselves, others, and the world around us.

How I think about four-wheelers doesn't cause me strife in my daily life, and that's probably true for you too. But other files—your files on who you are, what you believe, the rules you live by, your life roles, your past, or your sense of responsibility—are likely the root cause of the issues you're experiencing at work and at home. Those are the files we're going to explore together because they are the ones most likely showing up as problematic patterns throughout your life. For example, if you have a tendency to act out when your authority or intelligence is challenged at work, you likely do that at home with your family and friends. If you tend to be disconnected from emotion on the job and approach your coworkers transactionally, you do that in other places as well.

You might not care so much if your coworker feels dismissed, but that same behavior might do damage in relationships where you care deeply about the other person. If you are fortunate enough to get feedback in one life role, it would make sense to explore how that same pattern is showing up—and doing harm—in other life roles.

All models are wrong, but some are useful.

—GEORGE BOX

No model perfectly represents reality, and their usefulness outweighs their imperfection. Even imperfect models can be valuable for prediction, understanding, and decision-making. The good news is that you have immense power to shape your own life, and this transformative process begins with reshaping outdated mental models—those automatic thought patterns that operate in the background and contribute to the challenges you're facing. Your mental models can either support your dreams and goals or hinder them. Our goal is to adjust these models so they work in your favor.

Your Thoughts Dictate Your Results

Now that you understand the concept of mental models, let's explore the relationship between your thoughts and your results and look at how they connect to your models. I am going to share a framework I use extensively in my coaching practice that has the power to radically change your life; it has profoundly changed mine. While this framework is applicable in most situations, it does not apply to trauma. Even though this framework is inspired by psychology, it is designed to be used in a coaching environment, which is about taking forward action in your life. When working through trauma and trauma responses, therapy might be a better alternative.

When you experience something, it passes through your personal subconscious filing cabinet. The mental models in your filing cabinet produce your thoughts: conclusions about your current reality. Sometimes these thoughts are automatic and unconscious (we are unaware of them), and sometimes they are conscious (we are aware of them). Your thoughts evoke emotions, and your emotions in turn fuel your actions. Those actions create your results. In this way, what you think becomes what you feel, what you feel becomes what you do, and what you do creates your results. The sum of your results is your life. Your results are fed back to your filing cabinet, where they are stored for future use. They have the power to reinforce or reshape existing models or shape new ones.

MIND MANAGEMENT MODEL

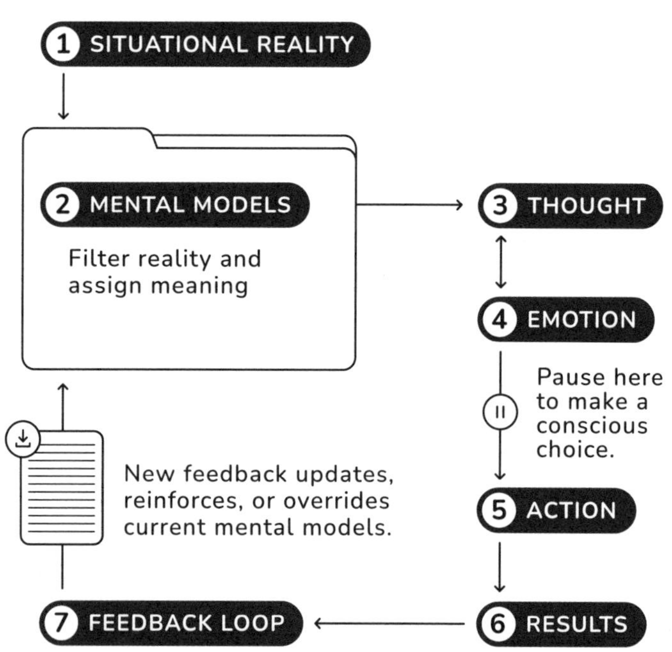

Mind Management Model

As I covered earlier, your greatest power lives in your ability to pause before taking action. This entire book is about helping you learn how to make the most of this pause. Let's play out an example using the model illustrated in figure 2.0.

Your reality: Katie, a member of your team, sends you a document for a client meeting that starts in thirty minutes, and you spot a handful of data errors.

Your mental models: You value personal accountability and believe things should be done right. You experience some dissonance because your previous experience of Katie doesn't match your current experience—you are starting to notice a pattern forming where her work contains errors.

Your automatic thought: *I can't trust anyone. I should have done this myself.*

Your emotion: Frustration

There is no intentional pause or awareness around how your thoughts and emotions are influencing your actions.

Your action: You send your team member a brash email pointing out the errors and ask for the original file so you can make the edits yourself.

Your results: You did the work yourself and humiliated your team member. Katie didn't learn anything except to defer to you.

Your feedback loop: You reinforced your belief that *if you want something done right, you have to do it yourself*, and you've labeled Katie as someone who does sloppy work.

This scenario is probably not foreign to you. In this situation, your reaction is causing a negative result for all the stakeholders involved.

The fortunate thing about our thoughts is that—with training and an intentional pause—we can choose them.

Let's play out the same scenario, but this time let's assume you took a moment to think about your impact as a leader and choose a different thought:

Your reality: Katie, a member of your team, sends you a document for a client meeting that starts in thirty minutes, and you spot a handful of data errors.

Your mental models: You value personal accountability and believe things should be done right. You experience some dissonance because your previous experience of Katie doesn't match your current experience—you are starting to notice a pattern forming where her work contains errors.

Your automatic thought: *I can't trust anyone. I should have done this myself.*

Your emotion: Frustration

You pause, and with awareness of what seems true to you in the moment, you choose to carefully consider your impact, expand your perspective, and think something new on purpose.

Your conscious thought: *Katie is a competent team member, and this isn't the first time Katie's data has been inaccurate. I wonder what we can do to remedy this pattern.*

Your emotion: Curiosity

Your action: You pull Katie aside and inquire about the data errors. She shares that your organization's CRM has been malfunctioning for the past six weeks and that she hasn't been able to escalate the problem so that it can be remedied. You work with Katie to make the necessary adjustments before the document is distributed and make plans to escalate the CRM issue so it can be fixed.

Your result: You partnered with Katie to solve the challenge together and built trust with her in the process.

Your feedback loop: Your opinion of Katie is restored. Your values and beliefs are still working for you.

This process seems easy when you read it on paper, but in practice, it's quite challenging, and that's mostly because your mental models are working so quietly and diligently in the background to ease your mental load. Their job is to make your life more efficient so you don't have to consciously think about every small action you take. The problem is that they can make us lazy, and we might not consciously think about the bigger actions we take either. Remember, your thoughts are optional and alterable. They're not happening *to you*; they're something you have the control to work with, change, and make work *for you*.

When we are not consciously in control of our minds, we end up focusing on what we can't control (reality and results) instead of what we *can* control (our models, thoughts, emotions, decisions, and actions). By directing our mind and choosing our thoughts, we are in the best position to produce desired outcomes.

Taking Inventory

In this chapter, we aim to establish the crucial connection between your thoughts and your results. I invite you to challenge what you believe to be true and realize that **you don't have to believe everything you think**. We will do this by evaluating what's working, shedding what no longer serves you, and updating the files in your mental models that need a refresh.

Think of this chapter as taking inventory. It will help you decide which beliefs and thoughts you want to carry forward and which ones you wish to challenge, change, or replace. The beauty of this process is that who you are and what you believe is largely your choice. Your sense of self is a mental model, and with the right tools, you can examine, edit, and replace those files whenever you choose.

This chapter might be uniquely frustrating for you, and I invite you to participate in this process from a place of nonjudgment. In the work on the next several pages, you're going to be confronted with learning things you're going to wish you'd found out when you were a child—and that can be irritating. You'll also uncover things you don't like about yourself that you want to be different.

Acknowledge them, but don't do more than that just yet. Before you attempt to create change in your life, you need to study what isn't working, what it stems from, and what you're attempting to change. This is the only way to create change that sticks—to tune in to the factors you're trying to shift and the driving forces behind them. If you jump to change, you'll only solve at the surface level, and the problem will likely return.

Envisioning the Change: The Power of Increased Consciousness

Your Unmanaged Mind

- You operate without awareness of your own motives, assumptions, beliefs, and emotions.
- You limit yourself to what is safe or familiar, avoiding risks and new experiences.
- You lack a true sense of self, often underestimating the power you have to shape your reality and drive your desired outcomes.
- You respond defensively and reactively, often without understanding the reasons behind your reactions.

Your Mind Managed

- You understand the connection between your thoughts, emotions, and actions, allowing you to respond thoughtfully rather than react impulsively.
- You are mindful of your actions, understanding what you do, how you do it, and why.
- You are unapologetically authentic, living with a strong, healthy sense of self.
- You take ownership of your conscious and unconscious thoughts and actively examine and reshape them, enhancing your life and achieving better outcomes.
- You recognize and challenge limiting beliefs, enabling you to break free from patterns that no longer serve you.

THE PATH TO MANAGING YOUR MIND

In this next section, you'll learn very practical strategies for overcoming some common barriers to managing your mind. In doing so, you will positively impact your capacity for answering the question "What is true for me?"

BARRIER	OVERCOMING STRATEGY	DESCRIPTION
LOW SELF-AWARENESS	Strategy 2.01: Audit Your Self	If you struggle to recognize your own motives and beliefs, strategy 2.01 can guide you through a self-audit to enhance your self-awareness and your ability to recognize your mental models.
STUBBORN BELIEFS	Strategy 2.02: Challenge Beliefs That No Longer Serve You	If you find it challenging to question long-held beliefs, strategy 2.02 will help you systematically dissect those beliefs, exploring their origins and impact on your life.
OVERTHINKING PATTERNS OR COGNITIVE DISTORTIONS	Strategy 2.03: Watch Your Mind at Work	If you notice your mind racing with negative or repetitive thoughts, strategy 2.03 encourages you to observe these thoughts as an impartial witness, fostering awareness and insight.
EMOTIONAL REACTIVITY OR INSTABILITY	Strategy 2.04: Neutralize Unhelpful Thoughts	If your emotions often cloud your judgment, strategy 2.04 will help you neutralize unhelpful thoughts, allowing you to focus on observable facts rather than emotional interpretations.
BELIEVING EVERYTHING YOU THINK	Strategy 2.05: Become a Just-in-Time Architect of Your Thoughts	If you tend to be unaware of whether your thoughts are supporting or detracting from your desired outcomes, strategy 2.05 teaches you to be flexible and adaptive in your thinking.

Strategy 2.01: Audit Your Self

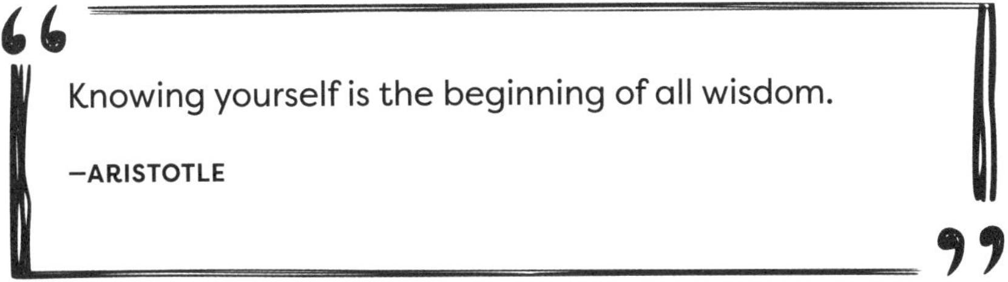

> Knowing yourself is the beginning of all wisdom.
>
> —ARISTOTLE

On their leadership journey, many high performers find themselves stuck—not due to a lack of talent but because their ability to perform exceeds their personal growth. It's often their social and emotional skills rather than their technical competencies that hold them back. With a strong track record of success, they tend to rely on what has always worked for them. However, they eventually realize that they cannot outwork the problem. Instead, they must engage in self-reflection, raise their awareness, and be willing to change.

In this strategy, I invite you to explore your true self for the sake of your growth, relationships, and performance. When I refer to *your self*, I mean your essential being and identity—what makes you uniquely you. My choice to use *your self* instead of *yourself* is intentional, emphasizing the distinction between your core identity and the actions you take.

Let's explore some of the key components of a healthy self:

- **Self-awareness:** You understand how you perceive yourself and recognize that this perception often mirrors how others view you.
- **Self-regard:** You respect and appreciate yourself just as you are.
- **Self-acceptance:** You feel comfortable embracing your true self without needing to change.
- **Self-assurance:** You stand firm in your identity, even in the face of judgment or criticism.

- **Self-actualization:** You are capable of realizing your full potential and pursuing meaningful goals.

Without self-awareness, you may repeatedly encounter challenges in your personal and professional relationships, failing to see how your emotions and behaviors impact others.

If you lack self-regard, you might struggle to advocate for yourself, missing out on valuable opportunities and relationships because you don't believe you deserve them.

A deficiency in self-acceptance can lead to chronic dissatisfaction, as you seek external validation to fill the emptiness you feel, regardless of your many accomplishments.

Without self-assurance, your decision-making may suffer from excessive rumination and doubt, causing you to second-guess yourself frequently.

Finally, if you don't pursue self-actualization, you might remain in your comfort zone, avoiding engaging in pursuits that could lead to a richer, more rewarding life.

Here are some ways to get started with your self-audit. Beware, you might have to exercise some constraint here. Just pick a good starting point and keep going!

Increase Your Self-Awareness Through Personal Assessments: Assessments are an effective way to learn more about your strengths, weaknesses, motivators, stressors, fears, preferences, and tendencies. There are so many to choose from, but here are a few ideas to get you started. Just remember, assessments are tools you can use to elevate your self-awareness, but they are not meant to diagnose or pigeonhole you—nor are they meant to be an excuse for anything.

- Personality assessments: I use many in my practice, and you should have no trouble finding free and paid varieties. Some of my personal favorites are DiSC, Enneagram, and Myers-Briggs Type Indicator (MBTI).
- Attitudinal assessments: An example is the Energy Leadership Index Assessment.

- Values assessment: An example is the Life Values Inventory.
- Strengths assessment: An example is the Strengths Finder.
- Emotional intelligence assessment: An example is EQi-2.0.

Improve Your Self-Regard by Seeking Constructive Feedback: Because you hold yourself to high personal standards, you might struggle to fully appreciate your unique talents and contributions. To gain a better understanding of your strengths, consider seeking feedback from trusted friends, family, or colleagues who can tell you what they appreciate about you or highlight the skills they believe you excel in. This approach can help you recognize and value your strengths more fully.

When seeking constructive feedback, it's important to be specific in your request and provide context about the areas you want to explore. For instance, instead of simply asking others how you can improve, you might share a particular skill or project you're looking to enhance, such as your presentation skills. You could say, "I'm working on making my presentations more engaging. Could you provide specific feedback on my last presentation?" This approach not only clarifies your intent but also encourages more targeted and useful feedback. To ensure that the experience is beneficial for both you and the person providing feedback, here are two recommended responses when you receive their insights:

- ***"Thank you."*** Acknowledge the effort they took to share their insights.

- ***"Please tell me more."*** This invites further discussion and deeper understanding. During this process, avoid defending or explaining yourself; instead, focus on listening and absorbing the feedback.

Grow Self-Acceptance Through Mindfulness: Meditation, prayer, and journaling are superb outlets for discovering and appreciating all your qualities, positive and negative.

Develop Your Self-Assurance Through a Beginner's Mind: Quiet your negative self-talk and bolster your resilience by taking on new things or stretching yourself with the understanding that you don't need to have the answers or perform perfectly when doing something new. Putting yourself in new and uncomfortable situations without all the heavy expectations can be freeing.

Achieve Self-Actualization Through Continuous Learning: Seek opportunities for growth and learning through guided or self-directed study. Choose something meaningful that expands your potential, like a life skill or hobby that expands your knowledge. Consider classes, book clubs, online courses, master classes, and podcasts; the opportunities are endless.

Strategy 2.02: Challenge Beliefs That No Longer Serve You

Your belief system is closely tied to the mental models you developed in childhood, as many of your values and beliefs were formed before you had the critical thinking tools to challenge what you were seeing and experiencing. This belief system began to take shape early in life and continues to evolve today; the cultures you engage with at work and home, your closest relationships, social media, and even the shows you watch all inform and reinforce your beliefs.

The challenge arises when we fail to pay attention to and consciously choose our beliefs. In such cases, our minds may store these beliefs as if they were facts, making it difficult to distinguish between what we believe and the actual truth of a situation.

What we believe shapes our reality, and if we're not conscious of it, we live on autopilot—in the driver's seat but unaware we are at the wheel.

For example, let's say you have long held the belief that timeliness means that being early is on time and that being on time is late. When a colleague arrives late to a meeting or a family member is late for a holiday dinner, you might conclude that they don't care or are being disrespectful—neither of which is necessarily true. However, this belief leads you to treat your interpretation as a fact. Your perception of time assigns meaning and motive to another person's behavior before your conscious mind has the chance to consider other possibilities.

In this case, believing your thoughts may leave you feeling disrespected or annoyed, causing you to respond coldly or dismissively, which could harm the mood or break trust in the relationship. This scenario may sound familiar, echoing what we covered in the previous chapter about understanding your emotions. Now, we're building on that emotional self-awareness to help you trace back to the source of your feelings, giving you the chance to make adjustments. This approach can relieve some of the emotional suffering in the moment and help prevent it in the future.

While the example above illustrates a belief about time, you also have beliefs about yourself and your own abilities that can create a false or altered sense of reality and unnecessarily constrain your capabilities and the capabilities of others.

Now I'm going to ask you to explore some of your own beliefs using this simple seven-step framework for examining any belief that is undermining your life or your relationships. In the following table, I have included some common themes you can choose from, or you can choose one of your own. An example around the theme of success is woven into the prompts to help you along.

Time	Family	Business
Money	Politics	Education
Success	Religion	Health
Conflict	Marriage	Other

Step 1: Identify the Limiting Belief

- Clearly articulate the limiting belief you want to explore.
- *Example: "I believe that I must work hard (borderline excessively) to be successful."*

Step 2: Explore Its Origins

- Reflect on where this belief originated. Consider your upbringing, past experiences, and cultural influences.
- *Example: "I learned this belief from my parents, who always worked long hours. They taught me that nothing in life is free and that success requires hard work."*

Step 3: Assess the Impact

- Evaluate how this belief affects your relationships, results, and overall potential.
- *Example: "This belief has caused me to neglect my personal life, leading to strained relationships and burnout, which ultimately decreases my productivity."*

Step 4: Weigh Costs and Benefits

- List the costs of holding on to this belief versus the benefits of releasing it.
- *Example:*
  "Costs: Increased stress, poor health, lack of fulfillment in personal relationships."
  "Benefits: Sense of security, perceived achievement, and productivity."

Step 5: Reframe the Belief

- Create a handful of realistic options that consider your values and long-term goals, your readiness to embrace the option, and whether the belief can be sustained over time. After your exhaustive list, circle the option that is most aligned with your values and long-term goals.
- *Example:*
  "I can achieve success while working smart and prioritizing my well-being."
  "Prioritizing short breaks for rest and play can enhance my productivity and creativity, making me more successful in the long run."
  "Success means that I also find personal fulfillment and happiness along the way."

Step 6: Test the New Belief

- Implement small changes based on your new belief, and observe the outcomes.
- *Example: Set boundaries around work hours, prioritize self-care, and take regular breaks to see if your productivity improves without burnout.*

Step 7: Reflect and Adjust

- After testing, reflect on the experience. Assess whether the new belief is working for you, and make adjustments as necessary.
- *Example: "After a month of prioritizing balance, I feel more energized and connected with my family, and my work quality has improved. I will continue to find new ways to incorporate this new belief into my actions."*

In previous chapters, we explored the five beliefs most likely to keep you stuck at *good* because they can promote the overuse of control, manipulation, and force to get things done. They rarely solve problems or create lasting change. Whether your limiting beliefs are about you, others, or the world at large, this is a great time to revisit chapters 2 to 6 and spend some time pulling forward the ways in which those core limiting beliefs are showing up for you. Let me be clear: I am specifically asking you to focus on where these beliefs have outgrown their usefulness and have started working against you. It is likely that some of them are working quite well for you.

Strategy 2.03: Watch Your Mind at Work

We can't change what we aren't aware of, so the first step to changing your reality is to raise your awareness. Watching your mind at work is a form of mindfulness where you actively—and without judgment—observe your own thoughts and mental processes as they unfold in real time. The goal here is for you to act as a detached observer of your own mind as it goes through various thoughts and emotions throughout the day.

This requires that we study what is and isn't working in our life and extract the thoughts driving those results. As with all lag measures, we can't change what has already occurred, but we can learn from it.

In my early work with new clients, I often assign them the work of simply *noticing*. Most of them are annoyed by the passive nature of the assignment and get further agitated when I suggest they continue noticing and resist the temptation to start making changes. I share this because I fully appreciate (and share) your preference for action—and there will be time for that. But for now, I encourage you to keep noticing until it is a habit. This is an essential step and cannot be skipped or rushed. I recommend that you stay in this phase for weeks, or even months, before trying to change your thoughts.

> Nothing can harm you as much as your own thoughts unguarded.
>
> —GAUTAMA BUDDHA

Consider the following recommendations for developing your skill of watching your mind at work.

Take Notes: It is important that you actually write them down somewhere. Please don't underestimate the difficulty of this skill because of its simplicity. It takes time and lots and lots of practice. Listed below are a couple of ways to collect your thoughts that work well using a notebook, journal, app, or any other method for capturing notes:

Make a list of your daily headlines—the big thoughts from the day. Sit with those headlines, and see if you can connect them to the results they created without judging the outcome. Just notice.

Pause when you notice you're experiencing stress. Write down all the thoughts you are having in response to the stressor—all of them. Don't judge; just write them all down. You will likely see themes in how you label your situation.

Study Your Findings: Once you've gathered some data, here are a few questions to help you study what's going on:

- What thoughts do you notice you're repeating?
- What themes are you spotting?
- What thoughts are attracting the most success?
- What thoughts are creating stress for you?
- How do you talk to yourself—are you critical and demanding, or are you candid and compassionate?
- How often do you see evidence of the five self-limiting beliefs?

Initiate Change: Once you have sufficiently studied your thoughts and identified any patterns that are undermining your success, then it makes sense to initiate change, using the next couple of strategies in this chapter.

A word of caution: When we begin to see how we are the cause of our suffering and undesirable results, it isn't uncommon to feel badly about it. Instead of judging yourself as bad, wrong, broken, or messed up, remind yourself that you are human and extend yourself some grace.

You are a human with an ego, and your ego's job is to protect you. Normalize that we all have patterns of thought that undermine our goals and sabotage our relationships, all in the spirit of keeping us safe from real or perceived threats.

Strategy 2.04: Neutralize Unhelpful Thoughts

One way to neutralize unhelpful thoughts is to strip away the drama, judgment, and noise, focusing instead on what is observable and factual. This practice helps eliminate unhelpful or unfounded meanings, motives, and blame, making it an effective way to quickly defuse situations that require your immediate attention.

Start by documenting your thoughts and then systematically remove any emotions, adjectives, and descriptors until you arrive at the neutral facts of the matter. You'll know you've succeeded when you can articulate the thought aloud without feeling a strong emotional charge.

For example, let's say you receive a phone call from your boss after missing an important deadline, despite multiple factors contributing to the delay. Your boss says, "I'm terribly disappointed that I didn't get the presentation on time. We're going to look foolish turning it in late, and it will probably hurt our chances of winning the work!" Initially, you might feel defensive and think, *That's unfair. I'm being blamed unjustly; they're attacking my work ethic and clearly don't respect my personal time.*

Let's begin by stripping away the emotional charge from your response:

> *My boss expressed frustration about the late presentation and seemed to attack my work ethic. She clearly doesn't respect my personal time.*

Now, let's remove any assumptions about motives:

> *My boss is concerned about the impact of the late presentation on our team's reputation and the potential loss of the project.*

Finally, shift the focus to your own experience and accountability:

I feel upset that we missed the deadline for the presentation, and I recognize that there might be unintended consequences that need to be addressed.

By reframing your thoughts in this way, you create a more neutral statement that is easier to digest. Instead of feeling defensive, you can approach the situation with a mindset geared toward problem solving. This new perspective empowers you to take constructive actions, such as discussing the challenges you faced with your boss, proposing a revised timeline, or implementing better time management strategies in the future.

Recognizing that your boss's frustration stems from genuine concern rather than a personal attack allows you to respond more thoughtfully and maintain a positive working relationship. Ultimately, this process not only helps you manage your emotional response but also positions you to improve your performance and communication moving forward.

A word of caution for those of you who really like to be right: Your brain will fight you on this. You are in charge of you (and your brain), so don't give in to the temptation. You will find more help on this in chapter 12.

To effectively apply this practice, follow these five steps to neutralize an unhelpful or emotionally charged thought. I've included examples to illustrate how to make each shift:

1. Strip away the adjectives.
    - *Before: My boss was aggressive in that meeting.*
    - *After: My boss shared some opinions in the meeting.*

2. Strip away the words that carry meaning and produce an emotional charge.
    - *Before: Becky was hostile at the all-company update.*
    - *After: Becky didn't seem like herself at the all-company update.*

2. Strip away motive.
    - *Before: Peter has been out to get me since our last project failed.*
    - *After: I felt a shift in my relationship with Peter after our last project.*

4. Strip away blame.
    - *Before: It's the sales team's fault we couldn't close that deal.*
    - *After: We couldn't close the deal.*

5. Make sure the thought is from your point of view and not offered as a statement of fact.
    - *Before: My husband doesn't understand me.*
    - *After: I often feel misunderstood in conversations with my husband.*

None of these steps will change reality. In fact, they are designed to help you stop trying to alter the reality that exists and guide you closer to seeing it clearly. Remember, suffering is optional.

Strategy 2.05: Become a Just-in-Time Architect of Your Thoughts

I used to believe it was my responsibility to have all the answers and to have them readily available. Convinced that my value stemmed from what I knew, I relied heavily on—and rarely questioned—my assumptions, especially if doing so risked slowing down progress or compromising results.

If you find yourself in a similar mindset, pay attention: This tendency can be dangerous, particularly in a leadership role. The power associated with your position may discourage others from challenging you, and even if they do, you might not be inclined to listen. One of the key responsibilities of leadership is to regularly evaluate and update your thoughts and beliefs to ensure they foster the best outcomes for both yourself and those around you.

Great leaders who have learned to observe their minds at work can identify when their thoughts are serving them and when they are holding them back. This awareness allows them to craft new, intentional thoughts designed to propel them toward success. I refer to this as becoming a "just-in-time architect" of your thoughts.

If you aspire to create meaningful and lasting change in your life, you must be willing to invest the effort required to change your thinking—and this process takes time. I understand that this can be a tough pill to swallow; you want results, and you want them quickly. However, transforming your life is a long game, and it will become easier with practice.

Merely understanding the concepts I'm sharing with you on an intellectual level isn't enough; you must commit to taking action every single day, even when it feels inconvenient or uncomfortable.

Here's a repeatable process for achieving intentional results in your life by adjusting your thoughts. This approach aligns with many popular coaching and self-coaching models, providing a structured way to guide your mindset and actions toward desired outcomes.

- **Step 1: Establish Your Desired Result:** Before choosing your new thought, consider what you want most. Your result should not include changing your circumstance, altering reality, or controlling another person. And further, it should be your result, not someone else's.

- **Step 2: Identify the Action Required:** Once you know what you want, consider all the actions that might bring you to the result you desire—then choose one.

- **Step 3: Identify the Emotion That Will Fuel This Action:** Once you know what you need to do, identify the emotion that will naturally produce it. The strategies in chapter 9 that support question 1 can help you with this.

- **Step 4: Choose a Thought**: If you are finding a new thought to serve you in the moment, decide what you will think about your situation. Even if your situation is imperfect, find a thought that has the potential to drive the required emotion and action you identified above.

If you are changing your thought to something more helpful, find a middle-ground thought (a click or two past the neutral thought) instead of going for the opposite thought; when you think, *This is wrong*, instead of trying to make yourself believe *This is right*, choose the more neutral *This is interesting*. Keep in mind that it doesn't have to be true; it just has to be believable—so don't swing for the fence.

If you are challenging a deeper mental model (such as a belief), commit to your new thought and repeat it often and on purpose—even if it doesn't feel natural or create results at first. Remember, this is a long game.

- **Step 5: Execute and Learn:** Dispatch your new thought at your first opportunity, and capture the result. If you achieve the desired outcome, congratulations. If not, repeat the process, knowing that you're one step closer to finding what works.

- **Step 6: Repeat:** The more you do this, the better you will become at the "just-in-time" part.

I can't emphasize it enough: When your new thought aims to change a mental model (such as a belief), it's crucial to consciously think this new thought repeatedly. Each new thought moves you closer to a belief that supports you, enhancing your ability to transform your results. You can apply this process to any aspect of your life, including your past. While you can't change what has already happened, you can shift how you think about those experiences now. I have helped countless leaders reframe past events into experiences that no longer cause pain, shame, guilt, doubt, anger, or resentment but instead propel them forward in ways they hadn't dreamed possible.

If you want to experiment with this framework, try changing how you think about any of the following mental models that may not be serving you:

- Any past experiences that still cause you suffering in the present
- Beliefs that are not working for you any longer (beliefs about time, money, success, etc.)
- How you think about yourself and what's possible for you
- Your identity
- Your negative self-talk
- How you think about (or judge) others
- Your interpretations and assumptions

FINAL THOUGHTS

Embracing the work of understanding what is true for you is a significant step toward achieving emotional maturity and personal fulfillment.

Stretching yourself to call more into your conscious awareness is where this question really gets traction, so resist the urge to stay on the surface when engaging with this question. This journey requires patience and commitment, but the rewards are profound. By aligning your thoughts and beliefs with your true self, you will find greater clarity, purpose, and satisfaction in your life.

Remember, the path to understanding yourself is not a linear journey; it is filled with twists, turns, and moments of self-discovery. As you commit to exploring your thoughts and beliefs, you'll likely encounter both enlightening and challenging revelations. Embrace them as part of your growth.

By implementing the strategies outlined in this chapter, you can develop a deeper awareness of your thoughts, emotions, and beliefs, allowing you to reshape your mental models to better serve your goals and cultivate a more authentic and empowered version of yourself.

APPLY YOUR LEARNING

Take a moment to reflect on what you've learned in this chapter. Use the prompts below to guide your thoughts, and make notes on how you can apply these insights moving forward.

Key Takeaways: What are the most important insights or concepts you learned in this chapter? Write down two or three key points that resonated with you.

Areas for Change: What is one thing you are most interested in doing differently as a result of what you learned in this chapter? Consider how this change could impact your decision-making or approach to challenges.

Commitments to Practice: Identify two specific actions or practices you are committed to implementing based on what you learned. These could be new habits, questions to ask yourself, or approaches to decision-making.

Erika's recommendations:

- ☐ *Identify one limiting belief that you recognize in your life. How can you apply the strategies in this chapter to challenge and reframe this belief?*
- ☐ *Consider a situation where you've reacted impulsively due to emotional triggers. How might you use the insights from this chapter to respond differently in the future?*
- ☐ *Schedule time to reflect on your thoughts and emotions to better understand your mental models.*
- ☐ *Practice the technique of stripping away judgment from your thoughts to see the clear facts in challenging situations.*

Reflection on Impact: How do you believe these changes will affect your life, leadership, or relationships? Take a moment to visualize how understanding your mental constructs and their impact might transform your life, leadership, or relationships. What changes do you anticipate as a result of this commitment? Consider how this clarity will enable you to make more intentional choices in alignment with your values and desired outcomes.

Chapter 11

QUESTION 3

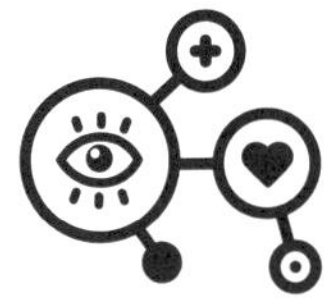

What Might Be True for Others?

Purpose: *Compassionate curiosity offers the gift of an expanded perspective. By setting aside judgment and engaging in meaningful inquiry—especially under pressure or in challenging situations—we open ourselves to a broader understanding of others' experiences.*

> Compassion is not a virtue—it is a commitment. It's not something we have or don't have—it's something we choose to practice.
>
> —**BRENÉ BROWN**

Wouldn't it be wonderful if other people's words, actions, and decisions truly reflected what was happening inside them? Relationships would be so much easier without the need to guess, read minds, check for understanding, or decode motivations and intentions. Imagine if we could take people at their word—when someone tells you "I'm fine," you could actually believe them.

But that's not how humans function; in reality, it's often quite the opposite. What we say or do is not always an accurate indicator of our internal experiences, and many of us lack the skills to see beyond the visible aspects—like words and actions. When we encounter behavior that seems questionable, we might quickly judge them and chalk it up to a character flaw. Ironically, while we prefer to be judged by our intentions, we tend to judge others based on their actions, behaviors, or words.

Fortunately, there is a better way: **practicing compassionate curiosity**.

When you approach yourself and others with compassionate curiosity, you refrain from judging and avoid assuming you already know the answer; instead, you engage in the process of discovery. You listen not just to respond but to learn, understand, and connect more deeply. This involves asking curious, open-ended questions with the intent to learn rather than seeking to confirm your preconceived biases. Above all, it's essential to come from a place of love—always.

I can almost hear you now: "But Erika, I was told that when people show you who they are, believe them . . . and don't actions speak louder than words?" I understand where you're coming from—and it's important to acknowledge what people show us. However, staying open and curious allows us to consider the context behind those actions. There are many reasons people may act out due to stress or personal challenges we know nothing about. Engaging in dialogue can help us understand their true intentions. With that additional perspective, we can make more conscious choices.

This is where the question "What might be true for others?" becomes vital. By asking ourselves this question, we shift from a judgmental perspective to one of genuine curiosity and discovery. This shift encourages us to explore the underlying reasons behind someone's behavior, prompting us to consider their feelings, experiences, and challenges. For example, if a colleague snaps at you, instead of immediately feeling offended or defensive, you might pause and ask yourself, *What might be going on in their life that led to this reaction?* This curiosity can lead you to consider that they may be dealing with personal stress, a heavy workload, or other pressures that you are unaware of. By recognizing that their behavior may not be about you, you can respond with empathy rather than judgment.

Compassionate curiosity not only enhances your understanding of others but also strengthens your relationships. When you approach interactions with the mindset of wanting to understand what might be true for someone else, you create a space for open dialogue where both parties can express their perspectives. This can lead to resolution, collaboration, and ultimately deeper connections.

Moreover, staying open to the experiences and emotions of others empowers you to influence them positively. The more you allow yourself to be influenced by their circumstances, the more effectively you can engage with them and support their needs. This reciprocal relationship amplifies trust and leaves everyone feeling valued and understood.

In this chapter, you'll learn practical strategies you can use during that critical pause between judging another person's behavior and taking action. The pause is similar to the calm before a storm. It's where the environment is rich with energy and information—if you are prepared to take it in. It's the time to ignite all your senses and direct your energy toward learning, discovering, and controlling yourself instead of the situation or the other person.

Compassionate curiosity is a skill all great leaders must develop to lead themselves and others to greatness. That's the work we're here to do in this chapter.

WHY COMPASSIONATE CURIOSITY MATTERS

Judith E. Glaser was an American author, academic, business executive, and organizational anthropologist. She was the founder of the CreatingWE Institute, and in her book *Conversational Intelligence*, she reminds us that getting to the next level of greatness depends on the quality of the culture, which depends on the quality of the relationships—and that depends on the quality of our conversations.*

As part of an inaugural group of coaches who were certified in her construct Conversational Intelligence, I was fortunate to learn from her before

---

* Judith E. Glaser, *Conversational Intelligence: How Great Leaders Build Trust and Get Extraordinary Results* (Routledge, 2016).

she passed in 2018. I learned so much from her, but what sticks out the most is that *words matter, conversations matter, people matter,* and *we is greater than me*. That last concept helped me see that moving from an *I*-centric focus to a *we*-centric focus means shifting away from protective behavior into partnering behavior that prioritizes success for all, not just individual success.

Letting go of control and moving out of overresponsibility is what creates space for others to flourish, making it more likely that our relationships and results will also flourish. And maybe you already know and agree with these premises, but working with leaders at all levels, I have come to learn that choosing our words, architecting conversations, and choosing to partner with others are learnable skills, but they take practice—and lots of it.

In my work across dozens of industries, I've found that there's one striking similarity among them: People struggle with the difference between leading and managing. Great contributors, like you and me, often get promoted into management roles because of our ability to perform. Our skills and abilities make us stand out in a crowd, and we get rewarded by being promoted. So we wake up one day in a new role with a track record of success yet no practical experience with the other half of our job: leading people. And worse, we keep leveraging the wrong set of skills, unaware that what got us *here* won't get us *there*.

At the root of most leadership issues is not a lack of skill or competency on the part of those you lead but rather a lack of compassion and openness on yours. It is also likely that you have a blind spot around the way your own ability has become a liability. That may sound harsh—perhaps you consider yourself a compassionate person—but go with me on this for a moment.

When people don't feel seen, heard, or understood, their natural tendency is to take on less, do the bare minimum, and disengage. When it feels like you and your work don't matter, why bother? We all want to feel that our contributions add value, and when we don't, we're never going to perform at our best.

This becomes a problem for you as a leader when your team is underperforming but you're still held to the standards and metrics set for them. Similarly at home, you might believe your kids are falling below their potential. Feeling the pressure, you may default to judgment, blame, or control—all of which exacerbate the problem.

There's a more effective approach to leading others under pressure: the powerful combination of curiosity and compassion. A key aspect of becoming a more conscious leader is resisting the urge to assume you know everything and instead remaining open and curious. Curiosity goes beyond simply asking questions; it means maintaining an open mind to the possibility that you may not know the full story or that someone else might have a better solution. And here's the kicker—you must be willing to be wrong.

The real power emerges when you blend curiosity with compassion. Compassion helps us move away from judgment and toward understanding, and at its best, it fosters appreciation. By practicing compassion, you can uncover the needs and concerns of others, increase trust and commitment, and promote higher levels of accountability.

Compassion differs from caring and empathy. While we can show we care by extending kindness to others and express empathy by imagining the world from another person's perspective, compassion goes deeper. Leading with compassion involves actively seeking to understand the source of another person's suffering and striving to alleviate it—without overreaching or overpowering.

To inspire others to reach their greatness, we must learn to bring out the best in them, draw out their wisdom, and unleash their potential. This means focusing on their needs rather than simply imparting our own wisdom or showcasing our potential. The best way to achieve this is by remaining open and curious, genuinely considering the needs, wants, and challenges of those we lead.

This practice requires us to shift our focus from our own stressors to the obstacles faced by others. Under stress, it's natural to concentrate solely on our own needs and challenges, but this can come across as insensitive or even cruel. By choosing compassionate curiosity, we broaden our perspective to include others, signaling that we care, want to help, and are committed to shared success.

This level of leadership demands a greater investment of time and energy than mere management. It's crucial to remember that while we manage tasks, we lead people. Knowing when and how to consciously switch between these roles is essential.

As you develop this practice, take a moment to check in with yourself after your initial attempts. Are you genuinely being curious and compassionate, or are you attached to a specific outcome or hoping the other person will change? If so, your intention may not be to understand but to serve your own interests, which can come across as manipulative—even if that wasn't your intent.

The goal is to remain considerate of others while also addressing your own needs; it's about shifting the focus from *me* to *we*. This approach isn't easy, but with time, patience, and commitment, these skills are learnable.

Envisioning the Change: The Power of Expanding Perspectives Through Compassionate Curiosity

Lacking Compassionate Curiosity

- You appear insensitive or indifferent to the needs and emotions of those around you, leading others to feel dismissed or invalidated.
- You display a lack of empathy, resulting in misunderstandings and unhealthy conflict.
- You erode trust and connection through judgment, criticism, and an overly practical focus on logic and facts.
- You prioritize your own needs and wants, exhibiting a me-first mentality, and stagnate due to a low desire to learn or explore new perspectives.

Harnessing Compassionate Curiosity

- You respond in ways that leave others feeling seen, heard, understood, and supported.
- You maintain an open mind, validating others' emotions and experiences.

- You deepen trust and connection through openness, curiosity, and a desire to understand.
- You weigh the needs, wants, and challenges of others as equally important to your own, fostering a *we-first* orientation and learning from the ideas and perspectives of your peers.

THE PATH TO COMPASSIONATE CURIOSITY

In this next section, you'll learn very practical strategies for overcoming some common barriers to expressing compassionate curiosity. In doing so, you will positively impact your capacity for answering the question "What might be true for others?"

BARRIER	OVERCOMING STRATEGY	DESCRIPTION
JUDGMENTAL MINDSET	Strategy 3.01: Find Compassion for Yourself	If you find yourself quick to judge others, strategy 3.01 can help you cultivate self-compassion, making it easier to extend compassion to others.
LACK OF EMPATHY	Strategy 3.02: Find Compassion for Others	If you struggle to relate to others' experiences, strategy 3.02 will guide you in listening and responding with empathy.
RIGID THINKING	Strategy 3.03: Be Mentally Flexible	If you have difficulty seeing multiple perspectives, strategy 3.03 encourages mental flexibility, prompting you to explore alternative viewpoints before making decisions.

BARRIER	OVERCOMING STRATEGY	DESCRIPTION
DISTRACTED LISTENING	Strategy 3.04: Direct Your Focus When Listening	If you often think about your response while someone else is speaking, strategy 3.04 will help you focus on the other person and enhance your listening skills.
IMPATIENCE IN CONVERSATIONS OR JUMPING TO CONCLUSIONS	Strategy 3.05: Ask More Than You Tell	If you tend to interrupt or rush to provide solutions, strategy 3.05 will support you in asking more questions and allowing others to fully articulate their thoughts.
PRESUMED UNDERSTANDING	Strategy 3.06: Establish Common Ground with Clarifying Questions	If you assume that everyone shares the same understanding, strategy 3.06 will remind you to ask clarifying questions to ensure alignment and shared meaning in conversations.
ASKING LEADING QUESTIONS	Strategy 3.07: Ask More Powerful Questions	If you find yourself asking questions that lead others to a specific answer, strategy 3.07 will empower you to ask more open-ended and thought-provoking questions, fostering genuine curiosity and learning.

Strategy 3.01: Find Compassion for Yourself

I'm curious: In what situations do you feel justified in withholding compassion from yourself? Do you actually benefit from doing so? What would need to change for you to not only believe you deserve compassion but also feel compelled to give it to yourself?

When we judge ourselves harshly, we're more likely to extend that judgment to others, projecting our self-criticism onto them. When clients come to me with issues in trusting others, it often stems from a lack of trust in themselves, particularly in interactions with those they struggle to trust.

Similarly, we cannot truly demonstrate compassion for others if we withhold it from ourselves. Cultivating compassion for others begins with practicing self-compassion—and you don't have to compromise your high standards or commitment to excellence to do this.

Self-compassion involves being kind and understanding toward yourself, especially during times of pain, failure, or feelings of inadequacy. In these moments, self-criticism often becomes the default. While judgment is a natural human response, it's crucial to have your own back. When you don't support yourself—either because you feel undeserving or hope for someone else to step in—you deny yourself compassion and inadvertently invite sympathy or pity from others. Not ideal.

There is no one-size-fits-all approach to self-compassion; the key is to find a practice that resonates with you. Some self-compassion practices that have worked for others include the following:

REFLECTION	Journaling or taking a walk to process your thoughts or feelings
MEDITATION	Focusing on the breath and body to create awareness of what you're experiencing
CONNECTION	Reaching out to friends or family and spending quality time with them
SELF-CARE	Doing something nice for yourself such as engaging in physical activities, hobbies, or relaxation
MINDFULNESS	Reminding yourself that you're human, monitoring your thoughts for signs of self-criticism, and neutralizing your negative thought patterns

Through biofeedback, your body will guide you in selecting the practice—or combination of practices—that best suits you. Pay attention to changes in your heart rate, breathing patterns, and body temperature. When you engage in one of the methods mentioned and notice a positive physiological change, that's your body's way of signaling that what you're doing is effective.

Strategy 3.02: Find Compassion for Others

Think about a leader or mentor who made you feel truly heard and supported. Their ability to create a safe space for your learning and growth likely left a lasting impression, paving the way for your continued development. What a gift that is!

Compassionate leaders set a powerful example by demonstrating behaviors that build trust and foster a safe environment for experimentation and failure. This approach cultivates relationships and cultures that thrive. As we've discussed, caring for others is different from showing compassion. By choosing to expand your capacity for compassion, you can develop essential skills.

Before moving forward, take a moment to reflect on the following questions:

- **Where do you withhold compassion from others?** What makes it difficult for you to express compassion in those situations?
- **Where do you freely extend compassion to others?** What makes it easy for you to show compassion in those situations?

It's important to understand that having compassion for others is distinct from pitying or feeling sorry for them. Pity often leads us to try to fix or rescue others, which can strip them of their personal power. The key difference lies in the level of judgment we hold, the meaning we assign to the situation, and whether we take others' experiences personally.

Compassion involves pausing judgment and creating space to genuinely care for and respond to others' needs, challenges, and emotional experiences. Here are six practical ways to experiment with extending compassion to others:

- Listening intuitively and empathetically
- Acknowledging that others' experiences may be different from your own
- Being conscious of how your words and actions impact others
- Offering support or encouragement
- Being tolerant and open minded
- Staying curious and judgment-free

It's important to note that you don't have to agree with a person's actions—how they got here—to express compassion. In fact, instances where you disagree with a person's choices or actions are a perfect opportunity to turn down your personal judgment and lean into empathy and understanding. Trust me—this will be difficult but well worth the effort.

Strengthening your compassion skills will help you develop a deeper level of trust, understanding, and connection with those around you. If you adopt a few of these behaviors into your routine, it will become more natural over time.

Strategy 3.03: Be Mentally Flexible

Think of a time when you faced a decision with competing perspectives or possibilities. The urge for certainty tugged at you, pushing you to make the "right" choice, yet this need for certainty held you back. It's in these moments of uncertainty that mental flexibility becomes a powerful asset, allowing you to pause, consider alternatives, and make more informed choices.

If your brain craves certainty, like mine, keep reading. Psychologist Virginia Satir once said, "We feel better with the certainty of misery than the misery of uncertainty."* However, your ability to remain mentally flexible—despite your natural inclination to seek certainty—is a leadership superpower.

---

* Virginia Satir, as quoted by Jerry Jampolsky, *Love Is Letting Go of Fear* (Bantam Books, 1979), 44.

Mental flexibility is the ability to hold differing or even competing thoughts simultaneously while remaining open to shifting your thoughts or actions based on new information. I like to think of it as hanging between two points on the monkey bars, each hand firmly gripping a different rung. These bars might represent differing perspectives, meanings, actions, emotions, or motivations—but more importantly, when in this position, you retain the option to shift or adapt before making a final decision on which direction to go.

This tool is powerful because when two or more thoughts compete, it compels us to broaden our perspective by seeking additional information. This expanded viewpoint increases our available options, enabling us to make more informed decisions, navigate setbacks or obstacles, manage difficult emotions, and function more effectively in challenging circumstances.

Moreover, staying open to being influenced by the very things you wish to influence can enhance your effectiveness as a leader and a collaborator. The degree to which you allow others' perspectives, feedback, and experiences to inform your own decisions and perspective directly impacts how much influence you can have in return. By being receptive to others, you not only gain valuable insights but also foster an environment of trust and collaboration, encouraging those around you to share their thoughts and ideas.

To harness this power effectively, start by becoming aware of moments when you assume you know—when you jump to conclusions without having the full picture. Next, imagine what it would feel like to entertain an alternative thought, one that differs from what you currently believe to be true. Explore your options. Visualize them side by side, allowing them to coexist. Finally, consider which option or thought aligns best with your goals or brings you closer to your desired outcome—what you truly want from the situation you're in.

Here are some questions designed to help you relax your judgment or conclusion and consider alternate options:

- *What conclusion have you formed?*
- *How valid are your assumptions?*
- *When you consider what is true for you, could the opposite be true?*

- *What else could be true?*
- *What would others say?*
- *What do the facts say?*
- *What did you ignore or not pay attention to?*
- *What other sources of data haven't you considered?*

By actively engaging with these questions, you open yourself up to new possibilities and insights that can transform your thinking. Embracing mental flexibility not only enhances your decision-making but also enriches your relationships and interactions with others. When you allow yourself to be influenced by different perspectives, you create a dynamic environment where collaboration thrives and everyone involved can benefit from shared insights. Ultimately, this willingness to adapt and grow will lead to more meaningful outcomes and a deeper understanding of both yourself and those around you.

Strategy 3.04: Direct Your Focus When Listening

Imagine being engaged in a conversation with a friend who is visibly stressed. As they share their troubles, you find yourself nodding, your mind racing ahead to solutions. You've been in this situation countless times before, armed with advice and eager to help. But as you interject with what you think is a brilliant suggestion, your friend's reaction isn't what you expected. Instead of gratitude, you notice a flicker of frustration or disappointment. It's a moment many of us have experienced—a reminder that listening is more than just waiting for your turn to speak.

You are a rich source of knowledge and wisdom, and people regularly come to you for help. This is beneficial in many areas of your life but can become a hindrance when it comes to listening.

If you're like most people, when listening, your brain is busy formulating a response long before the other person has finished speaking. This often comes from a good place; with your vast collection of knowledge and experience, you're eager to jump in and help.

However, in these situations, your inner dialogue can hijack your focus. You can't fully attend to the speaker if you're preoccupied with what you'll say next. Additionally, other thoughts may be swirling in your mind: *Did I leave the stove on? What time is the soccer game tonight? Did I reply to that email yesterday?*

Your ability to be genuinely and compassionately curious is tied to your capacity to direct all of your focus to the other person and listen intuitively, empathetically, and without judgment. This requires tuning out distractions and listening with all your senses to the entirety of what's being communicated, including body language, nonverbal signals, and what isn't being said.

When you approach conversations with this level of listening, you can practice compassion and nonjudgment and express genuine curiosity. If you struggle to maintain curiosity, you may still be holding on to judgment; in those moments, lean into compassion and find common ground or understanding.

Cultivating this skill is challenging; most of us don't naturally listen this way. Additionally, our personal biases and attachments to desired outcomes can interfere. We might ask questions to which we already know the answers, steer conversations in preferred directions, or inadvertently sabotage the dialogue.

To practice this skill, listen with all your senses and bring your focus back to the speaker whenever it drifts. Choose where your attention goes, and trust that when it's your turn to speak, you'll know exactly what to say.

Strategy 3.05: Ask More Than You Tell

Picture this: You're in a meeting, and a colleague is passionately sharing their idea. As you listen, your mind races with counterpoints and potential pitfalls. Before you know it, you've interrupted, eager to share your insights. The room goes quiet, and you notice a shift in the atmosphere. It's a common scenario where the impulse to showcase your knowledge can overshadow the opportunity to empower and learn from others. While it might not be intentional, it is no less disruptive.

Reflect on the last few times you chose to showcase your own talent or wisdom instead of empowering others, learning, or discovering. How might the other person have benefited from solving their own problem? What reasons did you use to justify your decision to take charge?

Leaders who tell more than they ask become less effective over time. Period.

Consider these scenarios: You walk the production floor and notice a team member not following procedure, so you immediately point out their mistake. In a meeting, a colleague shares an idea, and you jump in to explain why it won't work. After coming home from work, your spouse begins sharing challenges from their day, and you rush to tell them how to fix it.

The issue here is jumping to conclusions without understanding the full story, lacking clarity and context. You might think you're helping, but without comprehending the other person's complete experience and needs, how could you truly be assisting?

While you might think you're helping to solve the problem as you see it, rushing to give advice without context causes two more of them—you end up solving the wrong problem, and you create dependencies.

1. **Solving the wrong problem:** A common issue I observe when working with teams is the tendency to bury the lede when surfacing issues. Often, people do not present the real problem up front, yet leaders may jump to offer advice before fully understanding the core issue. As a result, they end up addressing the wrong problem, allowing the true issue to persist and resurface later.
2. **Creating dependency:** When you rush to solve someone else's problem, you prevent them from working through it themselves. By taking ownership of the solution, you inadvertently foster dependency, making them reliant on you for future problem solving. This pattern encourages learned helplessness and hinders their growth and critical thinking. Meanwhile, you might find yourself frustrated, wondering why you seem to be the only one capable of getting things done or figuring things out.

In one of my favorite books, *The Advice Trap,* author Michael Bungay

Stanier addresses the natural tendency in us all to compulsively give advice instead of coaxing out the brilliance in others. He suggests we suffer from one of three distinct personas*:

- **Tell-It:** This persona is the loudest and most obvious, and it convinces you that you add value by having all the answers. It can make you believe that if you don't have all the answers, you're letting everyone down.

- **Save-It:** This persona is a little quieter than Tell-It, and it convinces you that your job is to keep everybody safe. It can make you believe you're responsible for making sure nobody ever stumbles, struggles, or fails.

- **Control-It:** This persona is the most subtle and elusive, and it convinces you that the only way you win is to maintain control at all times. It can make you believe you shouldn't trust or assume the best in others.

Your intentions are good when you give advice. Your heart is usually in the right place, and if you're being completely honest, offering advice and solving other people's problems feels good.

I can almost feel your objection here: "But Erika, I do know more or have more experience. I can save others the time and aggravation of learning something I already know. Isn't that just a big waste of time?"

It's almost as if you've been training for it your whole life and you're finally getting a chance to step up to the plate and showcase your batting skills, and I'm telling you to take a pitch. It's tough watching a perfectly good pitch go to waste, but that's leadership, my friend. Being quick to solve others' challenges robs them of a development opportunity and encourages their reliance on you. It might solve the problem of the day,

---

* Michael Bungay Stanier, *The Advice Trap: Be Humble, Stay Curious & Change the Way You Lead Forever* (Page Two, 2020).

but then they're back tomorrow with a similar problem, and this keeps you *and them* stuck at *good*.

Let me be very clear: There is a time for giving direction. Your job is to know when direction is needed—generally when confidence, willingness, or competence is low—and when to seek additional context, expand the conversational space, or encourage others to experiment and find their own answers. Given the chance, most people will surprise you and themselves. It must be said that this is another one of those patterns that shows up across your life roles: If you do this at work, you do it at home too.

Strategy 3.06: Establish Common Ground with Clarifying Questions

Imagine a simple conversation about commitments for a work project. You say, "I'll handle it later," assuming everyone understands your timeline. But days pass, and your team is frustrated, having expected "later" to mean something entirely different. It's a common scenario where assumptions about shared meaning lead to misunderstandings and conflict.

Think about the last few times you encountered a misunderstanding that led to conflict. What context would have helped prevent the misunderstanding?

> In a world where you can be anything, be kind—and when in doubt, ask for clarity.
>
> —UNKNOWN

We often assume the words we use carry shared meaning with others. We use words to convey meaning, but we often forget to pause and confirm understanding. A relatable example is the word *later*. In my house, "later" means very different things for each member of my family, and when we don't stop to check for understanding, it inevitably leads to frustration, resentment, and conflict.

Establishing common ground means creating shared understanding and alignment, and reaching it is as simple as asking clarifying questions.

There are a few reasons you might not naturally be inclined to do this. You might assume you already have common ground, or you might worry that asking a question will waste time or make you look incompetent or disruptive. Regardless of your reasons, the likelihood is that not seeking common ground will lead to misunderstandings.

While the solution is straightforward, this is a significant issue for many people and organizations I've worked with. The primary cause of team dysfunction I observe is poor communication—specifically, a lack of shared understanding. Teams, including families and personal relationships, that fail to seek common ground will always struggle.

Seeking clarity can be as simple as asking, "Could you tell me what you mean by that?" Pay attention to the use of extreme words—like *always*, *never*, and *everyone*—and ask for specific examples. Other effective strategies include using open-ended questions to draw out more context, such as "Tell me more" or "What else?"

Here are my recommendations:

- Make a list of insightful questions that will help you gather additional context or meaning.

- Practice feeding back the following two crucial pieces of information to clear up misunderstandings and ensure alignment:

    - What you heard
    - What meaning you assigned—*how you interpreted it*

By combining these practices with a willingness to be corrected, you can foster better communication and strengthen your relationships.

Strategy 3.07: Ask More Powerful Questions

Imagine sitting in a meeting, having just posed a question to your team. The room falls silent, and you feel the urge to fill the gap with your own insights. It's a familiar scene where the discomfort of silence tempts you to provide answers instead of allowing others the space to think and respond.

Think for a moment about how long you are typically willing to wait for an answer after asking a question—and consider how you might benefit from becoming more comfortable with enduring long, awkward silences.

If you're honest with yourself, asking questions you already know the answer to might be your default. It's a common approach: You appear to ask insightful questions but instead offer your idea or solution disguised as a question.

This pattern is more about showcasing what you know than genuinely being open to learning. Even worse, it's leading, manipulative, and judgmental, potentially hindering both you and the other person.

Compassionate curiosity arises from a genuine willingness to understand another person's perspective, opinion, or ideas with an open mind and heart, facilitated by asking open-ended, thought-provoking questions. These questions typically begin with *what*, *how*, or *when*. In contrast, questions starting with *why* or *who* or those beginning with *have you* or *should you* often trigger defensiveness and hinder open dialogue.

While empowering questions are not the only type—clarifying questions serve to gather necessary information, which is different—they are highly effective in helping people discover their own answers. This may require patience, allowing questions to go unanswered in the moment. And that's okay: The answer is meant to benefit the other person, not you.

There's an art to this practice. You need to know when to use discovery questions (those that begin with *what* and expand the conversational space), solution questions (those that begin with *how* and lead to action), and innovation questions (those that spark big thinking and ideation). Knowing when to use each type is a mission-critical skill for anyone aspiring to be a leader. It's also essential to be situationally aware—there are times when people need direction, validation, or acknowledgment. Being attuned to others' needs allows you to support them effectively.

To put this into practice, try replacing *should* and *shouldn't* with open-ended, thought-provoking questions to which even you don't know the answer.

Your work ahead is twofold:

- Resist the urge to tell, and instead, ask one more question than you normally would—one you don't know the answer to—and observe how this transforms your conversations and, by extension, your relationships.

- Wait longer than you typically would before speaking or asking another question. It may be uncomfortable, but I know you can do it.

FINAL THOUGHTS

Understanding what might be true for others is a powerful skill that enriches both personal and professional relationships. This approach allows you to step outside your own experiences and consider the thoughts, feelings, and motivations of others. When you do this, you create opportunities for deeper connections, enhanced collaboration, and more effective problem solving. By recognizing that everyone has their own unique perspectives shaped by their experiences, you can cultivate empathy and understanding in all your interactions.

When you seek to understand what might be true for others, you become a more empathetic and effective leader, friend, and family member. This chapter has illuminated the importance of compassionate curiosity in shaping our interactions and decisions, providing a framework that encourages you to see the broader picture.

As you apply the strategies outlined here, remember that every interaction is an opportunity for growth and connection. By prioritizing understanding over judgment, you can create meaningful relationships that empower both yourself and others to thrive.

APPLY YOUR LEARNING

Take a moment to reflect on what you've learned in this chapter. Use the prompts below to guide your thoughts, and make notes on how you can apply these insights moving forward.

Key Takeaways: What are the most important insights or concepts you learned in this chapter? Write down two or three key points that resonated with you.

Areas for Change: What is one thing you are most interested in doing differently as a result of what you learned in this chapter? Consider how this change could impact your decision-making or approach to challenges.

Commitments to Practice: Identify two specific actions or practices you are committed to implementing based on what you learned. These could be new habits, questions to ask yourself, or approaches to decision-making.

Erika's recommendations:

- ☐ *Identify a recent interaction where you may have judged someone too quickly. How can you apply the strategies in this chapter to foster a more compassionate understanding in future interactions?*
- ☐ *Consider how this heightened awareness of others' perspectives could alter your responses, especially in stressful situations. What specific actions can you take to approach these situations differently?*
- ☐ *Make a conscious effort to listen without formulating a response while someone is speaking, focusing instead on understanding their viewpoint.*
- ☐ *In conversations, prioritize asking questions that encourage others to share their thoughts and feelings, fostering a deeper dialogue.*

Reflection on Impact: How do you believe these changes will affect your life, leadership, or relationships? Take a moment to visualize how engaging in compassionate curiosity might transform your relationships and interactions. What specific changes do you anticipate as a result of this commitment?

Chapter 12

QUESTION 4

What Is the Whole Truth, Even If It's Inconvenient?

Purpose: *Seeing and accepting the whole truth provides the gift of being grounded in reality. By distinguishing your thoughts and emotions from the facts, you achieve a clear understanding of the situation at hand. This clarity allows you to embrace the truth, even when inconvenient, positioning you in your most powerful stance for taking meaningful action.*

> "Reality is that which, when you stop believing in it, doesn't go away."
>
> —PHILIP K. DICK

As you explore this question, it's essential to recognize that uncovering the whole truth requires balancing the objective facts of a situation with the subjective experiences of those involved. It's easy to get caught up in your perceptions, but understanding that both perspectives matter is crucial. This question encourages you to cut through the noise and drama, allowing you to see the situation clearly and acknowledge the uncomfortable realities that may exist.

In a scene from the 1992 legal drama *A Few Good Men*, Colonel Nathan R. Jessup (played by Jack Nicholson) famously asserts, "You can't handle the truth!" to defense counsel Lieutenant Daniel Kaffee (played by Tom Cruise) during a pivotal courtroom scene.* This highlights a common human tendency to avoid confronting uncomfortable truths.

I don't know whether he could handle the truth or not, but I do know that ***the truth***—especially when inconvenient, uncomfortable, or negative—is something many people avoid, ignore, and resist. It's a common defense mechanism we use to protect our self-esteem and comfort, but it isn't keeping you safe. Quite the opposite—avoiding the truth is causing your suffering.

To truly embrace the whole truth, you must be willing to confront what is uncomfortable and examine your own biases and assumptions. This requires intentional self-reflection and a commitment to understanding the realities of your situation.

In chapter 1, I told you there were two difficult truths you needed to accept, and this is the chapter in which we tackle them.

The first truth was that you don't have a *how* problem; you have a *who* problem, and that *who* is you. More specifically, your problem is that the judgments, beliefs, and stories you create are keeping you from acknowledging and accepting reality, and that leaves you in a personal power deficit.

Let's play out a hypothetical scenario: You're sitting in a leadership status meeting and share the challenges you're experiencing with a particularly difficult client. Unprompted, Jack, a colleague from another department, asks a few follow-up questions and then offers recommendations for how you could address it.

After the meeting, as you walk back to your office, you're fuming. *Jack has no experience in my department. How could he possibly solve the problem? How dare he have the nerve to challenge me in front of the leadership team! He's out of his lane and needs to get back in his place.*

---

* *A Few Good Men*, written by Aaron Sorkin, directed by Rob Reiner. Columbia Pictures, 1992. Film.

In this situation, you've made Jack the villain of the story—and there can't be a villain without a victim, and by extension, that victim is you. By painting Jack as the villain, you've made yourself the victim, thereby rendering yourself powerless to change the situation.

In this story, the source of the stress is not Jack, his questions, or his recommendations. Even if Jack had been an outrageous asshole, he still would not have been the source of the stress. The stressor here is the judgmental, critical, and self-righteous story you created in your own head—and that is the source of your suffering.

Suffering often stems from our unawareness of the truth, our avoidance of it, or our resistance to it. In this example, you were resisting reality because you felt that Jack was out of line. By believing that he should have acted differently, you created your own stress and drama, ignoring the simple fact that he did not.

This is good news for you because, as I mentioned in chapter 1, if you are the problem, you are also the solution.

The challenge lies in the stories and thoughts you create about reality, but you have the power to change these narratives. By releasing judgments, reframing facts, and telling a different story, you can alleviate your own suffering through your mind. We covered this in chapter 10, but it is worth repeating.

The process of controlling your thinking can be incredibly challenging, as the brain is skilled at crafting stories and treating them as facts. The danger of your brain treating a story as a fact is what happens next—you stop challenging those thoughts.

Your mental models continuously form judgments and conclusions about reality to help make sense of what's happening. Even in unfamiliar situations, your brain will draw conclusions and treat them as facts, driven by a desire for certainty. Your ego, which often thrives on drama, further complicates this by adding to the turmoil. All this happens automatically unless you consciously intervene, which is exactly what you must do.

The goal here is to strip away the drama, judgment, and self-righteousness to uncover the reality of the story—the objective, neutral truth that is free from emotion and ego.

From this neutral standpoint, you have the opportunity to rewrite the story. Instead of interpreting Jack's behavior as a personal attack, consider giving him the benefit of the doubt and viewing his questions as a genuine attempt to help. Alternatively, you might choose to remain neutral, refraining from assigning any motives to Jack's actions. You could even decide to be brave and ask Jack for more insight into his comments, opening yourself to learning from them. How might these reframes influence your behavior or treatment of Jack in the future? How could they reduce the stress and drama you've created for yourself?

Your ability to resist your brain's tendency to jump to conclusions and your ego's inclination to create drama—and instead ground yourself in reality—offers the greatest opportunity to alleviate your suffering and transform your life, relationships, and outcomes. It's essential to seek out the actual facts in your situation, even when they are not immediately obvious or clear. This process may require digging deep, asking probing questions, and examining the evidence before you, as uncovering these truths is crucial for making informed decisions and fostering genuine connections.

WHY GROUNDING YOURSELF IN REALITY MATTERS

The work involved in this practice may be the most challenging task I ask of you in this book. That's why it's crucial to understand the benefits of investing your effort here. By grounding yourself in reality, separating emotions from facts, and deepening your connection to the truth, you can do the following:

- Be present and find power in focusing on what's happening *now*.
- Decrease the resentment you experience with others when you fail to share your expectations.
- Increase your self-awareness and ability to identify whether your thoughts and feelings are rooted in reality.

- Calmly and consciously make decisions that are based on fact, not stories you've created.
- Achieve a new level of mental and emotional stability.
- Deepen your sense of self.
- Stay grounded in what's happening without getting carried away by your thoughts and emotions.

This work requires you to develop two foundational skills: seeing reality clearly (awareness) and making peace with reality (acceptance). Failing to cultivate these skills will significantly reduce your ability to make conscious choices. While we will explore both concepts in depth, let's first look at them from a high level.

Awareness: Seeing Reality Clearly

The first step to grounding yourself in reality is to perceive yourself, others, and situations without the distortions, stories, and biases that often cloud our judgment. This mental clutter can obscure what's truly happening. By stripping it away, you empower yourself to respond to your environment thoughtfully rather than reactively or feeling victimized by it. Leaders who operate from this clearheaded perspective tend to be more successful because they avoid getting caught up in narratives; instead, they focus their time and energy on the truth, maximizing outcomes, and enabling others to perform at their best.

Acceptance: Making Peace with Reality

Being grounded in reality also necessitates acceptance. Acceptance means acknowledging situations as they are without an immediate urge to change or control them. When you close the gap between reality and your expectations of reality, it expands what is possible in any situation.

GROUNDING YOURSELF IN REALITY

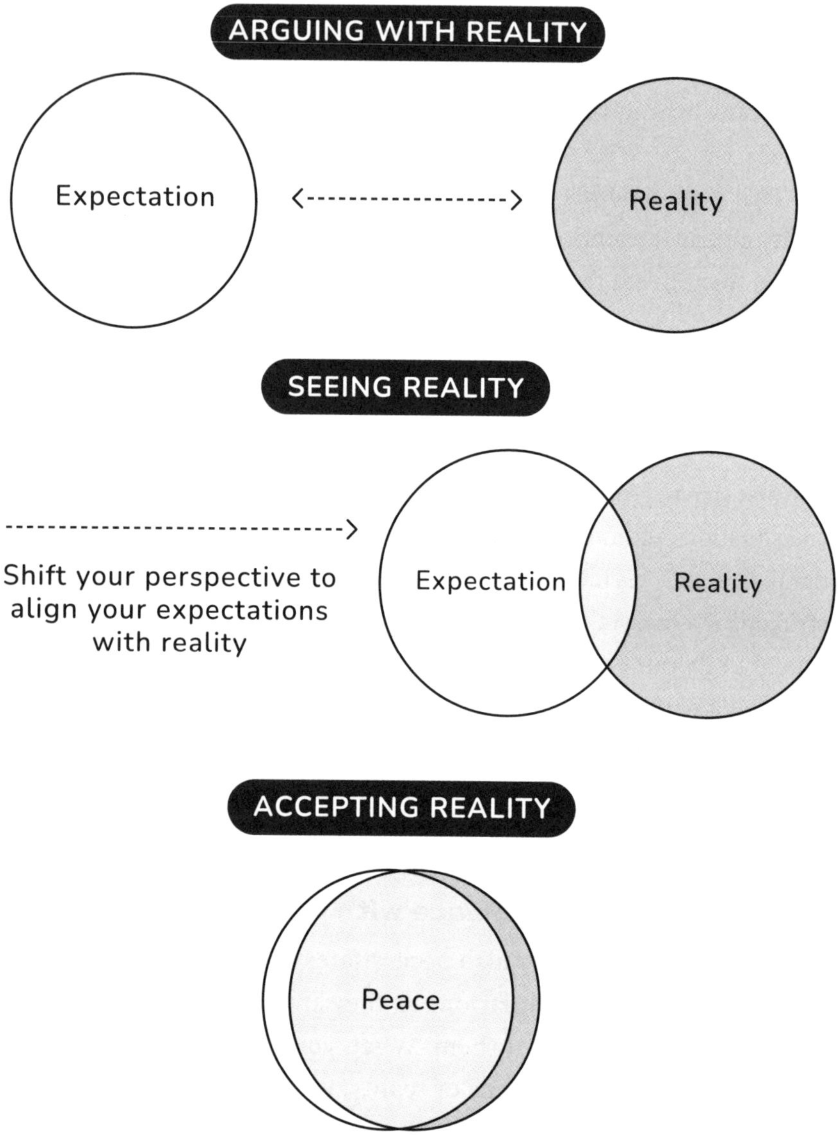

ARGUING WITH REALITY

Expectation <-------------------> Reality

SEEING REALITY

-------------------------------->

Shift your perspective to align your expectations with reality

Expectation Reality

ACCEPTING REALITY

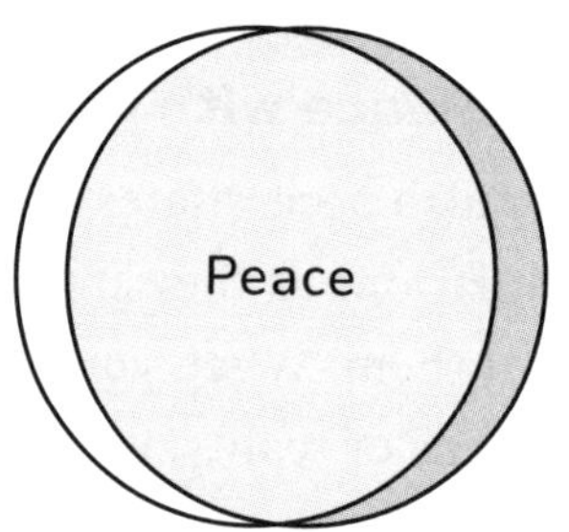

Figure 4.0

Keep in mind that you can embrace the present while still aspiring toward change in the future. However, if you resist what is real, hoping for something different in the now, you undermine your ability to effectively influence outcomes and rob yourself of the peace you crave.

It's important to note that acceptance is not agreement, permission, weakness, or conformity. Your acceptance of your team member's missed deadline is not a signal that you agree with their behavior. Your acceptance of your teenage son missing his curfew is not a permission slip to do it again.

The strength in both these approaches lies in being firmly rooted in reality. By accepting what is, you conserve time and emotional energy instead of ruminating or wishing things were different. This shift allows you to redirect that energy toward taking action and addressing the issue at hand.

Envisioning the Change: The Power of Embracing Reality

Resisting Reality

- You deny or refuse to accept inconvenient truths, leading to feelings of powerlessness.
- You filter out context that contradicts your beliefs, resulting in a distorted view of situations.
- You project your ideas onto others, assuming they share your perspective.
- You create emotional stress and drama by avoiding the discomfort of facing reality.

Being Grounded in Reality

- You accept truths, even when they are uncomfortable, enabling informed decision-making.
- You recognize that your perspective is just one of many, prompting you to seek additional context.

- You deepen your relationships by testing assumptions and seeking clarity rather than projecting your beliefs onto others.
- You experience less emotional drama and stress by aligning your expectations more closely with reality and objective facts, allowing you to respond more effectively to challenges.

THE PATH TO GROUNDING YOURSELF IN REALITY

In this next section, you'll learn very practical strategies for overcoming some common barriers to grounding yourself in reality. In doing so, you will positively impact your capacity for answering the question "What is the whole truth, even if it's inconvenient?"

BARRIER	OVERCOMING STRATEGY	DESCRIPTION
AVOIDANCE OF UNCOMFORTABLE TRUTHS	Strategy 4.01: Don't Believe Everything You Think or Feel	If you find it difficult to confront unpleasant realities, strategy 4.01 can help you detach from your thoughts and emotions, allowing for a more objective view of the situation.
TENDENCY TO MANIPULATE INFORMATION FOR YOUR OWN BENEFIT	Strategy 4.02: Don't Weaponize the Truth	If you struggle with presenting information selectively, strategy 4.02 will remind you to be mindful in how you communicate truth to maintain trust and credibility.
FEAR OF VULNERABILITY	Strategy 4.03: Acknowledge the Inconvenient Truth	If acknowledging inconvenient truths about yourself feels daunting, strategy 4.03 encourages you to embrace personal responsibility, revealing the power you have to influence outcomes.

BARRIER	OVERCOMING STRATEGY	DESCRIPTION
INABILITY TO COMMUNICATE FEEDBACK EFFECTIVELY	Strategy 4.04: Don't Omit the Truth When Sharing Your Opinion or Feedback	If you find it challenging to share honest feedback, strategy 4.04 will guide you in using the SBIC model to provide constructive feedback that promotes growth.
DISTORTING REALITY	Strategy 4.05: Separate *True* and *Truth*	If you often conflate reality with your interpretation of it, strategy 4.05 will help you clarify your thoughts by teaching you to distinguish between your feelings and beliefs, the objective facts at hand, and unhelpful drama that clouds decision-making.

Strategy 4.01: Don't Believe Everything You Think or Feel

Our inner world can be a rich source of data and self-understanding, but not everything that happens inside ourselves is factual. Mislabeling our thoughts and feelings as facts can cause stress and anxiety and have harmful consequences on our relationships, decisions, results, and well-being.

Before we go too far, let's get some things straight about thoughts and emotions:

- Your thoughts and emotions are valid.
- Your thoughts and emotions deserve your consideration and compassion.
- Your thoughts and emotions are not facts; you don't have to believe them. You can choose to believe them, but believing them doesn't make them factual.
- Widespread agreement does not make something a fact.

- Putting some space between you and your thoughts or emotions is the first step to loosening the hold they have on you.

The work you need to do here is to loosen your grasp on your thoughts and emotions. In doing so, you create an opportunity to separate what *feels* true from what *is* true while entertaining *what else could be* true.

Expand Your Perspective

Our brains naturally seek comfort, and few things are more reassuring than having our thoughts and emotions validated by others. However, problems arise when we seek affirmation only from those who share our views or rely solely on sources that reinforce our existing beliefs. This tendency is closely linked to our need to be right.

Expanding your perspective enables you to recognize and confront your biases, increasing your awareness of how these biases influence your thoughts and behaviors. This awareness is a crucial first step toward meaningful change. By actively considering multiple viewpoints, you can make more informed and balanced decisions, cultivate stronger relationships, and achieve better outcomes.

To break free from the echo chamber, engage in conversations with trusted individuals who challenge your thinking, and explore diverse research and resources that broaden your understanding. Make a conscious effort to engage with ideas and opinions that differ from—even contradict—your own.

Test Reality by Seeing Beyond Yourself

While looking inward for answers is a crucial first step, it's equally important to understand how your actions impact others, especially those you care about. Doing so positions you to deepen your empathy, expand your appreciation for their challenges, and make more positive contributions to their lives—all of which strengthen relationships. Viewing situations from others' perspectives also helps you recognize the limitations of your own viewpoint.

Shifting away from a self-centered mindset is an effective way to test your reality against that of others, ultimately reducing the grip your thoughts and emotions may have on you. By embracing this practice, you can cultivate a more nuanced understanding of the world and enhance your interpersonal connections.

By engaging in this strategy, you will find yourself in one of two positions:

1. **Reinforced conviction:** You may emerge even more convinced of your thoughts and emotions. If this is the case, congratulations—you can now move forward with greater confidence, armed with more evidence to support your beliefs.
2. **Increased openness:** Alternatively, you might feel open to new ideas and curious about different possibilities. This openness allows for exploration and growth, encouraging you to consider alternative perspectives and continue expanding your understanding.

In either scenario, you are taking a positive step toward deeper self-awareness and informed decision-making.

Strategy 4.02: Don't Weaponize the Truth

Consider a team meeting where you're presenting a project update. You're eager to showcase success, so you highlight data that supports your narrative while conveniently omitting less favorable metrics.

It's a common temptation to use information selectively to bolster our position, but in doing so, we risk undermining trust and credibility and may come across as a know-it-all.

Since you've gotten this far, I'm guessing that's not your intention. Weaponizing the truth might look like this:

- Selecting facts or data that support your position while ignoring data that doesn't (like citing studies that prove your point while leaving out those that refute it)

- Taking information out of context to give it a different meaning (like sharing an alarming statistic without sharing the factors that shaped the conclusion)

- Presenting a fact as an absolute truth without considering nuances (like making a blanket statement that one diet works for everyone regardless of genetics or lifestyle)

- Oversimplifying a situation to manipulate the narrative (like suggesting all the organization's problems will be solved if sales can just get their shit together)

Each of these examples is an attempt to manipulate the truth, undermine another person, and create a win-lose outcome—none of which is acceptable if you want to lead others. Admittedly, it feels good to win an argument, but anytime somebody wins an argument, the relationship experiences a loss.

Weaponizing the truth isn't always this obvious and insidious. Sometimes it's even well intentioned, like in the following scenarios:

- Choosing only to share positive customer reviews at the board meeting because you want them to think things are running smoothly
- Claiming the organization has great work-life balance when you heard one team member say it
- Saying that the solution to the marketing problem is "clear and simple" because you want to motivate the marketing team

While your intentions might be good, each of these statements is a manipulation of the truth and undermines the felt experiences of others. The solution is to become more deliberate about what we say and how we say it.

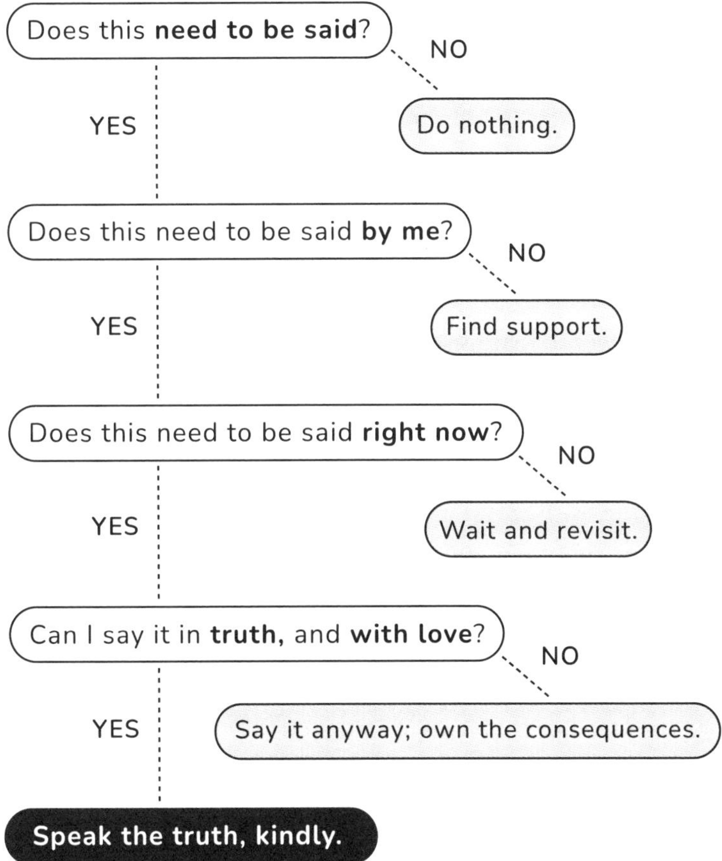
SPEAKING TRUTH KINDLY
Does this **need to be said**?
NO
Do nothing.
YES
Does this need to be said **by me**?
NO
Find support.
YES
Does this need to be said **right now**?
NO
Wait and revisit.
YES
Can I say it in **truth,** and **with love**?
NO
Say it anyway; own the consequences.
YES
Speak the truth, kindly.

Figure 4.02

Comedian Craig Ferguson has a great three-question framework to prevent saying things that are manipulations of the truth that you may later regret[*]:

- Does this need to be said?
- Does this need to be said *by me*?
- Does this need to be said by me *now*?

I like to add in a fourth question:

If the answers to the first three questions are yes, can I say it in truth and with love?

If the answer to that fourth question is no, take a pause before continuing to consider the costs and consequences.

Strategy 4.03: Acknowledge the Inconvenient Truth

Sometimes the truth hurts, and because it hurts, we might avoid, deny, or manipulate it. This is natural; hearing or accepting an emotionally painful truth can bring up some really unpleasant feelings.

The reason the truth hurts—particularly for highly responsible achievers like you and me—is that whether intentionally or not, we are at least partially responsible for an undesired result. Truths like this are inconvenient: They can make us feel vulnerable, disrupt our self-image, and expose our weaknesses, failures, or shortcomings. When confronted with inconvenient truths that threaten our sense of self, the brain scrambles to find fault or place responsibility elsewhere. While this is normal, it's not healthy—but you can intervene.

I was once working with a team that was struggling with trust, and I asked them to share an example of being truthful about mistakes or failures. One leader shared that he was truthful about why he had missed a deadline: He couldn't turn around the quote within twenty-four hours because he was in an all-day meeting. The team confirmed that this was,

---

* Craig Ferguson, *American on Purpose: The Improbable Adventures of an Unlikely Patriot* (HarperCollins, 2009).

in fact, truth. But was it the whole truth? I pressed him by asking whether he had a backup plan for turning around quotes when he wasn't available. This question exposed the inconvenient truth: He was responsible for the lack of backup plan for their proposal process when he was unavailable.

Taking personal responsibility for how you've contributed to an outcome is the hallmark of a great leader—and this means being skilled in owning and honoring the truth, especially when it's inconvenient. But arriving at the inconvenient truth isn't always easy. Your brain may be working against you to protect your ego, and the situation may be so complex that it's hard to suss out what's truly going on and how you contributed to the result.

To find the inconvenient truth in any situation, follow this simple five-question structure:

- *What was your direct involvement in the situation?*
- *What was your indirect involvement in the situation?*
- *What potential risks or outcomes of your action or inaction did you consider?*
- *What does the situation need that you have been unwilling or unable to give?*
- *Could you have reasonably acted differently to influence a different outcome?*

These questions are designed to help you expose the inconvenient truth and, in doing so, find the power you have to influence or change the situation.

The next time you find yourself resisting responsibility for an outcome over which you had influence, sit with these questions until you arrive at the inconvenient truth. And remember, an inconvenient truth is a gift; when you are part of the problem, you have power to influence the solution and create a better outcome for yourself and others.

Strategy 4.04: Don't Omit the Truth When Sharing Your Opinion or Feedback

When someone doesn't meet your expectations, how do you respond? If you're like most people, you might construct a narrative about the person's motives and intentions—usually unflattering—while keeping your thoughts to yourself and harboring a grudge. You might even decide to handle things yourself in the future. Alternatively, you could let resentment build over time, escalating tension in the relationship until you eventually act out in a way that conflicts with your true self.

There is a better approach, and although it may cause some short-term discomfort, it will ultimately lead to less stress, stronger relationships, and improved outcomes in the long term.

The key is to kindly share what's true for you—your experience—without omitting the factual elements of the situation.

When most people think about sharing opinions or feedback, they think about having "difficult conversations." But rather than think of it as difficult or burdensome, I'm going to ask you to reframe it as an opportunity to improve your relationship and results—which is exactly what it is.

When you invest in (kindly and thoughtfully) sharing your experience, expectations, and feedback with someone, you help them close the gap between their intention and their impact. You're helping them grow and improve. You're overcoming your own aversion to discomfort for the sake of their development.

This is only true when opinions and feedback are shared kindly. There's a difference between being honest and speaking a kind truth; you can be honest and also cruel. Candor ("It's the truth! I was just being honest!") is not an excuse to disregard someone else's emotional experience. When you choose to speak a kind truth, you are still committed to being honest, but you're doing so with the intention of growing the relationship and improving the outcome.

Before we go further, let me clarify a common misunderstanding between opinions and feedback.

An **opinion** is a personal belief or judgment that reflects an individual's thoughts and feelings about a subject. It is often subjective and may not be based on direct experience or evidence.

On the other hand, **feedback** is information or criticism grounded in specific observations and experiences, making it more constructive and actionable.

Often, we confuse sharing our opinions with providing constructive feedback. For instance, if a new requirement for using a CRM system is introduced, I might say, "This won't work; we tried it at my previous company and . . ." believing that I'm offering valuable feedback. However, if I haven't actually engaged with the new CRM process, my comment isn't feedback—it's simply an opinion.

I'm not suggesting that opinions are inherently bad. Rather, I encourage you to gain clarity around what the situation calls for. Understanding the difference allows us to contribute more effectively to discussions and decisions, ensuring that our input is relevant and constructive.

> The only way to know what someone intended is to ask them—and the only way to let a person know their impact is to tell them.
>
> —CENTER FOR CREATIVE LEADERSHIP

The Center for Creative Leadership has a method for sharing kind truths called Situation-Behavior-Impact (SBI). The model helps the person sharing the feedback prepare for a clear, productive conversation that leaves a positive impact.*

In my work with clients, I've found that the model is missing one final, crucial step—Change. With my addition and when thoughtfully prepared

---

* Center for Creative Leadership, *Feedback That Works: How to Build and Deliver Your Message*, 2nd ed. (Center for Creative Leadership, 2019).

and executed, the SBIC model is actionable, promotes constructive conversations, and minimizes defensiveness.

Here's how it works:

SBIC FEEDBACK MODEL

1 SITUATION

Anchor to the time and place that the behavior occurred.

2 BEHAVIOR

State the observed behavior using factual, impartial terms.

Share what you thought, felt, or experienced in this situation.

Share what you hope to be different in the future–your wants, needs, or expectations.

Figure 4.04

- **Situation:** Start by anchoring the conversation to a specific time and place where the behavior occurred. Be as specific as you can. This prevents getting lost in vague generalities or veering off course.

- **Behavior:** Provide an objective, observable description of the behavior (words, actions, decisions) you want to give feedback on.

   - **Objective:** It's evidence based and impartial, not an interpretation or assumption.
   - **Observable:** It's limited to what you saw, heard, or witnessed and is free of any preconceived motive.

- **Impact:** Share what you thought, felt, or experienced in the situation. Speak only for yourself, and if you want to bring others into the picture, share the fears or concerns you have but not what you assume they experienced.

- **Change:** Make visible your wants, needs, or expectations—what you hope to be different in the future.

SITUATION	BEHAVIOR	IMPACT	CHANGE
IN YESTERDAY'S STRATEGIC PLANNING SESSION . . .	. . . I noticed that you stopped sharing your input after Greg asked a question about your idea.	The brainstorm wasn't as productive without your ideas.	In the future, I'd love to see you continue to share your perspective, even when it's questioned.
WHEN YOU GOT HOME FROM WORK YESTERDAY . . .	. . . I asked how your day was, and without answering my question, you went to your office, shut the door, and made a phone call.	This hurt because it made me feel disconnected from you and less important than what was getting your attention.	Could we try to spend five minutes connecting with one another when we get home from work to invest in our relationship and connection before moving on to other demands?

This model is also great for proactively taking responsibility for behavior you want to address in yourself. Just remember to keep it free of excuses. Here's how that might play out:

SITUATION	BEHAVIOR	IMPACT	CHANGE
ON YESTERDAY'S SALES CALL . . .	. . . I was defensive when you asked about last month's sales numbers.	I noticed that my behavior changed the tone of the call. After I got defensive, everyone was walking on eggshells.	I'm sorry. I'm committed to working on not getting defensive, even when the conversation gets difficult or highlights a gap in my performance.

As you prepare to share your feedback, consider when the right time and place is to have the conversation. Perhaps you save your feedback for a face-to-face meeting rather than a virtual call where the other person might have their camera off. You might also review the other person's calendar and avoid days or times when they'll be feeling stressed. Even these small acts of consideration and kindness can make your time together more constructive.

Strategy 4.05: Separate *True* and *Truth*

I used to struggle with jumping to conclusions—and I still do at times—because I believed my perspective accurately reflected reality. In my defense, and perhaps in yours as well, I was never taught that my viewpoint could be limited or that I often relied on my unconscious mind to process experiences. It never crossed my mind that others might perceive a situation differently.

Looking back, it seems absurd to think that everyone around me would share the same interpretation of reality. Yet that belief persisted and significantly influenced my judgments.

Recognizing this pattern has been crucial to my growth, teaching me the importance of pausing to question my assumptions and seek additional perspectives. When I do, I avoid the pitfalls of my earlier overly simplistic thinking. You can too.

Earlier we dissected the difference between what feels true to you and what is the literal, factual truth—but just because you intellectually know the difference doesn't mean it's easy to spot.

Our brains assign meaning to experiences so quickly that it's incredibly difficult to strip away the stories we create to get to the truth. Yet your ability to dismantle your narrative and separate it from the truth strips away the noise and drama, clarifying where you have power and where you don't.

You might notice that some of the earlier strategies have prepared you for this one. That's by design. While my goal is to simplify the structures and frameworks I provide, it's important to underscore that this work won't be easy and will require practice. This exercise is a valuable resource for separating your story from the truth, and you can use it whenever you find yourself feeling stuck and unsure of how to move forward, not achieving the outcomes you desire, experiencing emotional distress (like frustration, anger, or sadness), or needing to pause before responding to a situation in order to show up more productively.

To get started, make a three-column table.

1. **Step 1:** Populate column 1 with the narrative in your head. List everything you can think of that is making the situation a problem for you or on your mind related to the situation. Don't judge your thoughts; just write them down—all of them. Include blame, judgments, excuses, and all the drama here. Be sure to include any other pieces of information you think might be relevant to the situation (how you feel, history, context, assumptions, results, etc.). Everything is fair game in this column.
2. **Step 2:** Convert each statement into what's true for you (column 2) and what the truth is (column 3). If gaps exist in your story, and they usually do, seek to close them by adding to this table until you have a very full picture.

True is about your personal experience and should be written from your point of view in the first person. This is where you call forward your beliefs, values, and emotional experience—which might not be factual but can help convey what's happening inside you. Refrain from making declarations about others that are not factual. In the example I provide below, we can all agree that Pat is selfish, but it is not a fact—it is a judgment. Declarations equal drama.

- This: *"When Pat didn't copy the team on an email reply to a customer today, it seemed selfish."*
- Not this: *"Pat is selfish. He intentionally leaves the rest of the team off every one of his email replies because he wants management to think he's the only one working so he can get all the glory."*

If you are struggling to articulate what's true for you in the first person, here are some tips:

- **Focus on *what* instead of *why*:** Document what happened rather than speculating, jumping to conclusions, or assigning motive.

- **Identify threats:** Consider the ways the situation is creating fear or threatening your values, beliefs, or identity, and include them. Turn your "what ifs" into statements. They might begin with "I worry that . . ." or "I'm concerned about . . ."

- **Own your interpretations and assumptions:** At any place where you're drawing a conclusion without all the information, preface it with "I assume . . ." or "The story in my head is . . ."

- **Admit your self-imposed limitations:** Sometimes we are unable or unwilling to take specific actions. Listing them lets you see where you might be holding yourself back and gives you the option to change your mind.

Truth is about the objective, observable, verifiable facts. There are no feelings, interpretations, or assumptions allowed in this column. There is no assignment of blame or motive here. This is pure, observable, non-negotiable reality. You'll be tempted to pick and choose what you put here to suit your argument, but don't. If you want this exercise to work, you need to be honest with yourself about what's really happening. I can almost guarantee that you are omitting facts.

- This: *"My wife and I got to the theater at 7:15 for a 6:55 showing and missed the first several minutes of the movie."*
- Not this: *"My wife is always running behind, and we end up being late for everything. No matter what I do to help her, we don't get out the door on time. I swear she does it just to make me mad."*

If you're struggling to find truth in your situation, here are some tips:

- **Seek neutrality:** Strip away any adjectives, descriptors, or labels and avoid extremes (*always*, *everyone*, etc.).
- **Stick to the facts:** Avoid subjective descriptions or judgments and concentrate on observable, verifiable information like dates, times, direct quotes, and specific actions.
- **Verify information:** Fact-check any speculations against credible sources. Go to the source of truth if you can.

You do not need to complete both the middle and right column in every row. Simply use this framework as a way to analyze what you're experiencing without being overly rigid.

THE SITUATION *What's on your mind or heart?*	**TRUE** *What feels true for you?*	**TRUTH** *What's the objective truth?*
Jane was late.	I think people should be on time.	Jane arrived at 8:13 for a meeting that started at 8:00. Everyone else was on time.
Jane is disrespectful.	I feel disrespected.	
Jane clearly doesn't value my time.	Timeliness is important to me.	I don't know what Jane values.
There is no excuse for being late. Jane obviously didn't plan ahead.	I assume Jane has no valid reason for being late.	I don't know why Jane was late.

In the example with Jane, I have very little information. I made several assumptions about Jane's behavior and character, but I really don't know why Jane was late, what Jane's values are, or what her intentions were. Now that I have separated true from truth, I'm better prepared to move forward. Rather than scolding Jane for being late, I might choose to pull her aside after the meeting and ask if everything was okay this morning.

I want to emphasize that all three columns hold significant value. This approach helps to alleviate emotional tension related to a situation, highlights any gaps in understanding, and enables more effective action by organizing all relevant information in a clear manner. From this vantage point, it is easier to move forward with intention.

With sufficient practice, you'll find that you no longer need the chart to navigate this exercise. You'll be able to discern the truth in any situation and manage your thoughts and feelings more effectively in real time. In the meantime, make it a habit to use the chart regularly. It will help train your brain to break down the narratives it creates and uncover the underlying facts. It also helps you to identify the mental models that might be tripping you up.

FINAL THOUGHTS

Grounding yourself in reality and embracing the whole truth is not just about facing discomfort; it's a powerful step toward personal empowerment and effective leadership. By practicing the strategies outlined in this chapter, you'll learn to navigate challenges with clarity and confidence, ultimately leading to improved outcomes in all areas of your life. You will also cultivate healthier relationships, as open and honest communication fosters trust and understanding. Remember, facing the truth doesn't always come easily, but it is an invaluable step toward living authentically and effectively.

APPLY YOUR LEARNING

Take a moment to reflect on what you've learned in this chapter. Use the prompts below to guide your thoughts, and make notes on how you can apply these insights moving forward.

Key Takeaways: What are the most important insights or concepts you learned in this chapter? Write down two or three key points that resonated with you.

Areas for Change: What is one thing you are most interested in doing differently as a result of what you learned in this chapter? Consider how this change could impact your decision-making or approach to challenges.

Commitments to Practice: Identify two specific actions or practices you are committed to implementing based on what you learned. These could be new habits, questions to ask yourself, or approaches to decision-making.

Erika's recommendations:

- ☐ *Identify one situation in your life where you have been avoiding an inconvenient truth. How can you apply the strategies in this chapter to confront that truth?*
- ☐ *Commit to engaging in regular self-reflection to separate your thoughts and emotions from objective truths to see how it shapes your decisions.*
- ☐ *Identify at least one opportunity to practice the SBIC model to give feedback with clarity and kindness.*
- ☐ *Set aside time each week to reflect on any inconvenient truths you may be avoiding and how they affect your life. Consider how acknowledging these truths could alter your interactions, relationships, and decisions.*

Reflection on Impact: How do you believe these changes will affect your life, leadership, or relationships? Take a moment to visualize how embracing the whole truth might positively affect your life, leadership, or relationships. What changes do you anticipate as a result of this commitment?

Chapter 13

QUESTION 5

What Do I Want for Myself, and Why Is That Important to Me?

Purpose: *Understanding what you truly want for yourself offers the gift of directional clarity. By pinpointing your desires and the reasons they matter, you can establish priorities that move you steadily and consciously toward what is most important to you.*

> Everything's in the mind. That's where it all starts. Knowing what you want is the first step toward getting it.
>
> —MAE WEST

As you contemplate this question, it's important to acknowledge that knowing what you want—and why it matters—often requires a deeper dive. Taking the time to cut through the noise and drama allows you to uncover your authentic wants, moving beyond surface-level insights that may reflect your ego's desires rather than your true self.

Reflecting on my own journey, I realize how easy it is to chase a vision of success that isn't truly yours. Have you ever pursued goals that others wanted for you, only to achieve them and feel an emptiness growing inside? I have. After countless late nights and weekends at the office and the endless pursuit of more, I found myself drained and disconnected from what—and who—mattered most. For years, the clarity of my own desires was drowned out by the noise of others' expectations. It wasn't that I lost sight of what I wanted; I never thought to define it. And without that clarity, I became a passenger in my own life, driven by goals that weren't truly mine. It was only when I paused to listen to my inner voice that I began to discover what truly mattered to me, paving the way to a life that was created by me, not for me.

If you regularly feel lost, disconnected from what matters, stuck, or if you struggle with feeling fulfilled, you probably lack directional clarity in some part of your life. I say "some part of your life" because it's completely possible to be crushing it in one part of your life and feeling completely lost in others. For me, there was a dull undercurrent that I couldn't shake. My life was great on paper—it checked all the boxes—yet something was off. And those signals from the universe don't go away; they get louder and more disruptive.

I learned I wasn't alone when I surveyed visitors to my website. In response to the prompt "I frequently feel moody, agitated, or cranky, and I don't know why," 40 percent of respondents answered, "Yes! All the time."

Maybe this is true for you too. If so, it's time to stop ignoring it and do something about it.

Finding directional clarity is entirely possible, but it requires regular and honest self-evaluation. For those of us who struggle to sit still and reflect, it means slowing down and engaging in the deep introspection necessary to identify what truly matters—or risk never feeling fully fulfilled.

Tuning in to our own desires isn't easy for most of us. When clients come to me in distress, I dedicate time to understanding their current situation and the challenges or opportunities they face. When they feel stuck or dissatisfied, my first question is almost always "What do you want?"

Many people struggle to answer the question. I get it—it's a big question. Yet not knowing what you want can be problematic for a number of reasons:

- You will lack focus and become vulnerable to distractions and emotional whims.
- You will be less efficient and waste time and resources heading in the wrong direction.
- You will settle for *good enough* when more is possible.

While lacking direction may be more noticeable in life's big moments, it's the small, everyday choices that quietly erode life satisfaction. Without taking time to gain clarity on what you truly want, you risk letting your priorities, tasks, and decisions be shaped by default rather than by design. Over time, as you live on autopilot, you accidentally create a life you don't actually want and drive yourself slowly and steadily toward dissatisfaction.

When you find yourself there—feeling devoid of purpose and meaning, craving connection, wondering what it's all for, or looking for fulfillment in all the wrong places—I recommend consulting your inner compass, a framework that defines your values, purpose, vision, and mission and represents what matters most to you.

When you're clear on these parts of your life, connected to them, and using them to guide your decisions, goals, and priorities, you're more likely to create a satisfying, authentic, and aligned life for yourself.

WHY DIRECTIONAL CLARITY MATTERS

Understanding your desires and motivations serves as a critical compass on your journey. Many clients I work with often settle for situations that don't truly fulfill them because they lack a clear vision of their goals or don't understand their motivations. They may convince themselves that their aspirations are out of reach, leading them to dismiss their dreams before they even explore them. To overcome this tendency, it's important to think about what you genuinely want without letting concerns about how to achieve it—or whether you deserve it—hold you back.

Even if you're unsure of your exact desires, you can still progress toward a deeply satisfying life by focusing on what you want for yourself rather than getting sidetracked by the expectations or needs of others. When contemplating your goals, concentrate on what you can influence, and avoid trying to control outcomes for others. For instance, while you may not be able to directly control your child's grades, you can create a supportive environment and establish structures that help them succeed.

Another common barrier is the reluctance to pursue bigger aspirations. Many people struggle with this limitation, including myself in the past. If dreaming without constraints feels daunting, try breaking your life into specific areas—such as home, family, career, health, and recreation—and identify what you truly desire in each. This exercise can open your mind to new possibilities. When doubts creep in—like "You're too old," "You don't have what it takes," or "You're not experienced enough"—acknowledge them, but don't allow them to stifle your exploration. Additionally, be wary of the sunk cost fallacy, which suggests that you should remain in a situation simply because you've invested time, money, or energy into it. This mindset can prevent you from pursuing what you genuinely want.

As you reflect on what you truly want, remember to dig deep until your answer resonates with your personal desires. Sometimes, what we seek is not just a specific outcome but the feelings associated with it. For example, you might desire your child to excel in school, not solely for the sake of high grades but also to feel the pride and happiness that their success brings you. Conversely, you may want them to succeed to avoid feelings of inadequacy regarding your parenting abilities. By identifying both the positive emotions you wish to cultivate and the negative feelings you seek to prevent, you can gain clearer directional clarity that aligns with your true self. This deeper understanding will provide you with greater insight into what you are ultimately striving for.

Gaining clarity on what truly matters to you can elevate both your life and your leadership. The work you're about to undertake in this chapter—leading yourself based on your true desires—has the potential to significantly enhance your satisfaction. It will empower you to make better decisions, define your version of success, and live and lead in ways that inspire pride and fulfillment.

Envisioning the Change: The Power of Articulating Your Desires

Without Directional Clarity

- You may feel stuck, unclear, confused, or uncertain about your goals and desires.
- You might run out of energy while aiming for a moving target, leading to frustration and disappointment.
- You could bounce from one pursuit to another, searching for satisfaction without a clear sense of direction.
- You may struggle to achieve your goals (or even define them), resulting in a sense of dissatisfaction with your life, career, or relationships.

With Directional Clarity

- You will believe that anything is possible and feel empowered to pursue your heart's desires, leading to a more fulfilling life.
- You will prioritize your energy and resources toward clear goals and objectives, enhancing your productivity and satisfaction.
- You will spend your time and energy on things that bring you meaning and joy, fostering a sense of fulfillment.
- You will set, adjust, and achieve your goals with confidence, feeling aligned with your true self.
- You will feel satisfied with where you are while leaving space to desire more, ensuring continual growth and development.

THE PATH TO DIRECTIONAL CLARITY

In this next section, you'll learn very practical strategies for overcoming some common barriers to finding directional clarity. In doing so, you will positively impact your capacity for answering the questions "What do I want for myself, and why is that important to me?"

BARRIER	OVERCOMING STRATEGY	DESCRIPTION
FEELING LOST OR CHRONIC DISSATISFACTION	Strategy 5.01: Dial In Your Inner Compass	If you lack awareness of who you are and what matters to you, strategy 5.01 will help you gain clarity by articulating your personal values, vision, mission, and purpose, directing you to make decisions that align with your true self.
SETTLING FOR LESS	Strategy 5.02: Set Well-Crafted Goals and Priorities	If you struggle with perfectionism and goal ambiguity, strategy 5.02 will help you define clear, actionable goals through a structured framework, reducing frustration, enhancing your sense of direction, and making it easier to prioritize your resources.
NEGATIVE SELF-TALK	Strategy 5.03: Make Sure You Are in Charge of You	If you are held back by a dominating inner critic, strategy 5.03 will help you reclaim control by fostering awareness of this voice, allowing you to make decisions aligned with your true self rather than succumbing to fear and self-doubt.

Strategy 5.01: Dial In Your Inner Compass

Your inner compass is the internal system that guides your decisions, helps you stay focused on what matters to you, and informs your goals, tasks, and priorities. When executed thoughtfully and updated regularly, it can lead you toward a meaningful, fulfilling life. A well-crafted compass includes your values, purpose, vision, and mission.

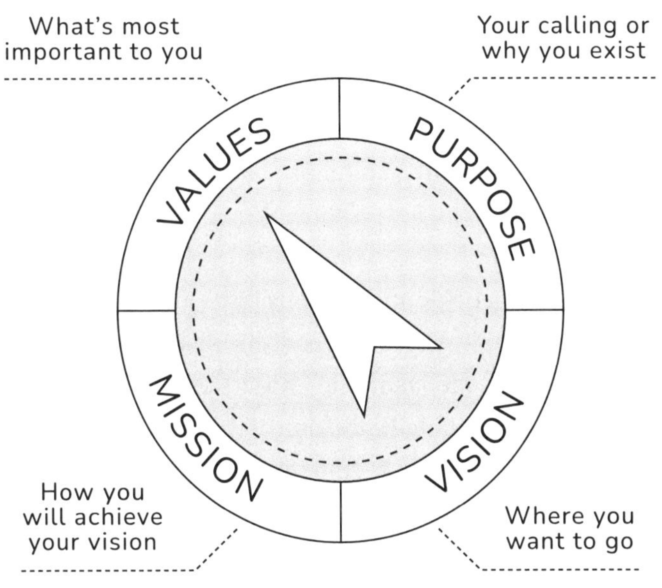

Figure 5.01

Your **values** are the most impactful part of your compass. Said simply, they define what's most important to you. Your values govern your behavior, illustrate your sense of right and wrong, influence your decisions, shape who you become, and have extraordinary power over the course of your life. The unfortunate reality is that most people are completely unaware of their values.

When you're not in touch with your values, it can seem like life is happening to you. You might struggle to make decisions or deal with the fallout of those decisions, and you may find yourself feeling victim to circumstance.

When you make your values visible and consciously choose how you express or honor them, you're able to claim agency over your life by making decisions that fully align with who you are and what's important to you.

Values are just words unless they stand up when tested.

Articulating your values will help you better understand yourself, give you the power to tame the values that are taking up too much space, and empower you to choose how you express and honor your values so they can best serve the life you want.

If I know you like I think I do, you place high value on responsibility; it's probably a value that's been a driver in your life for as long as you can remember. For me, my value for responsibility has created more success, more fear, more opportunity, and more havoc than any other value in my life. In working with highly responsible people, I've found that to be true for them too.

Responsibility is a noble and virtuous value and is widely celebrated as a positive trait. People who are responsible make life easier for others; they're reliable, they understand the impacts of their actions, and they tend to consider others in their decisions.

But every healthy value can become problematic when overexpressed. Overplaying your responsibility value is likely a large factor in what got you here. Your prioritization of (or even obsession over) being a highly responsible person might mean that you frequently take on more than you should, sacrifice yourself and your relationships to uphold your commitments, or assume responsibility for others. This can leave you feeling overworked and burdened and the people around you feeling helpless, disempowered, or even resentful.

Responsibility aside, you have only a few core values, and while exploring them, it's important to personalize them by giving them an identity that means something to you. They should also have guardrails: behavioral expressions of the value that help you avoid underexpressing and overexpressing it (too much of a good thing is, in fact, not a good thing).

The first step in leveraging your values is discovering them. Start by reviewing the list below and noting which of the values in the word bank stand out to you as important. Keep in mind that values are generally timeless and nonnegotiable, and do your best to think about your life as a whole. Your core values are not different across your life roles, although they might be expressed differently.

If you have more than four values circled at the end of the exercise, whittle your list down to the four values that are most essential to who you are and what you care about.

Values Word Bank

Accountability	Achievement	Adaptability	Adventure	Altruism
Ambition	Authenticity	Balance	Beauty	Belonging
Career	Collaboration	Commitment	Community	Compassion
Competence	Confidence	Connection	Cooperation	Courage
Creativity	Curiosity	Dignity	Diversity	Environment
Efficiency	Equality	Ethics	Excellence	Fairness
Faith	Family	Financial stability	Forgiveness	Freedom
Friendship	Fun	Generosity	Giving back	Grace
Gratitude	Growth	Harmony	Health	Honesty
Hope	Humility	Humor	Inclusion	Independence
Initiative	Integrity	Intuition	Joy	Justice
Kindness	Knowledge	Leadership	Learning	Legacy
Leisure	Love	Loyalty	Making a difference	Nature

Openness	Optimism	Order	Patience	Patriotism
Peace	Perseverance	Power	Pride	Recognition
Reliability	Resourcefulness	Respect	Responsibility	Risk-taking
Safety	Security	Serenity	Service	Simplicity
Spirituality	Sportsmanship	Stewardship	Success	Teamwork
Tradition	Trust	Truth	Uniqueness	Vulnerability
Wealth	Well-being	Wholeheartedness	Wisdom	Other

Based on your selections, reflect honestly on how true the following statements feel to you:

- These values truly define me at my core.
- I make decisions with these values in mind.
- I am honoring these values regularly in my personal life.
- I am honoring these values regularly in my professional life.
- Very little can prevent me from living in alignment with these values.

Your **purpose** articulates *why* you exist; it summarizes your unique talents and how you intend to use them to advance the greater good and create meaning in your life.

> When I stand before God at the end of my life, I would hope that I would not have a single bit of talent left and could say, 'I used everything You gave me.'
>
> —ERMA BOMBECK

Discovering your purpose takes some time and deep inner work, but you can start with a few reflection prompts that will help you discover how you make a difference in the world:

- *What brings you the most joy?*
- *What would you do even if you didn't get paid?*
- *How do you want to impact others or the world at large?*
- *What difference do you want to make?*
- *What will be your legacy?*

Make notes as you answer each question and use your answers to craft a single short phrase or statement that encompasses your purpose and calling. Ideally, your purpose is easy to recite and remember.

Your **vision** articulates *where* you're going. It is a summation of your most desired outcomes and provides direction for your life as you architect your future. Your vision can and should evolve throughout life's seasons. A great vision ignites the senses, speaks to the most relevant parts of your life, and aligns the head and the heart.

Start by finding some quiet time and considering a timeframe such as five or ten years into the future, and put yourself in that place physically, emotionally, spiritually, mentally, socially. From that place, answer the following questions:

- *Where are you?*
- *Whom are you with?*
- *What are you doing?*
- *What have you accomplished?*
- *Who have you become?*

Make notes as you go, knowing that you can refine it later. Your completed vision should be concise yet convey an inspiring, future-focused outline of your aspirations and desired outcomes.

Your **mission** is *how* you intend to make your vision a reality. It defines the repeatable actions you will take to achieve what you most desire. It is strategic, not tactical, and evolves as your vision evolves. A mission describes how you'll deliver on your vision but is more abstract than specific goals; think of your mission as the categories of actions you'll take. Knowing your mission helps you determine your priorities and set meaningful, actionable goals. When you're aligned with your mission, you are more likely to stay engaged, focused, and on track with your goals and tasks—even in the face of challenges or setbacks.

Once your vision is set, start to craft your mission statement by making an exhaustive list of what you might do to achieve your vision, resisting the urge to filter your list. Next, cross off anything that you are unable or unwilling to do. From there you can see what themes exist and weave them into a single statement.

Here is an example of what a completed inner compass might look like. I've included priorities and goals to highlight the differences in abstraction and how they work together:

VALUES	Mastery, Creativity, Responsibility, and Love
PURPOSE	To make a peaceful, more satisfied life possible for anyone who wants it.
VISION	To live in peace, knowing I gave my all and made a difference in the way I live, lead, love, and play.
MISSION	To champion greatness by weaving truth and love into the pursuit of purpose, passions, and profession.
PRIORITIES	Building community, strengthening relationships, creating content, praying, and practicing self-care.
GOAL	To publish a book on making conscious choices.

Once you've built out the elements of your inner compass, document them somewhere highly visible so they can assist you with everyday goal setting, decisions, and tasks—and especially with time management and planning. When you are clear about who you are, what you want, and what steps are required to get there, anything is possible.

Strategy 5.02: Set Well-Crafted Goals and Priorities

Setting goals is an important practice in building a meaningful life, but how we approach those goals—and our mindset about whether or not we achieve them—can work for or against us.

Reflect for a moment on your track record for setting and achieving goals. Do you have a track record of success, or are you more of a "Set it and forget it" person? Do you track and measure your progress while keeping your goals front and center, or do you hope to make progress while in reality make excuses?

As a high performer, you need a clear understanding of what you're striving to achieve. Without defining what success looks like, you might push yourself harder than necessary, fall prey to perfectionist tendencies, and start believing that *nothing is ever good enough* or *there's more you should be doing*. With high personal standards and hypercritical self-evaluations, you'll rarely (if ever) feel the sweet reward of achievement.

On top of that, ambiguous or ill-defined goals can lead to wasted effort and frustration—neither of which you have time for when you're already underwater.

Ideally, any goals and associated tasks you set for yourself describe *what* you need to do to achieve your mission. For them to produce results, they should be directly within your control and have a clear way to measure progress and indicate success.

This is why your process for setting goals matters. You've likely heard of SMART goals, but I'm going to introduce to you a simple framework that will help you combat your natural perfectionist tendencies by answering six questions:

- **WHO: Who do I want to become in the process?** Goal setting often discounts the important work of aligning what you want to accomplish with who you want to be. What part of you is being honored or shaped in the process of achieving this goal? What is the benefit to you for achieving it? What is the cost of not achieving it?

- **WHAT: What is it going to take to accomplish the goal?** Your goals need to be resourced. Create an exhaustive list; if done well, you will uncover all the resources you need to succeed—and potentially things you're unwilling to do that need to be reconciled.

- **WHEN: When am I committed to accomplishing the goal?** Determine your timeline for achieving the goal, and set milestones for larger goals by breaking them into smaller pieces. This will also boost your confidence as you acknowledge the progress you're making along the way.

- **WHERE: Where am I going?** Your goals should explicitly describe where you're starting and where you want to be. These measurements should include qualitative and quantitative metrics. At any point in time, you should be able to track against this goal and understand when you've achieved it. Having this clarity will build your confidence throughout the process while empowering you to measure backward.

- **WHY: Why am I doing this?** Your goals should be purposeful and in alignment with your inner compass. Does your goal support something bigger? If not, consider why you are doing it in the first place, and make sure you like your reasons.

- **HOW: How am I going to get there?** Clear plans of action are necessary for anyone setting out to accomplish a goal. Get clear on exactly how you're going to accomplish the goal and what you'll be doing to get there. It's imperative that you don't conflate activity with action. Lots of activity pretends to be useful but isn't. Your job is to know if what you're doing is taking you closer to your desired outcome or not and make adjustments in real time. The how is the most fluid part of your plan.

When all these elements are accounted for, you will be in the best possible position to succeed. If you are struggling to achieve any goals in your life, or if they're not providing the fulfillment they promised, combine this framework with the other strategies listed in this chapter and make necessary adjustments. Doing so will inch you closer and closer to the satisfaction you crave.

Don't Forget to Measure in Both Directions

As a high performer, you probably put much more emphasis on how much progress you still have to make to reach a goal than on all the progress you've already made. That's common, but this tendency can severely limit your potential and pushes satisfaction out of reach.

There is danger in only measuring forward. Measuring forward is the self-sabotaging pattern of looking only at how much distance stands between you and your goal. When you're measuring forward, you convince yourself that the extreme pressure you put on yourself to accomplish a goal is a good thing—it motivates and directs you to achieve something big, so what's not to like? You keep your head down, stay focused on how much work you have to do, and forget about the progress you've already made.

The problem with this orientation is that it directs you away from the bigger picture; you become fixated on reaching the goal and trade long-term change for a short-term win. Eventually, you realize you didn't actually achieve the long-term goal, and the cycle repeats. Meanwhile, while you were focused on the short-term win, you justified the path you took to get there, which meant operating outside your inner compass or compromising your values.

Measuring forward is even more damaging when you apply it to how you view other people in your life and downplay the progress they've made. For much of my life, I've struggled with measuring others against their potential. It took a couple of decades for me to realize this might have been my single biggest contribution to my first, and failed, marriage. I was more in love with my husband's potential than who came through the door each night. This behavior continued to play out in my current marriage and my roles as a parent (ouch), friend, volunteer, and boss. I still do this more than I want to, but now that I am aware of it, I can spot it and make adjustments before it gets me into too much trouble and damages the relationship. I'm also much better at acknowledging and celebrating the progress of others.

My recommendation is that you *also* measure backward. Measuring backward is what keeps you in harmony while pursuing goals and keeps you from having unrealistic expectations of others. It simply means that you also look at where you started, compare where you are to where you were, and acknowledge and celebrate the progress.

If you are using the goal framework mentioned earlier, your progress is tracked and measured in the *where* segment and will help you acknowledge how far you've come.

Poor Planning Can Derail Success

When everything is important, nothing is important—and that can lead to overwhelm, indecisiveness, and procrastination. It might seem a little paradoxical that you would be prone to procrastination, but that is exactly what happens when you don't prioritize well or overcommit and suffer the consequences of doing so.

By taking on more than you can reasonably get done in a timely manner (without great sacrifice, anyway), you become the opposite of responsible—and that is a problem.

Working over your capacity diminishes your ability to perform well over time. You might not notice it at first, but you'll see evidence of it soon enough. It also leads to lack of focus, poor time management, increased stress, and ultimately reduced productivity. This is likely the greatest source of pressure contributing to the near-constant feeling of having the weight of the world on your shoulders.

Chances are, you push yourself harder until you feel a little relief, but you never really address the source of the problem—your poor planning and inability to prioritize. I can already hear you: "But Erika . . . I work better under pressure." Maybe, but not this kind of pressure. Typically, pressure is a hack for people who can't—or won't—plan well.

Prioritizing is about more than just getting things done. It means accomplishing tasks in the right order and with the greatest impact on your goals, commitments, and assignments. Being clear about your priorities can reduce stress, anxiety, and overwhelm by helping you say yes to the right things and no to the things that don't support what is most important. When your priorities are straight, it's easier to ensure that you're using your resources—time, energy, money, and attention—wisely.

Sometimes our goals, tasks, and priorities are set *for* us instead of *by* us. You might have an annual budget or sales quota that's assigned to you, or perhaps a decision has been made and it's your job to execute on that decision, or a client moves up a deadline that already feels tight. These are imposed priorities, and most of us have our fair share of them.

Other times you say yes to being a coach for your child's sports team or the treasurer of your church even though your intuition tells you it's not a good idea and you haven't fully considered what you're taking on. When you say yes to those roles and their associated tasks, they impact everything else currently on your to-do list, and usually not in a positive way. While you may not have asked for these roles, they weren't imposed upon you.

Prioritization is part of the **planning process**. And before you tell me you don't have time for this, I would argue that until you find time for planning, your situation isn't going to change. There are so many systems and methods for planning—you just have to find what works for you.

Whatever system you choose, here is my recommendation for overcoming this barrier. Do this one at the start of each week:

Step 1: Consolidate all your tasks into a single to-do list. Time to get rid of the sticky notes. List everything you need to do that week along with the time you estimate each task will take. Use whatever method works for you. I like using a program that syncs with my inbox and my phone.

Step 2: Delete or delegate anything you're not committed to completing. By committed, I mean that you are going to schedule it and execute it. Your schedule is no place for good intentions. For example, don't list the gym five days per week if you struggle to get there twice. Don't accept meetings that aren't a good use of your time.

Step 3: Determine your hours and schedule. Will you work forty hours or sixty? Will you work four days per week or six? What time will you start, and what time will you end? Set a schedule and stick to it.

Step 4: Review and clean up previously booked calendar entries. This includes meetings, appointments, time off, etc. Reconcile any double (or triple) bookings. Move or delete anything that no longer works. Determine if a meeting could be condensed or become an email. Adjust meeting lengths to allow time to thoughtfully wrap up and take a few minutes to yourself before transitioning to the next commitment.

Step 5: Schedule your priorities. Put time on your calendar for everything that you need to do in order to advance the most important things and your goals. Your priorities get preferential treatment on your calendar.

Step 6: Schedule everything else. Get everything that's left on your to-do list onto your calendar (with start and end times) without exceeding your predetermined hours and schedule. Chances are that you will not have room in the coming week for everything. This will force you to make some decisions, such as deferring the task further out. Be sure to consider what will be required before deciding where to fit things into your week. Ideally your to-do list should be empty at this point. Unnecessary clutter on your to-do list adds to the pressure we're trying to relieve.

Step 7: Honor your calendar. The beauty of planning is that you make decisions ahead of time, presumably with a clear head, and all that's left is to do what you said you would do. Honoring commitments you make to yourself is equally important to those you make to others. When there are legitimate disruptions to your plan, and there will be, do the best you can and learn from it.

Step 8: Review your week, and apply any lessons learned. Even with excellent planning, things happen. Review your results, continue what's working, and make corrections to what isn't as you look ahead to the next week. If your reasons for not honoring commitments aren't legit, you might need to study your thoughts and feelings when you are choosing something different in those moments. You may also need to revisit your beliefs about time. Steps 2 and 3 can help you with that.

Strategy 5.03: Make Sure You Are in Charge of You

You might be wondering, *Who else would be in charge of me?* The answer is your inner voice—that judgmental whisper in the background, constantly setting moral standards and shaming you when you fall short. To be clear, this voice is not you, but it is inside you. (Before you dismiss the notion that you have one, please consider that if you grew up in an achievement-oriented environment, you may have learned to silence this voice, but it's still there.)

There are parts of you that exist to protect you from real and perceived threats, and they kick into action anytime you're facing a situation that puts you at risk of discomfort, failure, judgment, criticism, or uncertainty. This is the work of that inner voice.

In an attempt to help you avoid feeling inadequate, this subconscious whisper inside your head guides you to safety by directing you away from whatever is threatening you. Sometimes it's helpful, but sometimes this voice is sabotaging you by taking you further away from what you most want.

The thing about your inner voice is that it's not on the same page as your inner compass. Its only concern is protecting you, controlling the way others perceive you, and preventing any risk that might expose the gap between who you are and how you want to be seen. Here's how it might show up.

Let's assume—and I think this is a safe assumption—that you want to be seen as a high performer; you might have a fear that you'll fail and that others will judge you as incompetent or incapable. When faced with an opportunity to take on a new responsibility, your inner voice will actively work to prevent failure by chiming in with shame, criticism, and comparison; it's your way of protecting yourself from risk by discouraging it in the first place. You might feel compelled to numb out and binge a new show instead of preparing for your new responsibilities (procrastination), or you might obsess over the new responsibilities and completely lose sight of any other priorities (perfectionism). In either situation, you're disconnected from your inner compass and barreling toward self-sabotage.

In situations like these, your ego—your conscious self—steps in to mediate by running interference between your internal and external worlds and helping you make decisions. When the ego is healthy, you can make conscious choices that are directionally aligned and informed by your compass. When the ego is unhealthy, you will self-sabotage with procrastination and perfectionist tendencies.

> Our deepest fear is not that we are inadequate. Our deepest fear is that we are powerful beyond measure. It is our light, not our darkness, that most frightens us.
>
> —**MARIANNE WILLIAMSON**

This quote perfectly illustrates the fear our egos experience on a daily basis. I know you are burdened by a constant sense that you should be doing more. You hate it when you make mistakes or fall short. You want to take care of everyone and everything. But when you listen to this voice, you are not in charge of you.

To be in charge of you, you need to understand that the dull whisper in the background is normal, and rather than letting it run the show, choose instead to stay in control. Otherwise you risk being silently controlled by the whisper, and you'll never truly fulfill your purpose or reach your full potential with your negative inner voice at the wheel interrupting your sense of direction and priorities.

Protecting your directional clarity requires constant vigilance. A great place to start becoming attuned to your inner voice is sitting with the following questions to see what you can learn:

- *What are the messages on replay in your head?*
- *Whose voice is it?*
- *What is the voice in charge of?*
- *What strategies does the voice use against you?*
- *What is the voice protecting you from?*

FINAL THOUGHTS

Understanding what you want and why it is important to you is foundational for leading a fulfilling life. By engaging with the strategies outlined in this chapter, you will gain clarity on your desires and develop the ability to consciously prioritize your goals. This clarity will empower you to make better decisions, enhance your satisfaction, and ultimately lead to a more authentic and aligned life.

Embrace the journey of self-discovery as you explore your desires. Remember that it's okay to reassess and redefine what you want as you grow and evolve. This process will lead you to a more satisfying and meaningful life where you can confidently navigate your path and make choices that resonate with your true self.

Take the time to engage with these reflections and allow yourself to dream boldly about your future. Your clarity of purpose will be the guiding light that helps you achieve your goals and live a life filled with meaning and fulfillment.

APPLY YOUR LEARNING

Take a moment to reflect on what you've learned in this chapter. Use the prompts below to guide your thoughts, and make notes on how you can apply these insights moving forward.

Key Takeaways: What are the most important insights or concepts you learned in this chapter? Write down two or three key points that resonate.

Areas for Change: What is one thing you are most interested in doing differently as a result of what you learned in this chapter? Consider how this change could impact your decision-making or approach to challenges.

Commitments to Practice: Identify two specific actions or practices you are committed to implementing based on what you learned. These could be new habits, questions to ask yourself, or approaches to decision-making.

Erika's recommendations:

- ☐ *Identify one area of your life where you feel disconnected from your desires. How can you apply the strategies in this chapter to gain clarity and direction in that area?*
- ☐ *Schedule a weekly or monthly check-in with yourself to revisit your values, purpose, vision, and mission. Use this time to evaluate whether your current goals align with what truly matters to you.*
- ☐ *Dedicate time each week to reflect on your experiences, decisions, and feelings. Ask yourself questions like "Did my actions align with my values?" or "What steps did I take toward my goals?" This practice can help reinforce your commitment to what you want.*

Reflection on Impact: How do you believe these changes will affect your life, leadership, or relationships? Take a moment to visualize how gaining clarity on your desires and priorities might positively affect your life, leadership, or relationships. What changes do you anticipate as a result of this commitment?

Chapter 14

QUESTION 6

What Impact Do I Want to Make?

Purpose: *Thoughtfully identifying the impact you want to make provides the gift of making a difference with your decisions. By choosing to positively affect yourself and others, you align your words and actions with meaningful outcomes, contributing to a better world.*

Making a difference isn't about doing more or doing better. It's about being consistent, conscious, and deeply human.

Everything we do—or don't do—has an impact. Even the smallest choices can create ripples that affect others. Without consciously reflecting on the kind of impact we want to make, we may inadvertently cause negative consequences.

As you consider this question, it's crucial to envision the future you want to create through your actions today. Reflecting on what you want to be true in the future helps you recognize that your choices have a ripple effect, extending to others and influencing outcomes. This forward-thinking approach encourages you to plan ahead, ensuring that your efforts positively contribute to the lives of others and the greater good. When you are clear about the impact you wish to have, you can make decisions that serve not only your interests but also uplift those around you.

In one of my all-time favorite movies, *You've Got Mail*, Tom Hanks's character defends opening a book superstore that led to the demise of an independent bookstore owned by Meg Ryan's character by claiming that "it wasn't personal; it was business." Ryan's character replies that his claim makes no sense: "Whatever anything is, it ought to begin by being personal."*

I'm just doing me; you do you.
It's not personal; it's business.

What do we even mean by these phrases? Both the above statements serve to rationalize behavior that adversely impacts another person and marginalizes their emotional experiences.

I used to be attached to the belief that business wasn't personal. This single belief gave me permission to think only about myself and do the work I was paid to do without considering others. I cared about them deeply, but when there was work to do, I often couldn't see past my own need to get the job done. That is the job, right? Get it done at all costs?

Wrong.

Your job at home and work is also to see beyond yourself—especially if your job requires you to lead others and make decisions that impact others.

This might seem obvious if we are writing policy or determining where the family will go on vacation, but it's less obvious when we witness someone struggling or not living up to their potential and we choose to judge, blame, or shame them or prove a point instead of helping make things go well.

This practice is the reason I walked away from my corporate career after twenty-five years to become a coach. I knew there had to be a way to merge my for-profit brain with my genuinely well-intentioned heart. As I grappled with my beliefs and past, I questioned whether those things could coexist in the career space. It turns out that while it's not always easy, they very much can.

I've built my coaching business around helping leaders become better stewards of their influence so they can go beyond making money and move toward making a difference. In this chapter, I'll help you get there too.

---

* *You've Got Mail,* written by Nora Ephron and Delia Ephron, directed by Nora Ephron. Warner Bros. Pictures, 1998. Film.

WHY MAKING A DIFFERENCE MATTERS

To reach your fullest potential as a leader, it's essential to master the art of making confident decisions that **positively impact others**. It isn't enough to just make your point, or make money, or make things happen—true greatness involves making a meaningful difference in the lives of those you lead and love.

Making a difference isn't just for the wealthy, the noble, or the people in high-impact careers; it's for everyone, including you and me. You might wonder if one person can truly make a difference—and the answer is a resounding yes! No matter where you are in life, how much money you have, or how busy you are, you have the power to affect someone's life positively. And here's the bonus: When you make a difference for others, you also enrich your own life in the process.

This practice begins with recognizing that our actions, words, and behaviors directly influence those around us. Regardless of your intention, you are making an impact. The choice you face is whether that impact will be positive or negative. It's important to remember that simply avoiding harm to others isn't the same as making a difference; being neutral doesn't equate to having a positive effect.

When you actively choose to make a positive difference, you set an example for others. This not only helps them achieve greater results but also fosters a more supportive community, enhances emotional well-being, and enriches their work, relationships, and overall lives. And as a wonderful side effect, you'll find yourself experiencing these benefits as well.

> "The purpose of life is not to be happy. It is to be useful, to be honorable, to be compassionate, to have it make some difference that you have lived and lived well.
>
> —RALPH WALDO EMERSON"

This chapter is about helping you do better in those brief moments when stress abounds and your focus narrows, preventing you from seeing past your own needs, wants, and challenges.

Envisioning the Change: The Power of Intentional Impact

Without a Clear Focus on Impact

- You may make choices that distract you from your goals and what truly matters, leading to feelings of disconnection and dissatisfaction.
- You might react impulsively, making shortsighted decisions that do not consider the long-term consequences of your actions.
- You could struggle with feelings of resentment and disappointment, especially in relationships where expectations are unmet.

With a Clear Focus on Impact

- You will make choices informed by your values and higher purpose, leading to a more fulfilling and meaningful life.
- You will consider the short-term and long-term implications of your decisions, weighing your options carefully.
- You will feel empowered to create a positive impact on others, enhancing your relationships and fostering a supportive environment.
- You will be willing to face fears and uncertainties associated with making decisions that align with your desired impact.

THE PATH TO MAKING A DIFFERENCE

In this next section, you'll learn very practical strategies for overcoming some common barriers to making a difference. In doing so, you will positively impact your capacity for answering the question "What impact do I want to make?"

BARRIER	OVERCOMING STRATEGY	DESCRIPTION
JUDGING OTHERS' WORTHINESS	Strategy 6.01: Don't Discriminate Who's Worthy of Your Best	If you struggle to offer your best to those who may not seem deserving, strategy 6.01 will help you rise above your judgments by encouraging you to give your best regardless of others' perceived merit, fostering authenticity and compassion in your interactions.
REACTING DEFENSIVELY	Strategy 6.02: Be What's Missing	If you find yourself reacting defensively in tense situations, strategy 6.02 will help you transform the dynamic by choosing to offer kindness and understanding, thereby filling the void of what's missing in that moment.
HAVING UNMET EXPECTATIONS	Strategy 6.03: Don't Impose Your Rules on Others	If you often feel disappointed by others not meeting your expectations, strategy 6.03 will help you let go of your personal rules and focus on your responses, allowing you to foster healthy relationships based on mutual understanding rather than imposed standards.
RISING TENSION IN RELATIONSHIPS	Strategy 6.04: Set Boundaries	If you experience stress from others' behaviors or unmet expectations, strategy 6.04 will help you establish healthy boundaries that define your responses, empowering you to protect your well-being without attempting to control others' actions.

Strategy 6.01: Don't Discriminate Who's Worthy of Your Best

Let's imagine a situation where you're dealing with a colleague who frequently falls short of expectations. It's easy to feel they haven't earned your cooperation or kindness. Yet every interaction presents an opportunity: Will you rise above and offer your best or withhold your efforts based on perceived merit?

It's common to think things should be earned—especially when you value personal responsibility. While this belief often serves you well, if you're not careful, it can work against you when you want to make a difference.

You might hesitate to be kind to someone who isn't kind to you because they don't deserve it. Or you might resist sharing credit with a team member who didn't contribute equally because they haven't earned it. What I'm suggesting is that you do it anyway.

No matter the situation, this practice isn't inherently in conflict with your value of responsibility. I'm not advocating overlooking unmet commitments, brushing mistakes aside, or offering endless leniency. Instead, I suggest holding others accountable with compassion and recognizing that giving your best is about authenticity, not merit.

Once, while I was traveling and at a rental car counter, I encountered a seemingly rude agent who neither acknowledged me nor made eye contact. My initial reaction was to rush through the interaction, believing she didn't deserve my time or courtesy. Instead, I chose to shift my perspective and offer my best. I asked a friendly question, made eye contact, and smiled—and her demeanor transformed from agitated to friendly. Even if she hadn't responded kindly, I felt satisfied knowing I had given my best without expecting anything in return.

When we withhold our best from others due to unmet expectations, we become part of the problem, judging others for poor choices while making them ourselves.

You don't get to decide who is worthy of your best. You can choose to show up as your best self, but another person's worthiness isn't yours to judge. It's human to struggle with this practice, so I turn to my faith for guidance. After a moment of remembering "to be and see the face of Christ," I find the strength to show up.

I challenge you to find a mantra that redirects your best effort in those moments. Additionally, consider starting a "judgment journal" to uncover where you judge others' worthiness. Understanding and easing these judgments using other strategies in this book will help you improve.

Strategy 6.02: Be What's Missing

Imagine a team meeting where tensions are high. Your colleague, overwhelmed and stressed, snaps at you in front of others. What do you do? Do you defend yourself and snap back, escalating the tension? Do you get angry and withdraw, harboring resentment? Or do you take a moment to breathe and choose a different path?

Instead of reacting defensively, you decide to offer kindness and understanding. After the meeting, you approach them with genuine concern, acknowledging their stress response and offering support. This simple act of being what's missing—kindness in the face of harshness—transforms the dynamic, fostering a deeper connection.

As a highly responsible person, you're likely adept at identifying gaps in others and in situations. When you find yourself focused on these voids, let your judgment guide you—but instead of remaining in judgment, strive to be what's missing.

By tapping into your judgment, you can gain clarity on what you desire instead; judgment can reveal what you perceive as lacking in a situation. When you're willing to be what's missing, you provide what you believe the situation needs. This might look like the following:

- Extending patience to someone who is being demanding
- Offering kindness to someone who is being hurtful
- Be loving to someone who is angry
- Showing generosity to someone who is being selfish
- Expressing appreciation to someone who is being ungrateful
- Opening yourself up to someone who has shut down
- Offering forgiveness when you think you're owed an apology

Simply be what you wish was present without expecting anything in return. By giving what's missing unconditionally, you align with your inner compass—and although you shouldn't expect it, you might inspire someone to shift their energy and change the outcome.

Start small with this practice. Observe your tendencies, and note situations where you withhold your best self. Identify your excuses or justifications for this behavior. From there, explore what you fear might happen if you relax your judgment of others and give your best anyway.

Once you have this insight, I recommend revisiting the *true* versus *truth* activity in strategy 4.05. If you really want to challenge yourself, give freely even when it's difficult and observe the outcome.

Strategy 6.03: Don't Impose Your Rules on Others

We all have a personal rule book—a set of guiding principles that's shaped by your values and beliefs. Think of it as a mental manual; your rule book might include domestic rules like "Don't put dirty dishes in the sink if the dishwasher is empty" as well as more complex, relational rules like "If someone truly cares about me, they'll check in without me having to ask."

Most of the time, rule books make life easier. They eliminate the need to think about things repeatedly and make us more efficient. You simply put the dishes in the dishwasher after breakfast because it's your rule. The problem arises when you impose your rules onto others.

Let's say you value spontaneity, so after work one day, you see your neighbor grilling and decide to drop by unannounced. What's the big deal, right? What you might not see is that your neighbor has high value for privacy and experiences your drop-in as an imposition.

In this situation, your well-meaning behavior unintentionally invites resistance because you've violated a rule you didn't know anything about. While there is no right or wrong in these situations—your neighbor is not wrong for craving privacy, and you are not wrong for a benevolent attempt at connecting with him—it's important to acknowledge that we all have different ways of viewing the world. There are no universal values, beliefs, or rule books. (Even if we all had the same rules, adults will always do what they want to do; we cannot control anyone but ourselves.)

What if, instead of imposing unspoken and unrealistic expectations onto others, you threw out the rule book entirely? When I suggest this to my clients, they gasp: "How would people know what to do if I didn't spell it out?"

Let me challenge you with this: Think about all the disappointment you experience in your relationships with regard to unmet expectations. Chances are you've spent hours ruminating over chores you wish your spouse had done without being asked, conversations you wish your boss were having with you, information you wish your coworkers were sharing, grades you wish your children were receiving, and so on—all of which ties back to what *you* believe is important.

Now imagine a future where you allowed others to think, feel, and behave according to their values and you spent time and energy only on your response to them. That is the ultimate goal: focusing on what you can control and letting go of everything else. With this mindset, you decide whether you want to feel happy, sad, disappointed, worried, or angry. The only price you pay to get there is giving up control in the form of imposing your personal measuring stick on others.

It's time to take inventory of the rules you impose on others, and while they might work well when governing your own life, you might want to rethink the ones that are unnecessary or damaging your relationships.

Here's a ten-question framework for evaluating the thoughts and beliefs impacting any relationship. Start by listing your most significant relationships. For each person, answer the following questions honestly:

1. *Who is this person, and what is their relationship to you?*

____

2. *How satisfied are you in this relationship?*

Unsatisfied — *Highly Satisfied*

☐	☐	☐	☐	☐	☐	☐
1	2	3	4	5	6	7

3. What is the story you are telling yourself about why this relationship is not ideal or not where you want it to be?

4. Who are you around this person? Describe the way you feel and act in their presence. For example, are you a people pleaser? Do you try to control this person? Do you maintain your true sense of self when you're with this person? If not, why?

5. List everything you appreciate about this person. What are their gifts, talents, and unique qualities?

6. List everything that bothers you about this person. These are your judgments, assumptions, and interpretations of their behavior, the decisions they make, what they do, whom they do it with, how they do things, why they do things . . . you get the picture. Don't hold back, and don't filter.

7. Which of your judgments are a reflection of how you see yourself? Find at least one way you are mirroring these behaviors or emotions. Don't accept "I'm not." Be honest with yourself.

8. What are you taking personally about the way this person behaves or the choices they make?

9. *List every rule you have for how this person should be and why you find these rules necessary.*

____

____

10. *What thoughts, beliefs, or rules are you willing to revisit or reframe in service of this relationship?*

____

____

In previous chapters, you learned several strategies for reshaping thoughts and beliefs that are no longer serving you or your relationships. The beautiful thing is, you have the power to change them and improve your relationships for the long term.

Strategy 6.04: Set Boundaries

I have found in my work with clients that boundaries are generally misunderstood and misused—which is a shame, because they have the power to decrease your stress and significantly improve your life.

Before we dig into boundaries, let's clarify with a story the difference between a boundary and an ultimatum. Jessica and Emily were lifelong friends who found their relationship tested as they grew older. Jessica became more focused on her career, often working long hours, while Emily's focus was on her social life.

One weekend Emily surprised Jessica with a girls' getaway—but Jessica was up against a deadline and needed to finish a project. She asked Emily to reschedule. This left Emily feeling neglected and unimportant; she threw down what she called a boundary and declared that if Jessica did not come away for the weekend, she wasn't sure they could be friends any longer. This interaction left them both consumed with bitterness; Jessica felt misunderstood, and Emily felt unvalued. Their friendship, once unbreakable, was beginning to unravel due to miscommunicated and unmet expectations.

Emily was not honoring a boundary; she was offering an ultimatum. A boundary looks more like what Jessica offered, which was honoring a decision she had made previously to prioritize her career. This did not make her friendships unimportant, but it would take a back seat when critical career opportunities were on the line.

Boundaries are fundamentally straightforward. They are decisions you make in advance about how you will respond to specific situations. Here are some common scenarios that may require you to establish a boundary:

- **Unacceptable behavior:** Situations in which you encounter behavior that you find intolerable or do not wish to be around

- **Violation of values:** Situations that conflict with your personal values, which is a common reason for setting boundaries

- **Distress:** Circumstances that lead to mental, emotional, or physical discomfort

In situations like these, boundaries help us clarify and plan for how we will respond in the moment. Notice I have said nothing about what the other person will do; that's because boundaries govern your behavior, not theirs. Your boundary defines how *you* will respond, not how you'll attempt to change or control someone else. That's an ultimatum, and it will leave you frustrated and disappointed every time.

Here's what it looks like:

TRIGGERING EVENT (*The behavior you find unacceptable*)	**ULTIMATUM OR BID FOR CONTROL** (*What a bid for control might look like*)	**BOUNDARY** (*What a healthy, boundaried response might look like*)
Someone lights up a cigarette around you.	You tell them all the reasons they should stop smoking and cite the risks if they don't.	You excuse yourself and leave the space.
Your mother-in-law calls every night after the baby is asleep, even though you've asked her not to.	You insist your mother-in-law stop calling and expect her to change her behavior, or you ask your spouse to do something about it.	You turn off your mother-in-law's notifications on your phone and return calls when it's more convenient for you.
You get a calendar invitation on a completely packed day.	You try to institute a policy that requires all team members to honor existing calendar invitations.	You decline the invitation.

Now that you're clear on exactly what a boundary is, let's run through how to set one:

- **Begin only when you're ready:** Don't set out to create a boundary until you're 100 percent ready to enforce it. If you're secretly hoping your boundary will change the other person's behavior so you don't have to enforce the boundary, you are using boundaries to punish or manipulate another person, and that will never work. Come back when you're really ready.

- **Prepare your mindset:** Make sure you are operating from a place of compassion for yourself and others. Other people get to make decisions for themselves, and accepting that reality doesn't mean that you agree with their choices. Be ready for others to be unwilling to change without taking it personally. Remember, the boundary is for you, not against them.

- **Be specific about the trigger and your response:** Determine exactly what the triggering event is and what you will do. Get as clear and specific as possible so you can know exactly how you'll respond.

- **Honor the boundary:** In order to experience the power of boundaries, you must honor them. *Every. Single. Time.* Even when it's hard. Even when it's inconvenient. If you choose not to enforce the boundary, the person you'll be hurting is yourself. When you break trust with yourself, you invite unhealthy and unhelpful inner dialogue (*Why can't I say no? What's the matter with me? I'm such a pushover!*), and you'll cause your own emotional drama.

- **Choose whether you share the boundary—or not:** It's not necessary to tell people about your boundaries, but it is unfair to assume people naturally know your boundary exists; that will set you up for frustration and disappointment. You get to decide whether you share your boundary with the people who will be impacted by it. When shared, boundaries can prevent unnecessary relationship damage and help build trust and honesty in a relationship. But there are instances where it's not necessary or productive to share the boundary. You get to choose.

Task: Identify a recurring situation in your life that causes you stress and take the time to outline a healthy boundary for it. Start by reflecting on the specifics of the situation, the triggers involved, and the response you wish to establish. You don't need to enforce the boundary immediately; instead, focus on crafting a clear plan that you can implement when you feel ready. This preparation will empower you to set effective boundaries that protect your well-being.

> Love and kindness are never wasted. They always make a difference. They bless the one who receives them, and they bless you, the giver.
>
> —BARBARA DE ANGELIS

FINAL THOUGHTS

Understanding the impact you want to make is vital for living a purposeful and fulfilling life. By applying the strategies discussed in this chapter, you will not only clarify your desired impact but also empower yourself to act in ways that align with your values and aspirations.

As you engage in self-reflection and commit to making a positive difference, remember that every action matters. Even small gestures of kindness and understanding can create ripples of change, contributing to a better world for yourself and those around you.

Take the time to reflect on your experiences and consider how you can consistently align your actions with the positive impact you wish to make. Your clarity of purpose will guide you as you strive to lead a life that is not only successful but also deeply meaningful.

APPLY YOUR LEARNING

Take a moment to reflect on what you've learned in this chapter. Use the prompts below to guide your thoughts and make notes on how you can apply these insights moving forward.

Key Takeaways: What are the most important insights or concepts you learned in this chapter? Write down two or three key points that resonated with you.

Areas for Change: What is one thing you are most interested in doing differently as a result of what you learned in this chapter? Consider how this change could impact your decision-making or approach to challenges.

Commitments to Practice: Identify two specific actions or practices you are committed to implementing based on what you learned. These could be new habits, questions to ask yourself, or approaches to decision-making.

Erika's recommendations:

- ☐ *Identify one area in your life where you feel you could make a more positive impact. How can you apply the strategies in this chapter to enhance your influence in that area?*
- ☐ *Actively look for opportunities to be kind to others, especially those you might typically judge or withhold your best from.*
- ☐ *In challenging interactions, consciously choose to respond with empathy or support rather than defensiveness.*
- ☐ *Identify a situation in your life where you would benefit from a healthy boundary and determine how you can apply the strategies in this chapter to set and execute a clear boundary that protects your well-being.*

Reflection on Impact: How do you believe these changes will affect your life, leadership, or relationships? Take a moment to visualize how committing to make a positive impact could transform your life, leadership, or relationships. What changes do you anticipate as a result of this commitment?

Chapter 15

QUESTION 7

What Does It Look Like to Take 100 Percent Personal Responsibility, No More, No Less?

Purpose: *Taking full personal responsibility and allowing others to do the same provides the gift of shared power. When both sides take 100 percent ownership of thoughts, feelings, actions, results, and impact, it fosters an environment of mutual respect and accountability.*

> Personal power is directly tied to personal responsibility, which most people avoid.
>
> —BRENDON BURCHARD, *THE MOTIVATION MANIFESTO*

Understanding what you need to let go of or embrace in order to take 100 percent personal responsibility requires careful consideration of the implications of both exceeding and falling short of owning your thoughts, feelings, words, decisions, and actions. By finding the right balance, you not only position yourself powerfully but also create an environment where others can thrive.

You might recall the story I shared in chapter 1 about my son making the decision to switch high schools. A few years later, we had a similar exchange when he came to me expressing his desire to drop out of college—only this time, the stakes were higher. I felt a mix of fear, sadness, and anger. As a college dropout myself, I wanted more for him. However, I realized that allowing him to make his own decision was crucial to maintaining my 100 percent personal responsibility. My role in this situation was to determine whether to support him and his choice, even if I didn't agree with it.

In chapter 8, we discussed that a conscious choice presents two options: to allow it or to impact it. I decided I wanted to make an impact on it.

I told him it was his decision and that I would support him, but I needed him to help me understand how he'd arrived at that choice. It was important for me to know that he had thoroughly considered the short- and long-term consequences of his decision. I also asked him to listen to my concerns. He agreed, and we discussed his vision for the future. As I shared my worries, he listened attentively and promised to reflect on our conversation before making his final choice.

Ultimately, he chose to change schools and majors, graduating summa cum laude with a bachelor of science degree two years later. This experience reinforced the importance of allowing him to take ownership of his decisions, fostering mutual respect and accountability. I learned to trust that he had his own answers, and while I had a supportive role, it did not involve forcing, manipulating, or trying to control the outcomes. I effectively impacted the situation without exceeding what I could directly control or influence.

Personal Responsibility Is a Winning Strategy

At its core, personal responsibility means embracing complete ownership of your life—every thought, emotion, decision, and action, along with the results and impact they produce. Research suggests that prioritizing personal responsibility is a winning strategy; individuals who adopt this approach often achieve greater success than those who do not.

While taking full responsibility for our lives is essential, it's equally important to avoid becoming overresponsible. As highly responsible individuals, we often struggle to stop before taking on too much—tasks, problems, or emotional burdens that aren't ours to own. However, allowing others to take responsibility for their lives—even if it makes you uncomfortable—fosters their growth and autonomy.

When you take on others' responsibilities, it creates a power imbalance that can lead to several negative consequences, such as neglecting your well-being, setting yourself up for disappointment, and preventing others from finding their own power. Over time, this dynamic can lead to unhealthy dependencies, where others rely on you to solve their problems, ultimately stunting their growth and development. This cycle diminishes your personal power and undermines your effectiveness as a leader or collaborator.

Importantly, **control cannot be shared, but power can**. Understanding the distinction between control and power can profoundly impact how you navigate challenges and interact with others. While control often leads to stress, burnout, and strained relationships, embracing your power allows for a more flexible, empowering, and productive approach.

Control refers to the direct influence an individual has over specific situations or outcomes. It is often characterized by a desire to dictate how things should happen, leading to a focus on managing every detail to ensure that outcomes align with one's expectations. This need for control creates a barrier to collaboration; it cannot be shared or delegated, as it relies on an individual's effort and oversight. When control is centralized in one person, it can lead to negative consequences that impact individuals and the broader organization or team. An example of this is when a talented individual becomes a linchpin; without them, the entire system risks falling apart.

In contrast, **power** encompasses a broader scope of influence that goes beyond direct control. It includes not only what individuals can manage directly but also what they can influence indirectly, such as affecting others and outcomes through inspiration, motivation, and collaboration. **Power is inherently shareable**; it allows individuals to uplift and empower others, fostering an environment where everyone can contribute their strengths. When power is distributed among team members, it creates a culture of shared responsibility and innovation, enabling collective problem solving and enhanced creativity.

To achieve true success and foster a winning environment, it is crucial to embrace the 100/100 model of personal accountability, where each individual takes full responsibility for their thoughts, feelings, decisions, actions, and results. In this framework, power is shared rather than hoarded, allowing for collaborative problem solving and innovation that leads to better outcomes for everyone involved.

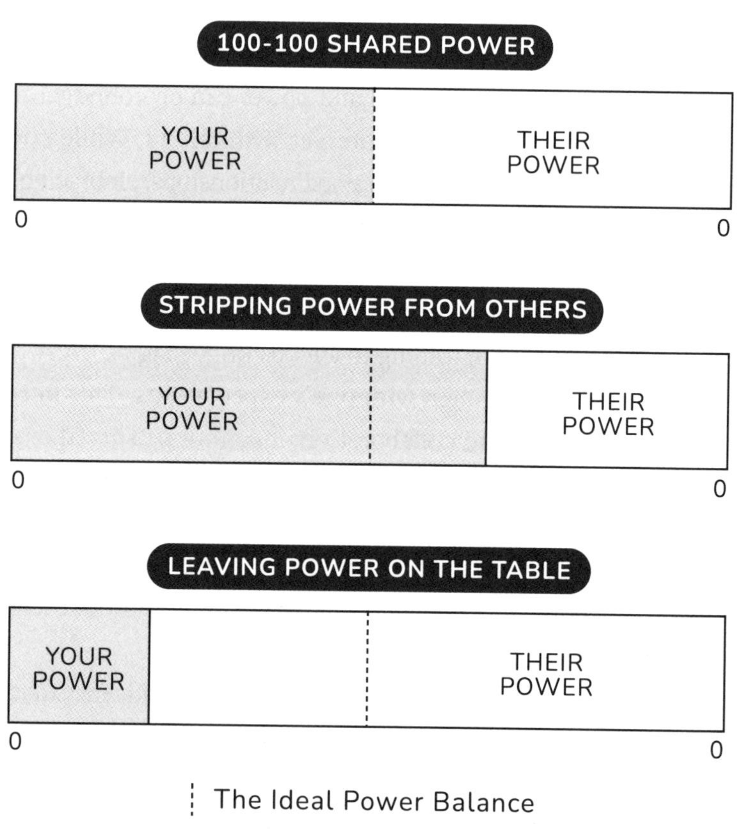

Figure 7.0

Consider the concept of shared power as a spectrum. On one end lies powerlessness, while on the other is the overpowering of someone else. The ideal position—shared power—exists at the center. Whenever you shift too far to the right, you push others toward powerlessness. Conversely, if you lean too far to the left, you forfeit your own personal power. This model is what every relationship and adult person needs to thrive.

With the exception of certain temporary situations that require a different distribution of power—such as when a team member is absent due to medical leave or vacation or when you are caring for an aging parent—maintaining a balance of shared power is critical in most situations. Ultimately, an individual's likelihood of success is defined by their commitment to personal responsibility and their ability to share power, which is the focus of this chapter.

WHY SHARING POWER MATTERS

If you love something, set it free—those words are easy to say but really difficult to do. As someone who hates losing control, I've struggled with how to find peace with relinquishing control of things that matter deeply to me. You might be wondering if the idea of letting go of control and submitting to what the universe has in store for you really holds up in practice. My experience says it does.

Love and fear might be the biggest contributors to forming attachments. The more something matters to us, the more difficult it is to let go of it or leave it to chance. On top of that, you may have been taught to fight for what matters to you—but even the good fight is a fight, and fights bear consequences.

Any form of letting go is a combination of releasing mentally, emotionally, and physically.

1. **Letting *someone* go**, while not the primary focus here, might be the greatest act of love. It signals unconditional, selfless respect for another person's right to choose for themselves.

2. **Letting *something* go** involves releasing the fear and worry associated with a situation or outcome. This includes the aspects of your life that undermine your results, disrupt your satisfaction, and hold you back because they no longer serve you or your relationships. Examples of what you might let go of include beliefs, assumptions, thoughts, emotions, part of your identity, expectations (of yourself or others), self-imposed limitations, deadlines, jobs, hobbies, goals, or even relationships.

I've historically struggled with this practice, and because I suspect you might, too, I want to share another example that beautifully illustrates what it looks like to overcome this natural tendency to strip power from others. The example I want to share with you involves my mom. I mentioned earlier that I lost her to cancer in 2018. To say we were close is an understatement—we spoke almost every day, sometimes twice. You can imagine how it hit me when she received a stage four cancer diagnosis in 2017.

My mom was fiercely independent, determined to make her own decisions, and a bit stubborn. In the months following her diagnosis, there were many times I disagreed with her choices, as did other family members who looked to me as the voice of reason to persuade her otherwise. Our fears, while understandable, were misguided. As I was her health advocate—and often the only one willing to stand up to her—family members urged me to change her mind when she refused treatments or disregarded doctors' orders.

Sharing power with her meant supporting her decisions even when I was acutely aware of the potential consequences. Instead of telling her what to do or pressuring her to listen to me, I expressed my thoughts and concerns with love and then offered to support whatever decision she made. This, after all, was how to offer her dignity in her final days. Although it still pains me to have lost her, I find peace in knowing she left this world on her own terms.

A Note on Letting Go of Relationships

Contrary to what you might assume, relationships involve letting go of something, not someone.

Relationships are a construct of your mind—they are nothing more than a collection of thoughts, like your opinions and judgments of the other person, what judgments and opinions you think they have of you, your thoughts about any history you have together, and all the thoughts, judgments, beliefs, and opinions you hold of yourself. You can also be in a relationship with someone you've never actually met; I have a very intimate relationship with Jesus, for example. Some people have relationships with artists, authors, celebrities, or loved ones they've never met.

What I see often in my work with clients is that the stress of letting go of a relationship has little to do with the other person and more to do with the grief that comes with losing what the relationship once was. The power of letting go of the relationship that no longer exists is that it frees you up to fully step into and appreciate the relationship as it is today; even if you can't find appreciation for it, you can experience power in accepting it for what it is.

Whether you're going from good to great, or great to optimal, you won't get there if you don't let go of what isn't yours to own. Not only does overresponsibility consume absurd mental and emotional bandwidth; it's exhausting and unsustainable.

Letting go not only reduces stress but also paves the way to greatness. By releasing negative emotions tied to overcommitment, you create space for positive feelings and new beginnings. Shedding unnecessary burdens enhances your focus and clarity, allowing you to prioritize what truly matters and concentrate on what you can control. This freedom from excess worry and drama improves your decision-making, aligning your choices with your inner compass. Additionally, honoring personal agency in your relationships fosters trust and connection, minimizing conflict and resentment.

Envisioning the Change: The Power of Personal Agency

Less or More Than 100 Percent Personal Responsibility

- You make excuses and blame circumstances, refusing to own your role in outcomes.
- You ignore the impact of your behavior on others and justify results without accountability.
- You fixate on outcomes and resist exploring new possibilities or solutions.
- You seek to control or change others, limiting their growth and agency.

100 Percent Personal Responsibility

- You empower others to grow and develop, enhancing collective intelligence.
- You acknowledge your role in situations and own your mistakes without justifications.
- You achieve results while respecting individual responsibilities and boundaries.
- You remain open to feedback and possibilities, fostering a collaborative environment.

THE PATH TO SHARED POWER

In this next section, you'll learn very practical strategies for overcoming some common barriers to sharing power with others. In doing so, you will positively impact your capacity for answering the question "What does it look like to take 100 percent personal responsibility, no more, no less?"

BARRIER	OVERCOMING STRATEGY	DESCRIPTION
FEAR OF LOSING CONTROL	Strategy 7.01: Understand What's in Your Control (and What Isn't)	If you struggle with relinquishing control to others, strategy 7.01 can help you understand your limits and recognize what is truly within your power.
NEEDING TO FIND FAULT	Strategy 7.02: End the Blame Game	If you find it difficult to take responsibility for your actions or outcomes, strategy 7.02 encourages you to acknowledge your contributions to outcomes, fostering personal accountability.
DESIRE TO BE THE HERO	Strategy 7.03: Leave Heroes to Hollywood	If you often intervene in others' situations to "save the day," ensuring outcomes or standards are met, strategy 7.03 will guide you in allowing others to own their responsibilities, promoting their growth.
FIXATING ON A SINGLE OR SPECIFIC OUTCOME	Strategy 7.04: Let Go and Detach from Outcomes	If you are overly focused on specific results, strategy 7.04 will help you practice detachment, enabling you to navigate challenges with a clearer mindset.
STRUGGLE TO ACCEPT OTHERS' CHOICES	Strategy 7.05: Don't Seek to Change People	If you find it hard to let people be themselves, strategy 7.05 will encourage you to accept others as they are, fostering healthier relationships and reducing frustration.
IMPERFECT CIRCUMSTANCES	Strategy 7.06: Find Realistic Solutions to Imperfect Circumstances	If you feel overwhelmed by challenges, strategy 7.06 will assist you in identifying realistic solutions to imperfect circumstances. By focusing on what you can control and acknowledging the limitations of your influence, you can approach problems with clarity and effectiveness, moving you closer to a conscious choice.

Strategy 7.01: Understand What's in Your Control (and What Isn't)

In his book *The 7 Habits of Highly Effective People*, Stephen Covey presents a simple but powerful model called the Circles of Concern, Influence, and Control. This model illustrates what is within our control and what is outside it.* I've adapted it for this discussion.

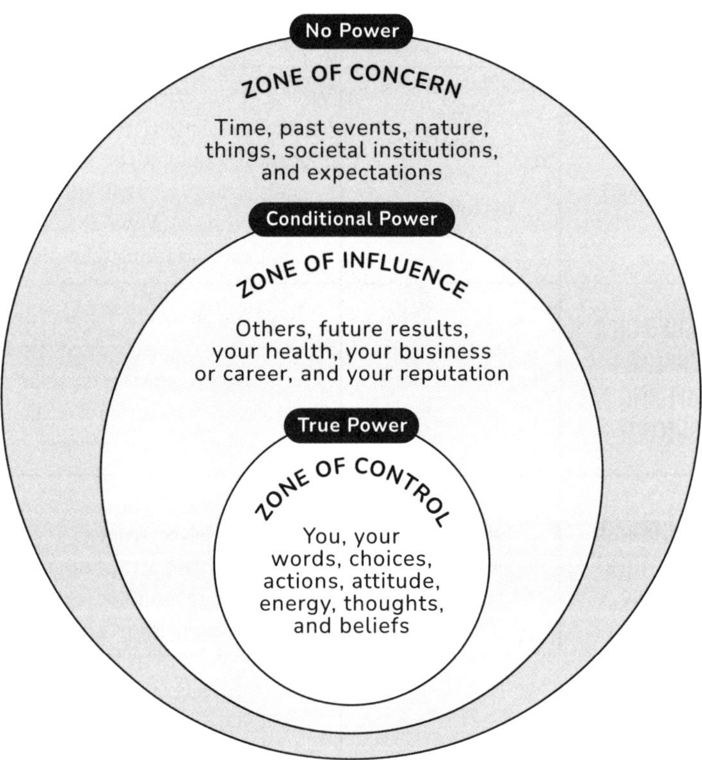

Figure 7.01

---

* Stephen R. Covey, *The 7 Habits of Highly Effective People: Powerful Lessons in Personal Change* (Free Press, 1989).

Direct Control (Zone of Control, True Power)

What you can control is very simple: you. You can control yourself as well as the following:

- What you think, believe, value, say, and do
- Your ideas, opinions, decisions, and effort
- Your commitments and agreements
- What you say no to
- Your priorities
- How you talk to yourself
- What gets your attention
- The degree to which you own your results and your impact
- How you respond to circumstances and experiences

This is the only area where you truly have direct power. However, be aware that some of these aspects can become limitations if you remain unaware or unwilling to change.

Indirect Control (Zone of Influence, Conditional Power)

This zone encompasses the things you can influence but not directly control, including aspects of your reality and results. It may be difficult to accept, but we cannot directly control anything outside ourselves. Thus, we must let go of the desire for control and embrace influence, understanding that attempting to change these external factors means trying to alter reality.

You do have influence over many areas, including your results and the actions of others. In situations where it makes sense, you can effectively impact outcomes even if you don't have direct control. For instance, in the earlier story about my role in my son's college decision, I demonstrated how to leverage influence without taking control. The challenge lies in finding peace if you cannot steer things in your desired direction.

While influence may be less effective in the short term—since force often yields quicker results—it proves to be much more effective in the long run. Those who choose to influence rather than control will consistently outperform those who seek control over their external circumstances.

No Control (Zone of Concern, No Power)

Most of what we encounter in the world falls into our zone of concern—issues where we have neither direct nor indirect control. Examples include medical diagnoses, traffic conditions, the weather, the economy, and events from our past. When we fail to recognize that these circumstances are beyond our control, we create unnecessary stress by fixating on things we cannot influence.

The opportunity here is to practice acceptance. By relinquishing control over what we cannot change, we can redirect our energy toward areas where we do have power. This shift allows us to focus on what we can influence, fostering a more productive and fulfilling approach to challenges.

I encourage you to identify which of these circles applies to any given situation. By understanding whether you have direct control, indirect influence, or no control at all, you can make informed choices to address your challenges effectively. This awareness will maximize your potential for success and is essential for applying strategy 7.06.

Strategy 7.02: End the Blame Game

Power and responsibility are often used interchangeably, and for good reason. Taking responsibility for your actions and choices increases your personal power and agency, putting you in the driver's seat of your own life.

The opposite of responsibility is blame: assigning fault to external factors when things don't go the way you wanted. When you blame someone or something else for your outcomes, you are claiming to have been completely unable to influence the result. This option leaves you in the unflattering position of being a victim to your circumstances.

While blaming someone or something might bring temporary emotional relief, in the long run, it's a distraction. When you place blame, you are focused on justifying what happened in the past—a place where you have no power or influence—rather than on taking ownership, learning, and making meaningful change now and in the future.

I have engaged in the blame game more than I care to admit, and I still do at times. I'm human, after all. I've left a marriage, a career, and friendships, bailed out on some big commitments, and even tried giving up on this book a few times, all because I was pointing to someone or something else as the source of my problems.

Blame happens in big ways—like the ones I listed above—but more often, it happens in small moments. Even though you are a highly responsible person, you are likely blaming more than you realize. Blaming might sound like this:

- *I meant to, but I got busy.*
- *I didn't mean to; it was an accident.*
- *I didn't have a choice; they made me.*
- *I didn't know; nobody told me.*
- *Everyone else is doing it.*
- *I can't help it; that's just how I am.*

The blame in each of these situations is covert; none of these examples explicitly points to a person or circumstance that's at fault ("Tom told me to work on something else instead!"). Still, each instance fails to acknowledge the choices you made that led to the result. You might have actually been too busy, but the fact is, you chose to prioritize other projects. You may really have not known, but you also didn't ask. It very well may have been an accident, but you still contributed to the events that led to that accident.

If you want to fully harness your personal power, you must stop playing the blame game and choose responsibility instead.

Choosing responsibility means acknowledging the inconvenient truth—our contribution to the situation—no matter how minor. Contributions aren't always obvious. Sometimes, our role in a poor result is minor or passive: perhaps you didn't actively do something, but you missed an opportunity to step in and change the outcome.

Regardless of the extent of your responsibility, you need to own it fully—every time. This is how you operate from a position of personal power. It's hard work, especially for the ego. Blame becomes an attractive option when our self-image is at risk; in moments when you fear you won't be seen as good, competent, smart, or successful, you might be tempted to place blame elsewhere to protect your identity and image. I urge you to resist that temptation and step into your personal power instead.

Let's explore some examples of blame and what it would look like to take full responsibility instead.

Situation: You missed a deadline, and your boss is asking why.

- **What blame looks like:** "I'm so sorry—I've been slammed all week and couldn't get to it. I got hit from every direction. And I'm not the only one who came up short, so that tells me we're not allowing enough time to get these things done."

- **What responsibility looks like:** "I committed to more than I could get done and prioritized other things ahead of this project. I also did not communicate that I was struggling to meet the deadline or ask for help because I was afraid of how it would make me look."

Situation: You made a mistake, and now a teammate is calling you out.

- **What blame looks like:** "I didn't have what I needed, and nobody told me how much research we had to do to complete this project. It was way too much work for one person. Somebody should have thought of that before assigning the deadline."

- **What responsibility looks like:** "I underestimated how much time it would take and didn't plan accordingly, which led to rushing and turning out sloppy work."

Situation: You told your child you'd attend their ball game, and you missed it.

- **What blame looks like**: "I'm sorry I didn't make it to your game, but something came up at work and I had to stay. I couldn't say no."

- **What responsibility looks like:** "I chose to stay late and help with a project instead of leaving in time to make it to your ball game because I didn't want to suffer the consequences of saying no. I'm sorry I broke my promise to you."

In each of these situations, there is a fine line between blame and responsibility, but the responsible path acknowledges your contribution and choices that got you here. This is what you must do if you want to harness the full scope of your personal power and live up to your leadership potential.

Strategy 7.03: Leave Heroes to Hollywood

Who doesn't love a good superhero movie? Humans are naturally drawn to heroes. They provide role models, help those in need, and often wear spunky outfits. While there is a place for true heroism in comic books and on the big screen, our everyday lives—especially in our workplaces, families, and communities—do not need heroes. Let me explain.

It can feel rewarding to be sought out for advice, help someone in need, or be chosen for special projects, even if it means taking on more than you can reasonably handle. The rush you get from solving a problem that no one else could can be intoxicating. Your ego thrives on this "hero" moment, making you chase it repeatedly—whether it's preventing a disaster, breaking a record, hitting a deadline, or closing a sale.

However, this relentless pursuit often leads to bitterness, resentment, and burnout. By setting the expectation that you'll always go the extra mile or that you know what's best, you risk overwhelming yourself. You may find yourself working late at the office, sacrificing your weekends, and watching the rest of your life slip away. You become a hero, but does it truly feel good?

Not only are you suffering; in your quest to help others, you may be doing more harm than good. Playing the role of the workplace hero can strip others of their power. When you constantly jump in to save the day, you prevent others from solving their own problems. Over time, they may develop an unhealthy dependency on you, expecting you to have all the answers. This reliance stunts their own learning and growth. You've become Batman, and without you, Gotham City feels vulnerable. Meanwhile, you're too busy rescuing everyone else to take care of yourself or pursue your own goals and priorities.

As with every other issue discussed in this book, you got yourself into this situation, and you're the only one who can get yourself out.

First, take a moment to reflect on the type of heroism you're most susceptible to. In general, there are two types of workplace heroes:

1. The "I'm Better" Hero
2. The "I'm Helping" Hero

Both types believe they are more capable than others and derive an ego boost from helping, but their motivations and methods differ.

	THE "I'M BETTER" HERO	THE "I'M HELPING" HERO
THEIR FOCUS	Self, and their need to intervene to solve what they see as the problem by taking swift action.	Others, and their need to step in and save, fix, or rescue them from their circumstances.
HOW THEY HELP	They leverage their talent or ability.	They leverage their emotional support.
THEIR MOTIVATION	They want to jump in and make problems go away, gaining esteem from others.	They want to feel good about themselves by being the one to solve problems for others.
THEIR DRIVING BELIEF	"I can't let others fail on my watch."	"I can't let others suffer on my watch."
THEIR APPROACH	They feel like they *must* jump in to help, and they justify their behavior after the fact.	They work to convince others that their help is the right thing to rationalize their actions.
THE THREAT TO THEIR IDENTITY	Being seen as someone who can't get the job done (incompetent).	Being seen as someone who doesn't care.
THEIR FEAR	Failure or poor results.	Rejection or irrelevance.
THEIR QUALITIES	Impatient Confident Unapologetic Driven	Intrusive (trouble honoring boundaries) Persistent or Insistent (helping even when it's not wanted)
THEIR WORK STYLE	They prefer to work alone and simply take over.	They prefer to work with others and insert themselves into everything.

Leaving heroes to Hollywood doesn't mean saying no every time a colleague asks for your help or advice, but it does mean changing a few unhelpful behaviors.

Process Your Motivations, Fears, and Threats

Reflect on the heroic tendencies listed in the table above, and identify which ones resonate with you. Examine the thoughts and beliefs that drive your workplace heroism. You can't change a pattern or behavior without first being aware of it, so take the time to cultivate self-awareness about why you feel compelled to jump in and save the day. This understanding will empower you to intervene and redirect yourself when you notice these patterns emerging. Additionally, the reflection prompts at the end of this section will further assist you in this process.

Reduce Others' Dependency on You

The fear of working yourself out of a job—or out of relevance—can be very real, but it isn't realistic. If you want to truly lead others to greatness, you must empower them to solve their own problems. This holds true at home as much as it does at the office. Tactical opportunities to reduce your dependencies include the following:

- Actively delegate tasks.
- Empower others by providing clear expectations and decision-making authority.
- Foster open communication.
- Encourage critical thinking.
- Give others space to fail safely and learn from their experience.
- Help others develop their skills and abilities.

Be of Service Without Trying to Fix

As a leader, you can most effectively serve others by empowering them to take ownership of their own situations rather than taking on their problems and attempting to fix them. Here are a few examples of how you might serve rather than fix:

- Actively listen and acknowledge without offering solutions.
- Normalize their emotional experience without taking it personally.
- Allow negative emotions without trying to fix them.
- Offer a supportive presence.
- Facilitate some critical thinking to assist in their decision-making process.
- Ask clarifying and empowering questions.
- Set clear boundaries while still offering genuine care.

Cut the Strings

Real heroes—the ones who make a difference in our communities and aren't celebrated or famous—don't attach strings to their contributions. They're motivated by kindness, courage, or selflessness, not getting something in return.

Workplace heroes, on the other hand, tend to attach strings to their help.

Strings are the contingencies we expect from others when we jump in to solve their problem. If your help comes with any kind of expectation ("Because I helped them, I expect this person will back my next project / stay late next week / give me credit, etc."), you have attached stipulations to your contribution, and that creates a power imbalance.

We can't share power if we attach strings to our relationships. Expecting something in exchange for help, without disclosing it, is holding power in reserve; you've created a dynamic where someone owes you something, and relationships can never be equal when debts are involved.

If and when you choose to be in service of others, you must consciously do so without any strings attached. If you find yourself wanting to attach strings, take a moment to do the following:

- Get clear about your role in the situation, if any.
- Face the fear you have that's preventing you from letting go.
- Reimagine the situation where you and the other person each have 100 percent power.

Honor Your Limits and the Limits of Others

Occasionally pushing yourself beyond your limits isn't a big deal, but when you consistently position yourself as the hero, you chronically exceed what's reasonable or realistic. This behavior can lead to stress, resentment, being taken advantage of, and ultimately burnout.

Just as crucial as knowing your own limits is respecting the limits of others, especially when they differ from your own. By honoring someone else's limits, you demonstrate empathy, build trust, and manage expectations more effectively.

Many people struggle with honoring their limits, but it doesn't have to be a grandiose or complex task. You can respect your own limits and those of others through small actions like these:

- Say no to additional tasks when you're already overcommitted.
- Admit when you've taken on too much.
- Allow a coworker to decline a project due to their workload.
- Ask for help.
- Admit you don't know the answer.
- Politely decline an invitation.
- Respect another person's privacy or boundary.
- Communicate clearly about your personal boundaries with others.

Now is the time for honest self-reflection to uncover potential blind spots. Take a moment to thoughtfully answer the questions below. As you respond, be sure to capture your answers clearly and consider how they might reveal insights about your default thoughts and behaviors.

- *What structures (praise, incentives, compensation, advancement) reinforce your heroic behavior, and what other options exist?*
- *What rewards (financial, spiritual, physical, emotional, social) encourage you to keep doing more (exceed your 100 percent), and are they worth it?*

- *Who pays the price for your heroism?*
- *What would it say about you if you didn't help or do so much?*
- *Where have you created dependencies?*
- *Where do you have strings attached to your contribution or your willingness to let go?*
- *What would it look like to know and honor your limits and offer the same to others?*

Strategy 7.04: Let Go and Detach from Outcomes

In a world that favors faster, better, and bigger, it's easy to get caught up in the pursuit of success and happiness by doing more, having more, and achieving more. We set big goals and map our paths to greatness—but too often this pursuit comes at the expense of our well-being and overall satisfaction.

Fortunately, I have the secret to elevating your success and satisfaction: **You need to let go**.

I'm not suggesting that you give up, settle for less, or become complacent. Instead, I encourage you to detach from specific outcomes and focus on what you truly want while remaining flexible about how you achieve it. By approaching your desires with greater fluidity and open-mindedness, you can release chronic frustration, resentment, and disappointment, paving the way for fulfillment, freedom, and inner peace.

Detaching from the outcome might feel counterintuitive; our results-obsessed culture often equates greatness with specific achievements. Letting go of a hyperfixation on results may seem like it interferes with achieving goals—but detachment doesn't mean abandoning the intention to realize your desires. Instead, it frees you to open your mind to possibilities, capitalize on better options as they emerge, and embrace the wisdom of uncertainty. Detachment means believing your desires are attainable even when the path to them is unclear. When you successfully detach from an outcome, you'll feel less pressure to act, force solutions, or manipulate situations in your favor.

You might not recognize how your attachment is causing problems in your life; you might even believe your expectations are reasonable—and yet you're still not getting what you want. A common pattern among clients is being so attached to an outcome that they lose sight of what they truly want. Here's a typical conversation I have with clients that illustrates this point:

> ME: What seems to be the problem?
> CLIENT: My kids.
> ME: What about your kids?
> CLIENT: They're selfish and disrespectful.
> ME: How so?
> CLIENT: They never include us in things.
> ME: Can you give me an example?
> CLIENT: The season is almost over, and I don't have a schedule for my grandson's baseball games.
> ME: And why don't you have this?
> CLIENT: Because they don't care enough to get me the schedule. I don't think they want me there.
> ME: Did you ask for a schedule?
> CLIENT: I shouldn't have to.
> ME: What do you want?
> CLIENT: I want them to be more considerate of us.
> ME: And what else?
> CLIENT: I want them to call and invite us to things.
> ME: And what else?
> CLIENT: Isn't that enough?
> ME: So is this about controlling your kids?
> CLIENT: [silence]
> ME: What do you most want for yourself?
> CLIENT: I want to have a relationship with my grandkids.
> ME: Are you open to what you can do to achieve that?

In this example, the client has alienated his kids and lost precious time with his grandkids because he's attached to how he's included in their lives.

He wants special invitations, placing all the responsibility on his kids. This attachment obstructs what he truly desires—to be close with his family—and prevents him from recognizing alternate paths to achieve that goal. While fixating on the baseball schedule he didn't receive, he overlooks the simple option of asking for it. He has surrendered his personal power to his attachment to being invited and included in specific ways.

Had he chosen detachment, he might have approached the situation with greater flexibility. By prioritizing his true desire—to be close with his kids and grandkids—he could have inquired about their sports schedule, initiated hosting a weekly family dinner, or explored other ways to nurture family closeness.

The real challenge is overcoming our natural predisposition for certainty. When we're attached, we're often seeking control for the sake of certainty. In this sense, detachment is a spiritual superpower: Choosing detachment means acknowledging that you don't know exactly how everything will unfold but trusting that it will. While detaching from someone or something can be difficult in the short term, it ultimately clears the path to better relationships governed and protected by healthy boundaries in the long term.

This work is not easy, but the rewards are many. Practicing detachment can help you to achieve the following:

- Experience less stress, drama, and emotional suffering.
- Cultivate a greater sense of inner peace.
- Improve your decision-making capacity.
- Be more adaptable and resilient.
- Nurture healthier relationships.

Enhancing your ability to detach requires honest self-reflection to uncover potential blind spots. For any situation where you feel deeply attached to a specific outcome, use the questions below to guide your exploration. Take your time to consider each question carefully, and write down your responses as they come to you.

- *What fears exist when you think about not achieving a specific outcome?*
- *What do you really want?*
- *What stops you from exploring other options?*
- *What limiting beliefs might be fueling your attachment to specific outcomes?*
- *What can you do in the present moment to contribute to a positive outcome, regardless of the final result?*

Strategy 7.05: Don't Seek to Change People

Think about a time when you wished someone in your life would change—perhaps a partner, a friend, or a family member. You envisioned how their transformation might improve your relationship and maybe even simplify your life. It's a natural inclination to want those we care about to align with our ideals, but what if the key to stronger connections lies not in changing others but in accepting and loving them as they are?

Take a minute to reflect on your most important relationships. Now consider what it would mean to love them without trying to change them. What fears arise when you think about allowing someone full agency over their life, decisions, and results, while they own the impacts of those choices?

If you're like most people, even imagining this is hard because you likely want others to be better or do more. You want your boss to be more supportive. You want your kids to take more initiative. You want your neighbor to take better care of their lawn. You want your sister to show up to family events on time. You want your spouse to spend more time with you. You want your coworker to mind their own business and get their work done faster. I know you can relate.

The situation varies, but the bottom line is the same: You want people to be different than they are. I see it all the time in my coaching practice: Clients are fixated on trying to change, fix, save, or control the people they care about most, usually because they see unmet potential in them or have convinced themselves that other people are the source of their suffering and that changing them will somehow make them feel better. In my experience, no one enjoys being controlled or feeling pressured to live up to the potential others see for them, even when it comes from a well-meaning place.

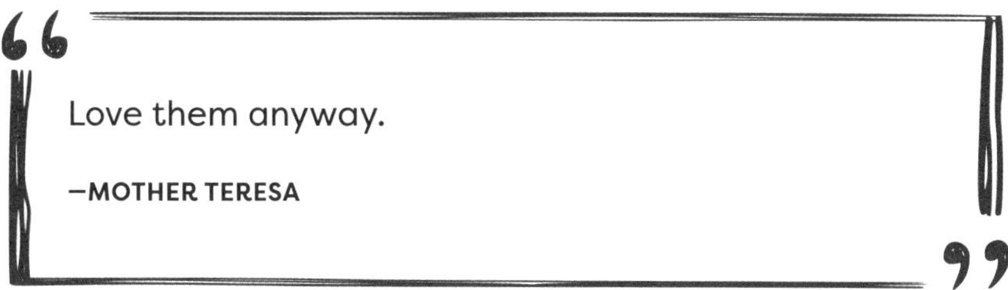

My advice—and the only advice I've ever found to be effective—is to let others be who they are (and who they aren't) and, in the words of Mother Teresa, to *love them anyway*.

Acknowledging that you can't control, change, or fix others frees you from the mental and emotional burden of taking on more than your share of responsibility. You have the free will and personal agency to make decisions about your life, and so does everyone else. Even when their choices affect you, those decisions remain theirs to make. While you can choose how to respond to their actions, you cannot make their choices for them.

I am no stranger to the urge to change people; this desire was a significant factor in the failure of my first marriage. To be honest, I've probably tried to change everyone I care about at some point. Through my personal development journey, I've learned that it is far more sustainable and rewarding to accept people as they are and love them unconditionally.

This practice can become challenging, especially when dealing with people who make self-destructive choices or whose actions conflict with our beliefs. Allowing others to make decisions you disagree with doesn't mean you don't care or that you consent to their behavior. Ultimately, adults will make their own choices, and believing we can control them is an illusion.

For instance, I have an older brother who has battled drug addiction throughout his adult life. My family and I have tried every possible approach to change him—helping, saving, forcing, manipulating, and rationalizing. At times, I've even put my own safety and well-being at risk in the process. And you know what? Every one of those attempts failed. The only approach that has brought me peace is allowing him to own his choices entirely. I can love and care for him without trying to control what isn't mine.

There are some recurring patterns I see in people struggling with this practice. First, the use of *should* and *shouldn't* when referring to others. These words signal obligation, duty, and consequences for not doing what they deem right or correct, and while we might intend to inspire or motivate others, they usually produce guilt, shame, doubt, and resentment.

Another unproductive pattern is cheating on the person in front of you with their potential. Reflect honestly about whether you are interested in who another person *actually* is or who you want them to be. When you are fantasizing about what someone could or should be, you are in a relationship with their potential, and you're missing out on enjoying and appreciating who they are in the present.

Other patterns that signal you have work to do here are as follows:

- Being overly critical, fault finding, or pointing out flaws in others
- Excessively offering unsolicited advice
- Believing your own well-being hinges on another person's character, behavior, or results
- Feeling frustrated when others don't meet your expectations
- Feeling resentful when others don't change according to your wishes
- Feeling guilty over how you've impacted others
- Taking responsibility for how others feel
- Using force or fear to get your way
- Using guilt or emotional manipulation to influence someone's behavior

This work is not for the faint of heart. I've counseled countless clients who struggle with the desire to change others in their relationships. Without a commitment to release that urge, I often find that I can't help them effectively. You'd be surprised at how many engagements stall at this point.

However, for those who allow others to be themselves without the pressure to change, the success rate is high, and the rewards are substantial. When you genuinely embrace people as they are, you maintain your 100 percent personal power while enabling them to own theirs. This approach is crucial for building sustainable, harmonious, and deeply loving relationships.

Let people be who they are (and who they aren't), and then decide how you want to think, feel, and respond to them. That's it.

If you want additional help on this, refer back to the ten-step framework in strategy 6.03.

Strategy 7.06: Work with Reality, Not Against It

The moment you stop resisting what is, you can start shaping what's next.

The struggle is real—and the stakes are high. Life presents no shortage of challenges that can get in the way of your success: unexpected setbacks, resource limitations, or interpersonal conflicts, just to name a few. We all face days when it feels like the deck is stacked against us, with new constraints appearing at every turn. In those moments, it's easy to fixate on what's not working or wish for conditions to be different. But fixating on things you can't change is an argument you'll never win—it only drains the energy you need for progress.

Life is hard. Succeed anyway.

Reality is rarely convenient, but it's always honest. It offers you data. When you learn to see that data clearly—and recognize what you can and can't control—you stop wasting energy trying to bend the world to your will and start using your power and influence to create change within it.

Every challenging situation contains a mix of forces presenting as limitations or constraints:

- Imposed fixed elements—the facts, past events, and external requirements you cannot change. These are the non-negotiables: what's already happened, what's mandated, or what exists outside your control.

- Imposed dynamic elements—the conditions, people, and systems you cannot control directly but may influence through communication, collaboration, or time. These are the shifting realities where influence—not force—creates movement.
- Self-imposed elements—your beliefs, interpretations, emotions, and choices that shape how you experience and respond to the situation. These are the levers of personal agency and growth.

When these factors block your progress, your task is to categorize them according to your level of direct control so you can direct your effort where you have the most power. The goal isn't to eliminate limits—it's to work with them, and often to be effective because of them. Constraints can clarify priorities, sharpen focus, and reveal what truly matters. The ones that hold the most power are often the ones outside your awareness. Making those constraints visible—especially the self-imposed kind—expands your options for impact and helps you see how much power you actually have.

WORK WITH REALITY, NOT AGAINST IT

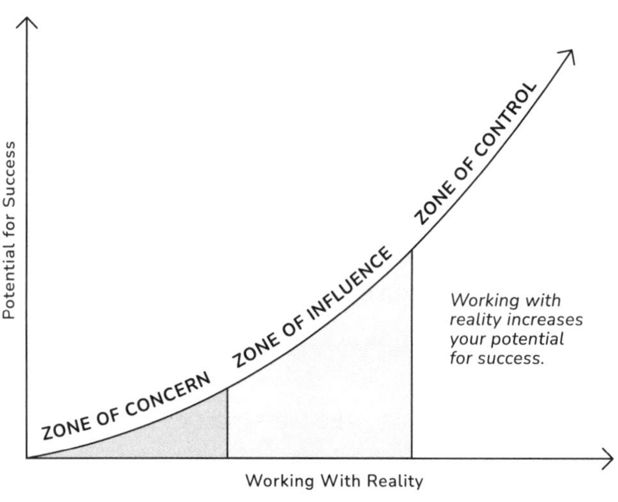

Figure 7.06

When you work *against* reality, you waste your precious energy fighting a battle that can't be won. The biggest trap is getting stuck fantasizing about options that simply don't exist—usually wishing that an imposed, fixed constraint were different. Every moment you spend wanting things to be other than they are keeps you busy but not effective. It's like shifting into neutral and revving your engine—you burn fuel, make noise, but go nowhere.

When you work *with* reality, you put yourself in your most powerful position—even when your circumstances are imperfect or undesirable. You intentionally direct your energy toward what you can control and your influence toward what you can only shape conditionally. Conditional influence requires patience, relationship, and collaboration; it's the art of creating movement without demanding control. You engage with the facts as they are, not as you wish them to be. You make peace with what's true, then move into intelligent action aligned with your goal.

Working with reality also requires that you stay clear about what you want and ensure your aim is realistic. Look at the conditions you've been given—constraints, people, resources, timing—and ask:

> **What is unalterable?**
> These *imposed fixed elements* represent facts, events, and external requirements that cannot be changed. Think of it as a collective of what was, or what is. It does not represent the future. Here are some things to consider:
>
> - The past—anything that has already happened
> - Common law
> - Rules, policies, or requirements
> - Requests and expectations
> - Pre-determined duties, tasks, or assignments
> - Pre-determined Budgets and allowances
> - Decisions, commitments, or agreements
> - A diagnosis
> - Resource allocation or availability

- Environmental factors such as where you are, the weather, structures, or system

What is outside of my direct control but could potentially be impacted indirectly?

These *imposed dynamic elements* are areas where you have influence—but not control. They often involve other people, systems, or circumstances that require time, communication, or collaboration to shift. Here are some things to consider:

- What is true for other people (their ideas, beliefs, values, choices, needs, wants, efforts, or emotions)
- What other people do and the results or impact of those actions
- The pace of change or decision-making in your environment
- Organizational priorities, politics, or culture
- Shifting timelines, resource availability, or external dependencies
- The readiness, willingness, or capacity of others to engage or gro

What do I directly control in this situation?

These self-imposed elements make up your entire inner world—your thoughts, emotions, interpretations, and intentions. They represent the only domain over which you have full authority. How you manage and align these elements determines how you experience life and the impact you create. They can limit or expand your available options. Here are some things to consider:

- Interpretations, assumptions, and ideas
- Values and beliefs

- Emotions
- Fears, concerns, or worries
- Motivation
- Perceived needs, wants, or expectations
- Choices
- Willingness, effort, or engagement
- Conditions (the strings you've attached)
- Priorities—what gets your focus or attention

As you work through these questions, your goal is to explore every limit or constraint and every available option until you identify the most realistic solution that can help you move forward.

First, expose what's true.

List everything—every fact, condition, or assumption—without filtering. Capture every limit or constraint, even those you'd rather not acknowledge. If you're tempted to skip something, don't. Anything you're currently unwilling to do, face, or consider goes in the *self-imposed elements* section. You may have good reasons for what you're unwilling to do, but they should still be documented. The purpose here is visibility. When you can see the whole picture, you can start working with it rather than against it.

Then, explore what's possible.

Once you've made your exhaustive list, revisit it with curiosity. Notice which elements are truly fixed, which are dynamic, and which are self-created through thought or choice. If you're unhappy with your options, revisit your self-imposed elements. Consider where your interpretations, assumptions, or expectations might be limiting you. Ask yourself what it would take to make peace with what you can't control or influence. You might discover that a shift in thinking—or a willingness to let go—opens new possibilities you hadn't seen.

If you're still not satisfied, look at your power to influence. You may not be able to control others, but you can often inspire, motivate, or create the conditions for movement—without being attached to the outcome or trying to change another person. As you identify areas where influence could be possible, make note of the conditions that would support change—trust, timing, shared purpose, and the quality of the relationship itself. Influence is conditional power; it only works when the conditions are right.

And if you remain stuck, revisit your goal. Maybe the goal itself isn't alterable. In that case, your most powerful decision might be to say no, to redefine success, or to rework the target altogether.

This shift—from resistance to responsiveness—is where transformation happens. It doesn't mean settling or shrinking your vision. It means moving from fantasy to mastery. You still pursue what matters, but you do it in partnership with the present moment rather than in conflict with it.

The most effective leaders don't ignore constraints; they integrate them. They turn limits into leverage. They see clearly, decide wisely, and act courageously within what's real. They don't wait for ideal conditions—they create impact with the conditions they have.

A final note: All solutions live on a spectrum. **Realistic solutions** exist fully within your control. **Conditional solutions** depend on your power to influence and the quality of your relationships. **Unrealistic solutions** require the world—or other people—to change before you do. The first two move you forward. The last one keeps you stuck. Choose accordingly.

Try This → Information Instead of Interference

Identify one constraint you've been fighting. Instead of seeing it as interference, treat it as information. Ask yourself: *What is this constraint showing me about what's true, what's possible, or what's next?*

When you stop resisting reality and start learning from it, you'll discover new ways to move forward—powerfully, peacefully, and on purpose—even when your circumstances are imperfect.

APPLY YOUR LEARNING

Take a moment to reflect on what you've learned in this chapter. Use the prompts below to guide your thoughts, and make notes on how you can apply these insights moving forward.

Key Takeaways: What are the most important insights or concepts you learned in this chapter? Write down two or three key points that resonated with you.

Areas for Change: What is one thing you are most interested in doing differently as a result of what you learned in this chapter? Consider how this change could impact your decision-making or approach to challenges.

Commitments to Practice: Identify two specific actions or practices you are committed to implementing based on what you learned. These could be new habits, questions to ask yourself, or approaches to decision-making.

Erika's recommendations:

- ☐ *Identify at least one recurring situation where you may be overstepping or taking on responsibilities that belong to others. Consider challenging your fears and concerns that rationalize this habit.*
- ☐ *Commit to asking a handful of trusted colleagues, friends, or family members for feedback on how you handle responsibility in different situations. Use their insights to guide your growth and adjust your approach.*
- ☐ *Practice using "I" statements to communicate your feelings and responsibilities.*
- ☐ *Change the habit of blaming others or external circumstances for your challenges. Instead, practice acknowledging your role in situations and recognize how your choices contribute to outcomes.*
- ☐ *Commit to a daily reflection, noting instances where you took responsibility for your actions and where you might have fallen short. After a period of time, see what patterns emerge.*

Reflection on Impact: How do you believe these changes will affect your life, leadership, or relationships? Take a moment to visualize what's possible when you keep from exceeding or falling short of taking 100 percent personal responsibility.

Chapter 16

YOUR FUTURE IS CALLING

Your future self wants you to pace yourself and stay the course. Whatever emotions you are experiencing now, my hope is that you are also feeling optimistic and hopeful about the promising, peaceful future that awaits you. This book was crafted with the intention of being a lifelong companion, one that you won't outgrow. It is not meant to be read once and then set aside. I invite you to engage with it continuously and discover the possibilities that unfold as you invest in developing yourself.

Each time you pause and work through these seven questions before taking action, you strengthen your ability to make conscious choices.

Let's Recap What You've Learned

Your biggest obstacle is you. Specifically, five beliefs often undermine your relationships and results. When you believe you are always right, that the ends justify the means, that you are inherently better, that you are always helping, and that situations are merely temporary, you default to force, manipulation, and control. This approach provides only temporary relief from the pressure of being overresponsible.

The solution lies within you, specifically in pausing to reflect on seven powerful questions and making conscious choices. These tools empower you to transform your decisions, improve your relationships, and pave the way for lasting change and fulfillment.

The Seven Conscious Questions and Their Purposes

Question 1: What Am I Feeling, and What Are My Emotions Signaling?

Purpose: Understanding your emotions and their underlying messages offers the gift of emotional maturity. By recognizing and learning from your feelings, you can better connect your inner world with your outer goals and strategies.

Strategies for Emotional Maturity:

- Expand your emotional vocabulary.
- Develop your emotional response skills.
- Learn from your negative emotions.
- Don't figure it out—feel it out instead.
- Understand your emotional triggers.
- Turn pain into power.
- Control your emotional impulses.

Question 2: What Is True for Me?

Purpose: Uncovering the mental constructs that shape your reality provides the invaluable gift of a managed mind. By identifying how your conscious and unconscious thoughts influence your experiences, you gain the power to redirect or reframe them to serve your best interests.

Strategies for Managing Your Mind:

- Audit your self.
- Challenge beliefs that no longer serve you.
- Watch your mind at work.
- Neutralize unhelpful thoughts.
- Become a just-in-time architect of your thoughts.

Question 3: What Might Be True for Others?

Purpose: Compassionate curiosity offers the gift of an expanded perspective. By setting aside judgment and engaging in meaningful inquiry—especially under pressure or in challenging situations—we open ourselves to a broader understanding of others' experiences.

Strategies for Expanding Perspective:

- Find compassion for yourself.
- Find compassion for others.
- Be mentally flexible.
- Direct your focus when listening.
- Ask more than you tell.
- Establish common ground with clarifying questions.
- Ask more powerful questions.

Question 4: What Is the Whole Truth, Even If It's Inconvenient?

Purpose: Seeing and accepting the whole truth provides the gift of being grounded in reality. By distinguishing your thoughts and emotions from the facts, you achieve a clearer understanding of the situation. This clarity allows you to embrace the truth, even when it's inconvenient, positioning you to take meaningful action.

Strategies for Grounding Yourself in Reality:

- Don't believe everything you think or feel.
- Don't weaponize the truth.
- Acknowledge the inconvenient truth.
- Don't omit the truth when sharing your opinions or feedback.
- Separate *true* from *truth*.

Question 5: What Do I Want for Myself, and Why Is That Important to Me?

Purpose: Understanding what you truly want for yourself offers the gift of direc-

tional clarity. By pinpointing your desires and the reasons they matter, you can establish priorities that move you steadily toward what is most important to you.

Strategies for Creating Directional Clarity:

- Dial in your inner compass.
- Set well-crafted goals and priorities.
- Make sure you are in charge of you.

Question 6: What Impact Do I Want to Make?

Purpose: Thoughtfully identifying the impact you want to make provides the gift of making a difference with your decisions. By choosing to positively affect yourself and others, you align your words and actions with meaningful outcomes, contributing to a better world.

Strategies for Making a Difference:

- Don't discriminate who's worthy of your best.
- Be what's missing.
- Don't impose your rules on others.
- Set boundaries.

Question 7: What Does It Look Like to Take 100 percent Personal Responsibility, No More, No Less?

Purpose: Taking full personal responsibility and allowing others to do the same provides the gift of shared power. When both parties take 100 percent ownership of their thoughts, feelings, actions, results, and impacts, it fosters an environment of mutual respect and accountability.

Strategies for Sharing Power:

- Understand what is within your control (and what isn't).
- End the blame game.
- Leave heroes to Hollywood.

- Let go and detach from outcomes.
- Don't seek to change people.
- Work with reality, not against it.

Remember: It's Supposed to Be Hard

I recently discovered Reformer Pilates and began my practice. I'm happy to report that I have found a form of movement that fuels my body and my soul. I think I'm drawn to it because it's hard—really hard. And I almost missed out on all of it.

In the beginning, I was skeptical—in part because I'm naturally skeptical but also because I was seemingly fielding signals from the universe that Pilates might not be the sport for me. Those signals calling out to me said I was too old, that my body doesn't move like it used to. Who was I kidding with this obsession, anyway? I wondered if I should just become a mall walker.

As it turns out, those signals weren't coming from the universe. The calls were coming from inside the house. Gasp! There I was again, sabotaging myself by considering leaving the game so I wouldn't have to admit defeat. I am a trained professional, but it doesn't exempt me from the natural design of being human. Fortunately, I practice what I teach and was able to see the pattern and make a conscious choice to continue, and I'm proud to report that I'm advancing in my practice and doing things I hadn't dreamed possible just a few months ago.

The use of these questions and strategies will be like that for you. It will be hard, and you will get signals from the universe telling you not to bother with this bullshit. It will be compelling, and you will want to listen to it. Please don't.

If you start to hear this:

- *I'm not at the end of my rope. Things are fine.*
- *I'm not an asshole; I'm a good person.*
- *I'm not at risk of losing anything big.*
- *I'm in good standing in my relationships.*

- *People respect me, even if they don't like me.*
- *I'm successful.*

Don't blindly accept those thoughts without considering the following:

- *Things might be fine, but do you deserve better than fine?*
- *You might be a good person, but are you effective?*
- *You might not have anything big on the line, but are the small things starting to pile up?*
- *Your relationships aren't broken, but are they thriving?*
- *If you're not well liked, but you feel respected, could it actually be that you are feared?*
- *You might have all the markers for success, but are you happy?*

I'm putting you on notice that selfish tendencies, while maybe effective in the short term, will eventually lead to burning out in your relationships, your career, or your life. You will wake up one day feeling alone and misunderstood with a broken "give a damn" and wonder how you got there.

But you made it to the end of this book, and that tells me you have what it takes. It also brings me great joy because I know that you, too, will be doing something you never thought possible if you commit to regularly reflecting on these seven questions and making more conscious choices.

Without knowledge, action is useless.
Without action, knowledge is meaningless.

Now that you know better, it's time to do better. Your new knowledge doesn't provide any real value until you execute. At the end of the day, the ones who can execute in spite of imperfect circumstances will go the furthest and experience the most happiness.

There Are No Do-Overs, Only Do-Betters

To date, nobody I know regrets learning these things—but they all wish they'd learned them sooner, me included. Let me reassure you that it's never too late, and it's certainly not too early. What matters is that you are committed and willing.

A willing participant will get busy, start taking small actions consistently, strive for progress, and ditch the perfectionist tendencies. Nobody is perfect at this. Nobody! And most importantly, a willing person will see failures and setbacks as a naturally occurring part of the process and celebrate the small wins, knowing they will soon add up to something meaningful.

When setting out to make changes in their lives, many of my clients start to feel a little discouraged at the following:

- They don't see immediate results.
- The amount of effort feels disproportionate to the initial return.
- Their "wins" are private or undetectable by others.
- Others aren't doing the same work, and it feels unfair.

If this happens to you, normalize it. Of course, it is natural to want some external validation when you're working so hard to change. Of course, your desire to see a return is normal, given given that you are a high performer and are used to seeing tangible proof of your effort. Stay the course, and remember that it's normal for others to want to see your change demonstrated over time before they'll believe it or give you credit, if at all.

In my experience, climbing out of the drama was a gradual process, and it took time for others to believe it was genuine—not just a facade to save my job. It was easy to backslide, and when circumstances were less than perfect, I often appeared disingenuous. You may experience this as well. Keep going, and extend yourself some grace.

While others might be part of your motivation for change, this is about you. You'll know that you are really making progress when a private win is as rewarding as a public win. And you don't need other people to participate for this to be effective. You'll just have to trust me on that.

Practice, Don't Preach

One of the most common comments I hear when training groups in these concepts is "Can I bring my [wife, husband, boss, kids]?" I love their enthusiasm for sharing what they've learned with those they care about, but I caution them to be thoughtful about how they share it.

When you start seeing results—and you will—you'll want to share your success with others. You'll also notice where others are suffering from those five beliefs and may feel the urge to point out the opportunity for change. Proceed with caution, because mastery is practiced, not preached. The most powerful advice is demonstrated consistently through your actions.

Your desire will be to motivate others, but remember that they won't be influenced by judgment, especially if you're measuring them against your new standards. Focus on your own growth, and you'll be amazed at how every action you take can influence those around you. You can change the world—especially your world—by changing yourself.

Stay or Go—Just Make Peace

When a client is at the end of their rope, burning out, or trying to recover, one of the first questions I ask is this: "Am I helping you stay or go?" This often elicits confusion because they haven't fully considered leaving, nor have they grasped what's required to stay. That's because they still hope to change others or perfect their circumstances to avoid making a difficult choice.

Another common hurdle is confusing quitting with completing. They are not the same. "Quitting" often carries a negative connotation of giving up entirely, which can prevent people from closing out things that aren't working or have outlived their usefulness. Remember, some things naturally come to an end; recognizing this can alleviate the guilt, shame, and fear associated with your decision.

When deciding whether to stay or go—whether in your job, relationships, or any other circumstance—your ability to flourish depends on moving toward something you desire rather than running from what you believe is the source of your suffering. Wherever you go, you'll carry the same judgments, beliefs, and habits with you. All that will have changed is your geography.

Neutralizing your circumstances—grounding yourself in reality—allows you to make a clear choice about staying or going. It helps you identify what's required of you in either situation. This is crucial, because we often seek to change our current circumstances or find better ones instead of taking personal responsibility.

If you stay, you must make peace with your current reality in order to flourish. This involves changing yourself instead of others or your circumstances, letting go of the need to be right in favor of being happy, and committing to compassion. You can find happiness and satisfaction anywhere if that's your choice. Remember, staying and trying to change others or perfect your circumstances is not an option—it never was.

If you go, you must make peace with your decision in order to flourish. This involves accepting what you cannot change, resisting the urge to feel guilty or justified, taking accountability for yourself and your decisions, and committing to compassion. Ensure that you extract every possible learning opportunity so your next situation is free of drama and emotional baggage.

Don't Go It Alone

This is hard work, and you don't have to go it alone, nor should you waste precious time hiding in shame because you've finally started to realize it might be you.

I know how hard it can be to ask for help. That voice in your head wants you to have things figured out before you risk exposing your weakness or vulnerability. Even if you're sure you can do this on your own, invite others into your journey. Doing so makes you stronger, increases your likelihood for success, and enhances your feeling of security.

If you are really serious about developing your practice, I recommend that you do the following:

- Engage with others and create community.
- Get one-on-one help in a private setting.

Find Others

Who are your people? Where are your people? Seek them out and connect with them. There are countless online and in-person communities, book clubs, communities of practice, peer groups, and similar opportunities for people with shared interests to learn with and from each other. You'll likely be surprised to discover that you're not alone in your challenges; many others are in similar situations, and you'll probably find some who are just a few steps ahead.

Work with a Coach

Did you know that you don't need to be broken to work with a coach, and their job isn't to fix you? In fact, almost all high-performing leaders work with a coach consistently. A coach is more than a mentor or adviser—they can help you get unstuck, move toward your goals, uncover blind spots, and identify limiting beliefs and other disruptive thought patterns that undermine your best life. Coaches can see things you can't (or won't) and provide a safe space for you to see and acknowledge them too. There are excellent coaches available in various price ranges and with different specialties. I suggest starting by seeking recommendations from people you trust. Most coaches offer free discovery sessions to check for a good fit.

Drum Up a Discussion

Like so many things, this book will be more fun when enjoyed with friends or colleagues. To that end, here are twelve questions designed to help you get the discussion started with other readers:

- Which of the five beliefs spoke loudest to you, and what stands out?
- What is currently at stake if you don't make some changes?
- Where does your overresponsibility show up the strongest? What are you afraid will happen if you don't overcommit, jump in, help, or take on something that isn't yours?
- What are the five most important things in your life right

now? How much of your time, energy, and focus are you giving them?

- What mental models are most in need of an update, and why?
- What emotions are hardest for you to process or regulate?
- How would your life be different if you didn't believe everything you thought?
- Where is it hardest for you to share power, and why?
- What prevents you from seeing beyond yourself in times of stress and expressing some compassionate curiosity?
- Where would giving your best unconditionally make the biggest difference?
- Which concept was toughest for you to face, and why?
- What strategy are you most excited to apply, and when is your first opportunity to do so?

SHARING THE LOVE (ACKNOWLEDGMENTS)

Really incredible achievements rarely happen flying solo; they are the product of a collective. This book came to be through powerful collaboration with and contributions from some of the most amazing people on the planet. To all of you, I am eternally grateful.

To my loving husband—my partner in everything: None of this would be possible without you. You have championed my life in countless ways by believing in me more than I believe in myself. I am better because you are by my side.

To Sam Parker—my developmental editor, friend, and colleague: I am forever grateful to you. Your strategic thinking, insightful words, and unwavering support have been invaluable to me throughout this journey. Having you by my side gave me the confidence to keep going. Thank you for challenging me and for being a constant source of encouragement and friendship.

To every person who physically worked on this book: My one big hope is that this work makes you proud to have been part of it. It would not exist without you.

To my family, friends, and colleagues: Your passion inspires me, your wisdom and experience humble me, your leadership guides me, your candor calls me to more, and your support and love fuel me in every way.

To my clients: Your courage drives me, your faith lifts me, your vulnerability makes me proud, and your achievements blow me away. Keep going! Thank you for inviting me into your lives and sharing so deeply. I've learned so much from you.

To all the thought leaders who've come before me: Thank you for generously sharing your time and talent, paving the way for so many of us who want to make the world a better place.

To you, my dear reader: Thank you. I am honored that you gave your time and consideration. I will eternally be cheering you on to the next level of greatness and praying that you find peace in everything you do.

And to Cameron: You are my *why*. Thank you for helping me understand unconditional love.

LET'S BE FRIENDS

It has been an honor to share this book with you. If it spoke to you, I hope you will take action and let me know how it goes. I also hope you help others find relief and amplify their success by sharing your experience.

There are a number of ways to connect and share:

- Visit the website www.maybeitsmebook.com to download free and paid resources.
- Purchase bulk copies of the book to share with your team or group.
- Host a book club using our digital resources for book club facilitators and participants.
- Tell your social circle what you're working on.
- Send an email to hello@maybeitsmebook.com and let me know what's working for you. I'd love to celebrate with you.

Even if this book wasn't for you, we can still be friends. Thank you for your kind consideration.

ABOUT THE AUTHOR

Erika is a passionate coach, facilitator, and author on a mission to make a peaceful, more satisfying life possible for anyone who desires it. With over a decade of coaching experience and a rich background in business, Erika empowers individuals and leaders to unlock their full potential and pursue a life filled with deep satisfaction.

Erika's professional journey began in the automotive aftermarket, where she spent twenty-three years, largely at the executive level, untangling the complexities of business operations, sales, and leadership. Her experiences during postacquisition integrations ignited her passion for coaching. She recognized that many well-meaning leaders faced challenges that left them feeling bitter, begrudged, and burned out. This realization fueled her commitment to champion greatness in others from the inside out, making it possible to achieve incredible results without paying the price mentally, emotionally, and relationally.

Erika believes in a coaching style that blends candor with compassion. She sees herself not just as a coach but as an ally—someone who supports and challenges her clients in equal measure. Her goal is to create a safe and supportive environment where individuals are encouraged to explore their purpose, passions, and profession. Whether you're a seasoned leader or someone seeking direction, Erika is here to partner with you on your path to transformation, helping you live in peace, give your all, and make a difference in the way you live, lead, love, and play.

Don't forget to support the author by leaving a review!